PAPERS

RELATING TO THE

COLLECTION AND PRESERVATION OF THE RECORDS

OF

ANCIENT SANSKRIT LITERATURE

IN

INDIA.

PAPERS

RELATING TO THE

COLLECTION AND PRESERVATION OF THE RECORDS

OF

ANCIENT SANSKRIT LITERATURE

IN

INDIA.

EDITED BY ORDER OF THE GOVERNMENT OF INDIA

ARCHIBALD EDWARD GOUGH; B.A.

GYAN

Published by

Gyan Publishing House
5, Ansari Road
Daryaganj, New Delhi-110002
Phone: 011-47034999, 9811692060
E-mail: books@gyanbooks.com

Distribution Network
gyanbooks.com
India, USA, Canada, UK, Australia, France

ISBN : 978-81-212-9468-3 (PB)
First Published, 1878

2nd Impression 2023

Printed at: Gyan Press, Delhi.

PAPERS RELATING TO THE COLLECTION AND PRESERVATION OF THE RECORDS OF ANCIENT SANSKRIT LITERATURE IN INDIA

Editor: ARCHIBALD EDWARD GOUGH

PAPERS

RELATING TO THE

COLLECTION AND PRESERVATION OF THE RECORDS

OF

ANCIENT SANSKṚIT LITERATURE

IN

INDIA.

EDITED BY ORDER OF THE GOVERNMENT OF INDIA

BY

ARCHIBALD EDWARD GOUGH, B.A.

PROFESSOR IN THE PRESIDENCY COLLEGE, AND PRINCIPAL OF THE MADRASA, CALCUTTA.

CALCUTTA:
OFFICE OF SUPERINTENDENT OF GOVERNMENT PRINTING.
1878.

CONTENTS.

COLLECTION AND PRESERVATION

OF THE

RECORDS OF ANCIENT SANSKṚIT LITERATURE.

Extract from a letter from PANDIT RÁDHÁKṚISHṆA, *Chief Pandit of the late Lahore Durbar, to His Excellency the* VICEROY *and* GOVERNOR-GENERAL *of India,—dated the 10th May 1868.*

YOUR EXCELLENCY has issued orders for collecting the catalogues of Sanskṛit, Arabic, and Persian books in existence in many parts of India. There are two things which would complete the information so much desired by the Oriental scholars of Europe and Asia. The Sanskṛit list will necessarily remain incomplete unless it contains the names of the books that are in the libraries of the Mahárájas of Jaypur and Nepal. The rarest books were collected by the liberal ancestors of the former, from the time of Rájá Mán Siṇh; and as the latter country has never been under the subjection of Mahomedans, the oldest Sanskṛit books are to be found there. A similar thing may be done with regard to the Sanskṛit books that are in the great libraries of England, Germany, France, and other Continental countries of Europe.

A list of these books should be published in English and Sanskṛit; and anything that Your Excellency is pleased to order for the furtherance of the cause of learning, will be highly and gratefully appreciated by the scholars both of Europe and India.

Note by WHITLEY STOKES, Esq., *Secretary to the Council of the Governor-General for making Laws and Regulations,—dated Simla, the 6th August 1868.*

THE Viceroy has received a letter from Pandit Rádhákṛishṇa, Chief Pandit of the late Lahore Durbar, suggesting the compilation of a catalogue of all the Sanskṛit MSS. preserved in the libraries of India and Europe, and stating that anything which His Excellency may order for the furtherance of learning,—that is, as I understand the Pandit, of Sanskṛit learning,—will be gratefully appreciated by Native and European scholars. The present Note on the subject has been drawn up at the request of the Hon'ble Mr. Strachey.

There can be little doubt that such a catalogue as the Pandit contemplates would be of use to a limited class of students. But there can, I think, be as little doubt that it could be only satisfactorily produced in Europe, or, at all events, by a European scholar capable of understanding the catalogues which European Sanskṛitists have already published in the Latin, German, and other tongues, and the extensive literature, in at least four European languages, which directly or indirectly treats of Sanskṛit MSS. The compilation of such a work, even if it were confined to the MSS. already known, would be the labour of a life-time. It has taken Professor Aufrecht, one of the most laborious of German scholars, more than ten years to catalogue merely the Sanskṛit MSS. in the Bodleian.

Now, I venture to assert that no one who has ever seen a Native list of MSS. would think of entrusting a Native with the preparation of such a catalogue. The titles of Sanskṛit works (which are all that Native lists present) are often fanciful and insufficient to identify the books referred to. Take instances familiar to every one. Who would know beforehand that the "Immortal Treasury" *(Amarakosha)* was a versified dictionary of synonyms, or that "Moonlight on the Established Truth" *(Siddhánta-kaumudí)* was a grammatical work of the school of Pāṇini, and not, as the Commander-in-Chief suggests, a Sanskṛit version of a speech of Mr. Disraeli's on the Irish Church? The lists, too, are often untrustworthy, "important works" (I quote from Professor Bühler) "being entered under wrong titles."

I know of no Native scholar possessed of the requisite learning, accuracy, and persistent energy. I know of no European scholar in India possessed of the requisite time, or who might not be more usefully employed in making original researches.

Under these circumstances, the work, if done at all, should be done in England, and, like Max Müller's edition of the Ṛigveda, under the patronage of the Secretary of State. But, in my opinion, the preparation of such a catalogue at present would be premature,—the muster-roll of a regiment can hardly be made until the men are enlisted,—and some years must elapse (even if the scheme which I am about to propose be vigorously carried out) before we possess even the names of all the extant Sanskṛit MSS.

I proceed to state what I venture to think would be the most practically useful course for the Government of India to follow in this matter, keeping within the pecuniary limits which I understand the Financial Member is willing to sanction. My scheme, I know, is quite incommensurate with the vastness and importance of the subject; but the problem is: given R2,000 a month, how shall we best employ that sum?

First.—We should print uniformly all procurable unprinted lists of the Sanskṛit MSS. in Indian libraries. Lists of the collections in State libraries, such as that lately procured by the Political Agent at Jaypur, might probably be obtained by all the Political Agents and Residents in Nepal, Central India, and Rajputana—perhaps even at Travancore and the other independent States of Southern India. There exists moreover, or shortly before I left Madras there existed, a Native list of the numerous Sanskṛit MSS. belonging to the late Rájá of Tanjore; and this the Madras Government would probably be able to procure. Then, the number of private libraries is very considerable, especially in the Presidency of Bombay; and though, as I have said, the lists of such collections are often untrustworthy, and books still figuring in them will sometimes, on enquiry, turn out to be lost, still they will frequently afford a clue to the discovery of unique or rare books. We should have the lists so printed, bound up in volumes; and I would send copies to the various learned Societies of Europe, and to individual scholars, such as Aufrecht, Cowell, Goldstücker, Hall, Max Müller, Muir and Rost in England, Benfey, Kuhn, Roth, Stenzler, and Weber in Germany, Regnier in France, Gorresio in Italy, Westergaard in Denmark, Böhtlingk in Russia, Whitney in America, Bühler and Griffith in India; intimating at the same time that the Government would carefully attend to their suggestions as to which of the MSS. therein mentioned should be examined, purchased, or transcribed.

Secondly.—We should institute searches for MSS. In order to this end, we should prepare from time to time lists of desirable codices, and place these lists in the hands of Native scholars and other persons willing to assist in the search. We might also send them to the principal officers employed in the Educational Departments of the various Local Governments. The lists should be printed both in Nágarí and Bengali: those intended for distribution in the Madras Presidency should be printed in the Telugu character. The recipients of these lists should be invited to report their discoveries to such officer as should from time to time be appointed by the Government of India (I venture to suggest the present accomplished Home Secretary as the first appointee); and scholars, such as Professor Bühler in Bombay, Mr. Burnell in Madras, Mr. Growse in the North-Western Provinces, Bábu Rájendralála Mitra or Mr. Tawney in Bengal, should every cold weather be sent on tours to examine the MSS. reported on, to seek new MSS., to explain to the Native scholars at the different places visited the objects and importance of the mission, and to purchase (for the India House library) such MSS. as the possessors are willing to sell at a reasonable rate. Some tact and management will be needed to lessen the aversion which Native scholars sometimes have to shewing and parting with their books; but here the Government might effectually aid by conferring titles of honour on such Śástrís and other Natives as exhibit conspicuous liberality in this respect. The gentlemen sent on tours should, of course, make reports to Government, and those reports, as well as extracts from the communications obtained from the recipients of the printed lists of MSS., should from time to time appear in the Supplement to the *Gazette of India*.

Thirdly.—Having thus gained some idea of the situation, extent, and nature of the stores of MSS. still preserved in India, we should proceed to copy those which are unique or otherwise desirable, but which the possessors refuse to part with. In selecting MSS. for transcription, we should bear in mind the subjects which European scholars deem most valuable. We should regard as of primary importance MSS. of the Vedas and Vedángas, and of their commentaries, law-books, grammars (especially those relating to the system of Páṇini), vocabularies, and philosophical treatises. We should regard as of secondary importance poetry, astronomy, medicine, treatises on mechanical arts, &c. The chosen MSS. should be copied in Nágarí, or, when necessary, transliterated into that character. This transliteration is absolutely essential. One of the largest and most valuable Sanskṛit libraries in existence is at Madras; but most of the MSS. being written in one or other of the four Drávidian characters (Telugu, Grantham, Malayalam, and Canarese), copies of them, in the original character, would be useless to European Sanskṛitists and to Native scholars in Northern and Western India. There would be little difficulty in procuring Telugu Bráhmans competent to make the transliteration. Where the whole of a MS. is not transcribed, the Śástrí should be instructed to copy its beginning and its end. The copies and extracts so procured should, from time to time, be sent to the library of the India House. Duplicates, which will doubtless be sometimes accidentally obtained, might be given to the British Museum, the Bodleian, or to one or other of the great Continental libraries. To Europe we should send everything obtained in working out this scheme,—original MSS., copies, extracts; for in Europe alone are the true principles of criticism and philology understood and applied, and, fifty years hence, in Europe alone will any intelligent interest be felt in Sanskṛit literature. There will then, it is safe to say, be as few Sanskṛit scholars in India as there are now Greek scholars in Greece.

Fourthly.—I would increase the grant made to the Asiatic Society at Calcutta for the publication of their *Bibliotheca Indica*. That grant now, I believe, amounts to the petty sum of R500 a month, and out of it the Society has to provide for the editing and printing of Arabic and Persian as well as of Sanskṛit MSS. The increase so proposed to be given should be devoted solely to the publication of Sanskṛit works hitherto unprinted; and of these the Society may well be trusted to make a good selection. I would also encourage the Bombay Government to persevere in the admirable efforts which it has lately made for the discovery and preservation of the Sanskṛit MSS. in Western India.

The expense of carrying my scheme fully into operation would be comparatively trifling: R24,000 a year would probably cover the whole cost at first, and the expense would, of course, gradually diminish as the collections were examined, or the desirable MSS. were purchased or transcribed. I would distribute the above-mentioned sum thus—

	Per mensem. R	Per annum. R
25 Copyists, at R20 each	500	
Stationery	100	
Total	600	7,200
Tour expenses—(1) North-Western Provinces, (2) Oudh and Central Provinces, (3) Rajputana, (4) Bombay, (5) Madras and Mysore, and (6) Bengal, at R1,000 each		6,000
Purchase of MSS.		6,000
Printing Native catalogues and lists of desirable MSS.		1,000
Additional grant to Asiatic Society		3,000
Sundries		800
Total		24,000

I venture to assert that the scheme above sketched out would result in important contributions to the history of religion and philosophy; that it would enable the Government to begin a work which should no longer be deferred, namely, the publication of critical editions of all authoritative Sanskṛit law-books relating to inheritance and adoption; that it would settle many important questions of philology; and that its effect, politically, would be beneficial, as tending to prove to the educated class of Hindus that the present Government of India is *not* neglectful of the claims of their literature; that it is *not* contemptuously satisfied to leave the preservation and elucidation of that literature to the efforts of Continental scholars and the support of Foreign Governments.

I submit that the scheme is elastic, economical, and practicable. It may be expanded in parts of India where the MS. material is unexpectedly large, and where available Native scholars are numerous; it may be contracted in places where the MSS. turn out to be few or worthless, or where the chosen MSS. have been transcribed or purchased. It will require no expensive staff,—no creation of new offices. I may perhaps mention that, during the greater part of my stay at Madras, I employed a Telugu Bráhman to transliterate into Nágarí Sanskṛit MSS. written in the Telugu.

Grantham, and Canarese characters, and chosen by Professor Bühler for transliteration. The Bráhman's work was excellently accurate, and his wages were only R20. There is no doubt that the Government could still procure many like him,—perhaps at a lower rate of stipend. I speak with confidence as to the practicability of the scheme; for, in its leading features, it is identical with that lately framed by Professor Bühler, which has resulted hitherto in obtaining from the Southern Mahratta Country and Canara alone the originals or copies of nearly two hundred valuable codices.

But whatever may be done, I trust that no time may be lost in doing something. The climate and the white-ants of India are fell destroyers of manuscripts. The old race of Śástrís is dying out; the younger Natives are losing their interest in the study and preservation of their national literature; and it is safe to say that in another generation, unless the Government bestir itself at once, much of value that is now procurable will have disappeared for ever.

SIMLA; W. S.
The 6th August 1868.

Minute by Major-General the Hon'ble SIR H. M. DURAND, C.B., K.C.S.I.,—*dated Simla, the 13th August 1868.*

OUR Administration has evinced no partiality for the encouragement of either antiquarian researches, or the preservation of the ancient literature of India. Some trifling and desultory investigations, such as those on which Major-General Cunningham was for some time engaged, are all that has been done in the purely antiquarian line; whilst, with respect to the ancient literature of India, I am aware of nothing except the grant of R500 a month to the Asiatic Society, and the volumes of the *Bibliotheca Indica* which are the result of this moderate grant.

In Bombay there has been some activity, which Mr. Stokes notices in his valuable Note, which suggests a much more systematic and comprehensive endeavour on the part of Government to ascertain the Sanskṛit works that exist, to compile a valuable index, and to print critical editions of authoritative texts of Sanskṛit law-books.

However practical our Government may be in its administration of this great Empire, and justly reluctant to apply its resources to measures which offer no palpable return of present or prospective advantage, it may,

I think, be questionable whether this utilitarian principle may not overshoot its mark, when it neglects the ancient literature of India, as an element having no sensible relation to the public mind of the masses of the Hindu population.

Mr. Muir has shewn in his publications what use may be made of the Sanskṛit ancient and authoritative works. Max Müller corroborates it; and though I with great regret confess my own inability, from my utter ignorance of Sanskṛit, to give an opinion of any positive value on the uses of the ancient literature of India in the hands of our modern scholars, and of all who take an interest in the phases under which religion and law take root in the institutions and character of millions under our rule, I must at any rate confess that I have, throughout my whole career, been painfully sensible that the main reason of the superficial knowledge which was observable in the great mass of our official men with regard to the root-feelings pervading Hindu society, was the fact that our British officials had no means, as a general rule, of becoming at all conversant with the literature which a formed priesthood and the habits of ages make the current pabulum of the Hindu mind almost from its cradle.

I am not in favour of devoting exorbitant sums to the sentimental nurture of Sanskṛit or Arabic literature; but, so long as both these languages remain what they are,—the radical sources of enormous spiritual influence on millions under our rule,—I am averse, even from a purely utilitarian principle, to neglect their ancient utterances; for they remain a living power among those millions.

I have long regretted the comparative neglect of Oriental studies among the members of the British Services in India. I am aware that very few can find the leisure for such studies; but this fact hardly justifies the Government in materially augmenting the hindrances to such studies, by neglecting even to indicate what works exist and are available. I am, therefore, much in favour of Mr. Stokes' moderate proposal, and of the publication of the best works gradually, and after careful examination and comparison of authoritative texts by competent scholars.

I am certain it will redound, not only to the enduring credit of Her Majesty's Government, but to many now uncontemplated practical uses and modes of effective leverage on the manifold masses and phases of the Hindu mind.

SIMLA; H. M. DURAND.

The 13th August 1868.

Extract from the Proceedings of the Government of India in the Home Department (Public),—No. 4338-48, dated Simla, the 3rd November 1868.

READ—

Extract from a letter from Pandit Rádhákṛishṇa of Lahore, to His Excellency the Viceroy, dated the 10th May 1868, suggesting the compilation of a catalogue of all the Sanskṛit MSS. preserved in the libraries of India and Europe, and stating that anything done towards the encouragement of Sanskṛit learning would be gratefully appreciated by scholars.

Note by Mr. Whitley Stokes, dated the 6th August 1868, containing his opinion as to the best course to be followed by Government in order to give effect to the recommendation of Pandit Rádhákṛishṇa.

RESOLUTION.—Mr. Stokes is of opinion that such a catalogue as the Pandit contemplates could be satisfactorily compiled only in Europe, and that any attempt to produce it at present would be premature. The following are the principal features of the scheme which he proposes for rendering the production of such a catalogue possible, and otherwise for the encouragement of Sanskṛit learning:

To print uniformly all procurable unprinted lists of the Sanskṛit MSS. in Indian libraries, and to send them to the various learned Societies of Europe, and to individual scholars in Europe and India, with an intimation that the Government will carefully attend to their suggestions as to which of the MSS. therein mentioned should be examined, purchased, or transcribed;

To institute searches for MSS., and, to this end, to prepare lists of desirable codices; to distribute these lists among scholars and other persons willing to assist in the search, with a request that they will report their discoveries to such officer as may from time to time be appointed by the Government of India; and to depute competent scholars on tours through the several Presidencies and Provinces to examine the MSS. reported upon, to seek new MSS., to purchase MSS. procurable at reasonable rates, and to have copies made of such MSS. as are unique or otherwise desirable, but which the possessors refuse to part with; and

To grant to the Asiatic Society of Bengal an additional allowance for the publication of Sanskṛit works hitherto unprinted.

2. The statement given in the margin shews the financial result of the scheme; and the total cost, R24,000 a year, which it would entail on the Imperial revenues, is not extravagant when compared with the importance of the object in view.

	Per annum. R
25 Copyists, at R20 per month . . .	6,000
Stationery, R100 per month . . .	1,200

	Per annum. R
Tour expenses,—(1) North-Western Provinces and Punjab, (2) Oudh and Central Provinces, (3) Rajputana, (4) Bombay, (5) Madras and Mysore, and (6) Bengal, at R 1,000 each . . .	6,000
Purchase of MSS. . . .	6,000
Printing Native catalogues and lists of desirable MSS.	1,000
Additional grant to Asiatic Society of Bengal . .	3,000
Sundries	800
Total per annum .	24,000

His Excellency in Council, therefore, accords his general approval to the scheme, and requests that the Secretary in the Home Department will, in communication with Mr. Stokes, draw up such further instructions as may be necessary for carrying it out.

ORDER.—Ordered, that copy of this Resolution, and of the papers referred to, be forwarded to the Governments of Madras, Bombay, Bengal, North-Western Provinces, and Punjab; the Chief Commissioners of Oudh and Central Provinces; and the Commissioners of Mysore and Coorg.

Ordered also, that a copy of this Resolution, and of the papers referred to, be forwarded to the Financial Department and to the Asiatic Society of Bengal.

Ordered further, that a copy of this Resolution, and of the papers referred to, be forwarded to the Foreign Department for communication to the Political Officers under its control.

From A. P. HOWELL, Esq., Officiating Secretary to the Government of India, Home Department, to the Secretaries to the Governments of Madras, Bombay, North-Western Provinces, Punjab, and Bengal; to the Chief Commissioners of Oudh and the Central Provinces,—Nos. 4349 to 4355, dated Simla, the 3rd November 1868.

I AM directed to forward copy of a Resolution this day recorded by the Governor-General in Council, in regard to the discovery and preservation of the records of ancient Sanskrit literature. His Excellency in Council has no doubt that the object in view will enlist $\frac{\text{the}}{\text{your}}$ zealous co-operation of $\frac{\text{the Governor in Council}}{\text{the Lieutenant-Governor}}$, and that among the servants of Government and other gentlemen in *, European and Native, several will be found able and willing to assist in its attainment.

* Madras, Bombay, N.-W. Provs. | Punjab, Bengal, Oudh, Central Provs.

The circumstances of each province differ so materially, that it is expedient only to lay down such general rules as may serve to secure the necessary degree of uniform and concerted action.

2. All procurable unprinted lists of Sanskrit MSS. in the Native libraries, situate within the territories under * , should be printed uniformly in octavo, in the Nágarí character, and under the superintendence of a competent editor, such as Bábu Rájendralála Mitra in Bengal, Mr. Burnell in Madras, and Dr. Bühler in Bombay. Fifty copies of each list so printed will be sent to the Government of India in the Home Department, and the remainder of the edition (which need not exceed 150 copies) may be sold to the public, or otherwise disposed of as the Local Government or Administration thinks fit.

* Madras, Bombay — the Government of; N.-W. Provs., Bengal, Punjab, Oudh, Central Provs. — your Administration.

3. Competent scholars should be sent annually on tours to examine the MSS. named in the Native catalogues so printed, to seek new MSS. (especially those named in the lists of desiderata hereinafter mentioned), to explain to Native scholars at the different places visited the objects and importance of the mission, to purchase such MSS. as the possessors are willing to sell at a reasonable rate, and to employ copyists to transcribe codices which are unique, extremely old, or otherwise desirable, but which the possessors refuse to part with. The gentlemen sent on tours will make reports to their respective Local Governments, and such reports will be transmitted to the Government of India in the Home Department. The annual expense of the several tours should be so arranged as not to exceed, in the case of each Local Government and Administration, the amount marginally noted.

	R
Bengal (L. P.)	1,000
Bombay	1,000
Madras and Mysore	1,000
N.-W. Provinces	500
Punjab	500
Oudh	500
Central Provinces	500
Rajputana	1,000

NOTE.—The officer sent by Madras will extend his researches to Mysore. The Governor-General's Agent will administer the sum appropriated for tours in Rajputana.

4. Scholars both in India and in Europe will be invited to transmit lists of desiderata. Those in Europe will be requested to communicate with the Government of India through the Secretary of State; those in India, through the Local Governments. From the suggestions so received, general lists of desiderata will be prepared and circulated annually, and the notice of Local Governments and Administrations will be drawn to entries in the catalogues received from them which seem to refer to any work in the lists of desiderata.

5. Subjoined is a specimen form in which, as far as possible, notices of MSS. ascertained to exist may be prepared. Quarterly lists of the MSS.

found during the previous quarter will be submitted in this form to the Government of India in the Home Department.

6. Local Governments and Administrations will use their discretion in purchasing or having copies made of the MSS. existing within their jurisdiction. His Excellency in Council would, however, suggest the desirability of bearing in mind the subjects which European scholars deem most valuable, and that MSS. of the Vedas and Vedáṅgas, and of their commentaries, law-books, grammars, vocabularies, and philosophical treatises, should be regarded as of primary importance. When transcripts are made, these should be in the modern Devanágarí character. Copies of the Sanskṛit MSS. existing in Southern India, if made in the Telugu or other Drávidian character, would be of little use to European Sanskṛitists and to the large majority of Native scholars.

7. The annual outlay in purchasing and transcribing MSS. should not exceed, in the case of each Local Government and Administration, the amount marginally noted. But if a valuable library be offered for sale, if any rare and rapidly perishing MSS. be available for transcription, or if there be any other ground for incurring extra expenditure, the local authorities should state the facts of the case to the Government of India, which will be ready to sanction any reasonable proposal in this behalf.

	Purchase. R	Transcription. R
Bengal (L. P.)	1,000	1,200
Bombay	1,000	1,200
Madras and Mysore	1,000	1,200
N.-W. Provinces	500	600
Punjab	500	600
Oudh	500	600
Central Provinces	500	600
Rajputana	1,000	1,200

NOTE.—The sum allotted to Madras and Mysore will be expended under the direction of the Madras Government. That allotted to Rajputana will be expended under the direction of the Governor-General's Agent.

8. The original MSS. and transcripts so obtained should be carefully preserved apart in the office of the Secretariat of each Government and Administration, pending the arrangements which may be made in each case for their ultimate disposal. Such arrangements will, from time to time, be communicated through the Government of India in the Home Department. Quarterly lists of the MSS. remaining undisposed of will be forwarded to the Government of India by each Local Government.

No. 4356.

COPY to Foreign Department, with request that, if there is no objection in that Department, orders to the above effect may be communicated to the Agent of the Governor-General, Rajputana.

No.	Name of MSS. in modern Devanágarí.	Name transliterated in Roman character.	Subject-matter and name of Author.	No. of pages.	No. of lines in each page.	Substance on which written, and character.	Where deposited and in whose possession.	REMARKS.
		Vikramorvaśí...	Urvaśí, gained by heroism. A drama by Kálidása.	80	24	Palm-leaf; in old Canarese character.	Temple in Conjeeveram; in the possession of the High Priest.	This MS. the High Priest refuses to sell. It is reported to be very ancient, and is said to have been copied direct from the original MS. of the author. The High Priest has consented to allow a copy to be made under his own inspection, and this is being done in the Devanágarí character.

Reported to the Right Hon'ble the Secretary of State for India, in letter No. 162 of 1868, dated the 5th December.

From Bábu Rájendralála Mitra, to Captain J. Waterhouse, B.S.C., Secretary to the Asiatic Society of Bengal,—No. 47, dated Calcutta, the 15th February 1875.

I have the honour to submit the following report on the operations carried on by me to the close of 1874 for collecting information regarding Sanskṛit manuscripts in Native libraries.

2. *Objects of the enquiry.*—Under the orders of Government, my attention has been steadily directed—*1st*, to enquire and collect information regarding rare and valuable manuscripts; *2nd*, to compile lists thereof; *3rd*, to print all procurable unprinted lists of such codices, with brief notices of their contents; *4th*, to purchase, or secure copies of, such of them as are rare or otherwise desirable.

3. *Enquiry for MSS.: Places visited.*—The work under the first head has been mainly conducted by a Pandit, who has been deputed to the Mufassil to visit the different private Ṭols or Sanskṛit colleges and private gentlemen who are reputed to possess collections of Sanskṛit MSS.; and I have been out on several occasions to help him. I have also been to Benares on three occasions to enquire for and purchase MSS. The places visited by the Pandit include the districts of Dacca, Nadiyá, Bardhwan, Hoogly, and 24-Pergunnahs. The large collections of Rájá Yatíndramohan Thákúr, of the late Sir Rájá Rádhákánt Dev, of the late Bábu Rámkomal Sen, of the late Rájá Pítámbar Mitra, of Bábu Subaldása Mallik, and of others in Calcutta, have also been examined. In Dacca Pandits are the only owners of MSS., no private gentlemen having anything like a large collection, and the few works they have being mostly such as have already been printed. In Nadiyá the library of the Rájá of Kṛishṇanagar contains the largest number of Tantras; but at the time when my Pandit visited it the MSS. were kept in a very neglected state, and most of them were found to be defective. In Bardhwan there are not many Ṭols, but Bábu Hitalál Miśra of Mánakara has a very choice collection of works, including a great number of very rare treatises on the Vedánta. In Hoogly the Serampur College has a small, but valuable, collection of MSS., procured principally by the late Dr. Carey, and there are also a few Ṭols owning MSS. In the 24-Pergunnahs several zemindars have good collections of the Tantras and the Puráṇas; and the numerous Ṭols on the left bank of the River Hoogly, and at Harinábhi and elsewhere, contain many old and rare works of which very little is known to European Orientalists. There are no Maths (monasteries) in any of the districts named which contain a collection of Sanskṛit

works: not even the Maṭh attached to the great temple of Tárakeśvara in the Hoogly district is noted for its literary treasures. The case is, however, different in Rájsháhi, Maimansing, Pabna, Tirhút, and Orissa, where some of the Maṭhs own large collections of great age and considerable value.

4. *Substance of MSS.: Paper.*—The manuscripts examined are mostly written on country paper, sized with yellow arsenic and an emulsion of tamarind seeds, and then polished by rubbing with a conch-shell. A few are on white Kaśmírí paper, and some on palm-leaf. White arsenic is rarely used for the size, but I have seen a few codices sized with it, the mucilage employed in such cases being acacia gum. The surface of ordinary country paper being rough, a thick coating of size is necessary for easy writing, and the tamarind-seed emulsion affords this admirably. The paper used for ordinary writing is sized with rice-gruel, but such paper attracts damp and vermin of all kinds, and that great pest of literature the "silver-fish" thrives luxuriantly on it. The object of the arsenic is to keep off this insect, and it serves the purpose most effectually. No insect or worm of any kind will attack arsenicised paper, and so far the MSS. are perfectly secure against its ravages. The superior appearance and cheapness of European paper has of late induced many persons to use it, instead of the country arsenicised paper, in writing *pothís;* but this is a great mistake, as the latter is not nearly so durable as the former, and is liable to be rapidly destroyed by insects. I cannot better illustrate this than by referring to some of the MSS. in the library of the Asiatic Society. There are among them several volumes written on foolscap paper which date from 1820 to 1830, and they already look decayed, mouldering, and touched in several places by silver fish. Others on John-letter paper, which is thicker, larger, and stouter, are already so far injured, that the ink has quite faded and become in many places illegible; whereas the MSS. which were originally copied on arsenicised paper for the College of Fort William in the first decade of this century, are now quite as fresh as they were when first written. I have seen many MSS. in private collections which are much older and still quite as fresh. This fact would suggest the propriety of Government records in Mufassil Courts being written on arsenicised paper, instead of the ordinary English foolscap, which is so rapidly destroyed both by the climate and also by white-ants. To guard against mistakes, I should add here that the ordinary yellow paper sold in the bazars is dyed with turmeric, and is not at all proof against the attack of insects.

5. *History of paper.*—It is well known that originally the Hindus used leaves of trees for writing upon, whence the name of letters in Sanskṛit has become *pattra,* and latterly newspapers have been designated by the same name. The oldest manuscript on paper I have seen is a copy of the Bhágavatapuráṇa, now in the possession of Bábu Hariśchandra of Benares. It bears date Saṃvat 1367 = A.C. 1310, and is consequently 565 years old. Its paper is of a very good quality; and judging from it, it is to be inferred that the people of the country must have, at the time when it was written, attained considerable proficiency in paper-making. Long before that time, in the reign of Bhoja Rájá of Dhárá, a work was written on letter-writing (the *Praśastiprakáśiká),* and in it detailed directions are given for folding the material of letters, for leaving a large space on the left side of such letters as margin, for cutting a portion of the left lower corner, for decorating the front with gold-leaf, for writing the word 'Śrí' a number of times on the back, &c., &c.—all which apply to paper, and cannot possibly be practicable on palm-leaf; and the inference therefore becomes inevitable, that paper was then well-known and in general use, though the word used to indicate it was *pattra,* probably very much in the same way as paper of the present day owes its name to papyrus. Again, a verse occurs in the Saṃhitá of Vyása, which must be at least two thousand years old, in which it is said "that the first draft of a document should be written on a wooden tablet, or on the ground, and after correction of what is redundant and supplying what is defective, it should be engrossed on *pattra;*" and it would be absurd to suppose that *pattra* here means leaf, for leaves were so cheap, that it would have been a folly to save them by writing on wooden tablets, which were much more costly. How long before the time of this verse paper was known, I have no positive evidence to shew; but the frequent mention in the old Smṛitis of legal documents *(lekhya),* of their attestation by witnesses, of their validity, &c., suggests the idea of there having been extant in olden times some material more substantial and convenient than palm-leaf for writing; and knowing that paper was first manufactured by the Chinese, long before the commencement of the Christian era, that the famous *charta bombycina* of Europe was imported from the East, and that block-printing was extensively practised in Tibet in the fourth century, I am disposed to believe that the Hindus must have known the art of paper-making from a very early date. Whether they originated it, or got it from the Chinese through the Tibetans, or the Kaśmírís, who have been noted for their proficiency in

the art of making paper and papier-mâché ware, is a question which must await further research for solution. *A priori* it may be argued that those who manipulated cotton so successfully as to convert it into the finest fabric known to man, would find no difficulty in manufacturing paper out of it.

6. *Palm-leaf.*—The palm-leaf referred to above is not now much in use, except in Orissa, and in the Mufassil vernacular schools, as a substitute for slates. In Bengal the Chaṇḍí is the only work which is now-a-days written on palm-leaf, as there is a prejudice against the formal reading of that work from paper MSS.—a prejudice in many respects similar to what obtained in Europe against printed Bibles in the first century after the introduction of printing. Formerly two kinds of palm-leaf were in use: one formed of the thick, strong-fibred leaflets of the *Corypha taliera (tiret),* and the other of the *Borassus flabelliformis (tálapátá).* The former is generally preferred for writing Sanskṛit works, as it is broader and more durable than the latter, and many MSS. are still extant which reckon their ages by five to six hundred years. The leaflet of the *Corypha elata* is sometimes used in lieu of those of the *taliera.* The leaflets of all the three kinds of palms are first dried, then boiled or kept steeped in water for some time; then dried again, cut into the required size, and polished with a smooth stone or a conch-shell. For school use no such preparation is necessary.

7. *Bark.*—The practice of writing on bark is of the greatest antiquity, and, from constant use, the Greek and the Latin terms for that substance,—*biblos* and *liber,*—have long since become the names for books, even as the name of the rolls of ancient parchment MSS. produced the term *volume,* and codes of laws have received their generic name from the bundles of boards on which they were written,—from *codex,* a tablet of wood. In the eastern districts this practice of writing on bark still prevails, and I have seen several codices of bark which formed thin sheets like veneer, eighteen inches by four; but I have not been able to ascertain from what species of tree the article had been obtained. Some say that the tree called *ugra (Morunga hyperanthera)* yields the best bark for writing upon; but I have not seen it. The birch bark, Bhúrjapattra *(Betula bhurja),* is extensively used as a material for writing upon; but only for amulets, it being too thin and fragile for books. I have by me a piece of this bark about a hundred years old, which, on a space of ten inches by eight, contains the whole of the Bhagavadgítá, written with letters so small that they are illegible to the naked eye, and require a magnifying glass to be read. It was evi-

dently intended to be worn as an amulet enclosed in a locket of gold or copper, but it had never been so used. Whether the *bhúrj* bark was ever pasted or glued into thick sheets I cannot say.

8. *Wood, metal, and skin.*—In the Śástras tablets of wood and metal have been recommended as materials for writing upon, and in former times copper-plates were usually employed for royal patents, and in Burmah they are still occasionally used for writing large works; but I have seen none now used by the Pandits of Bengal. Wooden tablets are confined to petty traders' account-books in Bengal; but in the North-Western Provinces poor people have some religious books written with chalk on blackened boards. In the Lalitavistara, or 'Legendary Life of Buddha,' mention is made of sandal-wood boards which were handed to Śákya when he first commenced to write. In Europe parchment and dressed skins of goats have been from time immemorial used as materials for books, and for durability they stand unrivalled; but I have never seen mention in Indian works of parchment, or dressed skin of any kind, as material for writing; and palimpsests are, of course, unknown.

9. *Pens.*—According to the Yoginſtantra, bamboo twigs and bronze styles are unfortunate, and gold and reeds are the best for pens; but the universal practice among the Pandits of Bengal is to use the bamboo twig for pens, and only rich householders employ the *vrinnala* or *khákrá* reed. In the North-Western Provinces the reed or calamus, whence the Indian word *kalama*, is generally used, and bamboo pens are all but unknown. The latter however, when well-prepared, is much more elastic and durable, and it has the further and supreme advantage of being everywhere procurable without any cost. Crow-quills were formerly used for writing very small characters for amulets, but never for ordinary manuscripts. In Orissa, where letters are scratched, and not written, on palm-leaves, an iron style with a pointed end and a flat top everywhere replaces the bamboo twig and the calamus reed.

10. *Ordinary ink.*—The ink used for writing *pothís* is of two kinds: one fit for paper, and the other for palm-leaves. The former is made by mixing a coffee-coloured infusion of roasted rice with lamp-black, and then adding to it a little sugar, and sometimes the juice of a plant called *kesurte (Verbesina scandens)*. The labour of making this ink is great, as it requires several days' continued trituration in a mortar before the lamp-black can be thoroughly mixed with the rice infusion, and want of sufficient trituration causes the lamp-black to settle down in a paste, leav-

ing the infusion on top unfit for writing with. Occasionally acacia gum is added to give a gloss to the ink; but this practice is not common, sugar being held sufficient for the purpose. Of late, an infusion of the emblic myrobalan, prepared in an iron pot, has occasionally been added to the ink; but the tannate and gallate of iron formed in the course of preparing this infusion are injurious to the texture of paper, and Persian MSS., sometimes written with such ink, suffer much from the chemical action of the metallic salts.

The ink for palm-leaf consists of the juice of the *kesurte,* mixed with a decoction of *áltá*. It is highly esteemed, as it sinks into the substance of the leaf and cannot be washed off. Both the inks are very lasting, and being perfectly free from mineral substances and strong acids, do not in any way injure the substance of the paper or leaf to which they are applied. They never fade, and retain their gloss for centuries.

11. *Coloured ink.*—To mark the ends of chapters, and for writing rubrics, colophons, and important words on paper, an ink made of cinnabar, or *áltá*, is sometimes used; and in correcting errors the usual practice is to apply on the wrong letters a colour made of yellow or red orpiment ground in gum-water, and, when it is dry, to write over it. Omissions of entire words and sentences, of course, cannot be rectified in this way, and they have therefore to be supplied by writing on the margin. Interlineation is generally avoided; but in old MSS., which have been read and revised by several generations, they are not altogether wanting. In commentaries the quotations from texts are generally smeared over with a little red ochre, which produces the same effect which red letters in European MSS. were intended to subserve; whence the term 'rubric' got into currency. These peculiarities, however, are more prominent in the MSS. of the North-Western Provinces than in those of Bengal, and in palm-leaf codices they are generally wanting, except in Burmah, where some sacred Pálí works are written with a thick black varnish on palm-leaves, throughout richly gilt, and wrought over with scrolls and other ornaments. Ordinary Burmese MSS. have the edges of the leaves painted and sometimes gilt.

12. *Illustrations.*—Illustrations are almost unknown in Bengal, but in Orissa they are frequently employed. The most noted place, however, for illustrations is Kaśmír, and the finest and richest MSS. are usually produced in that province, the illuminations consisting of flowery initials, grotesque cyphers, single figures, historical compositions, marginal lines, and scroll borders: most of the illustrations are in the Moorish style.

13. *Size, &c., of paper MSS.*—The size of paper MSS. varies from eight to twenty inches by four to eight inches. The paper is folded so as to mark the margins and regulate the straightness of the lines. In the North-Western Provinces the paper is sometimes so folded as to retain two leaves together; but in Bengal it is always cut into separate and distinct folia. Sometimes a board mounted with strong thread, tied at equal distances, is used for a ruler. The paper is laid flat on this board, and then pressed hard with a ball of cloth, whereby it receives an impression of the threads on its surface, and these impressions look very like waterlines. The leaves are written over lengthwise, leaving a uniform margin all round. The words are generally, but not always, separated by small spaces, and for punctuation the upright stroke, or *dándi,* is freely used. No breaks are made to indicate the ends of paragraphs or sections; and should the writing at the end of a work terminate in the middle of a line, the line is filled up by writing the letter *śrí,* or stars, or the name of some god several times, until the line is completed, so that all the lines may be of uniform length. In the case of codices which contain both a text and a commentary, the text is written in large letters in the middle, and the commentary above and below it in smaller letters. This arrangement is called the *trivalli* form, and some tact is necessary in engrossing it, so that all the commentary on the given text may be comprised on the same page. The copyist's name is frequently given at the end, and also the date in Śáka or Saṃvat—rarely in Jupiter's cycles. The name of the place where the copy is made, and that of the party for whom it is made, are also occasionally given, but never the name of the reigning sovereign. A protestation sometimes occurs at the end, saying that the copyist has faithfully followed his text and is not responsible for errors.

14. Size, &c., of palm-leaf MSS.—Palm-leaf MSS. are, from the nature of the material, narrower and longer, and they are never ruled or folded, the veins of the leaf serving the purpose of ruling. A square space is usually left blank in the middle of the page, and in the centre of it a round hole is punched for a string to pass through, for the purpose of tying the codex in a bundle. Very long MSS. have two such spaces and holes. The Tantras enjoin that the holes should always be punched—never cut with a knife, or produced by burning. The reason for this rule is obvious, as cutting or burning produces a hole with jagged sides, which are very apt to catch the string and cause a split in the leaf. A clean, punched hole allows the string to slide freely, and produces no injury. In Bengal some very old paper codices have the square blank space in the middle, but none has any hole bored in it. In the North-Western Provinces the blank space does not occur, and both in Bengal and the North-West the leaves are piled in a bundle between two boards, and then tied round in a piece of coarse cloth. Where the codices are small, with a view to economy several of them are usually tied in one bundle, and this causes much trouble in finding out any particular work when needed. For boards the spatha of the betel-nut tree, which yields a thick, coreaceous, pliant substance, is often substituted in the eastern districts, and they are found to be very useful, as they are not liable to warp, crack, or be attacked by insects.

15. Mode of preserving MSS.—In the houses of rich men a dry masonry room is generally assigned to MSS., where a sufficient number of shelves or chests are provided for the storage of the codices. But care is not always taken to open the bundles every now and then, and to expose them to the sun for a few hours. In pakká monasteries, the same mode of preservation is also adopted; and there being always some monk or other who can read, and who takes a delight in reading, the bundles are more frequently opened, aired, and dried. The Jains are very particular in this respect, and in their monasteries great care is usually taken of their literary treasures. The case is, however, very different as regards the Ṭols of Bengal. The men who own them are, with rare exceptions, very poor; they live in low, damp, thatched huts of the meanest description; they have no means of buying proper cabinets for their manuscripts; and their time is so occupied by their professorial duties, and frequent peregrinations to distant places for earning the means of their livelihood, that they cannot often look after their books. The receptacle they usually assign to their MSS. is a bamboo frame placed across the beams of their huts, exposed constantly to the damp emanating from the daily-washed mud floors of their rooms, and occasionally to leakage from ill-made and old thatched roofs; while mice and other vermin have full and free access to them at all times. The mice are particularly destructive, as they not only gnaw cloth, boards, and palm-leaves, but, by their liquid discharges, rapidly destroy the texture of arsenicised paper. The fact was first brought to my notice by a mukhtiyár when I was a boy. He asked my permission to put two sheets of fresh-looking, written, stamped paper for a night on the bottom of a cage of white mice, which were my pets. The permission was granted, and the next morning the papers were taken out, stained and decayed very like old documents, which they were. I then learnt, intended to pass for. I was also told and shewn that by careful and repeated washing with a mixture of the fluid discharge of mice with water, paper can be made to assume the appearance of any age that may be desired: the effect produced is not confined to the surface, but is perceptible even in the texture of the paper.

16. Copyists and copying.—Even as in mediæval Europe monks were the principal copyists of ancient works, so have their congeners been the principal preservers of Sanskṛit literature in India during the last ten or fifteen hundred years. Yatis, Sannyásís, Gosáins, and their disciples congregated in large Maṭhs, devoted all their leisure-hours,—the former to composing, and the latter to copying; and the monasteries benefited largely by their labours. In the Ṭols the pupils were, and still are, the principal copyists. In return for the board, lodging, and education they receive, free of all charge, from their tutors, they copy all such works as their tutors require, and thus the Ṭols are enriched. For the public, however, the principal copyists are the Káyasthas. Old and used-up men of this caste, when no longer fit to earn their livelihood by active exertion, generally betake to copying ancient works for householders and private gentlemen, and the bulk of the MSS. now extant are due to their labours. Poor Bráhmans also take to this occupation. Seated on their haunches, with the paper or palm-leaf resting on their raised knees, which serve for a table, and the pen and ink procured from materials everywhere available, they ply their vocation without making any outlay, or subjecting themselves to any exertion which would be unsuited to their habits and time of life. The remuneration they formerly derived ranged from one rupee to two rupees eight annas per thousand *ślokas* of thirty-two thousand letters, according to the quality of writing. The rates have now been doubled, owing principally to the demand for copyists being limited, and very few taking to the profession. As a class these copyists are men of limited literary knowledge; but generally speaking they are faithful to their duty, and reproduce the originals placed before them with fair accuracy.

17. Authenticity of MSS.—They rarely attempt to correct the errors and mistakes of the originals, and, to exonerate themselves from all charge of tampering the originals, they not unoften put a verse at the end of their works, saying, "As he has seen, so has he copied, and the copyist should not be blamed for mistakes." Clerical errors they are certainly liable to, and do commit; but such errors are not numerous. One serious mistake they, however, sometimes commit,—it is that of copying in the body of the text notes and parallel or remarkable passages, which often occur on the margins of old and frequently-read codices; and these consequently appear as parts of the texts in their works, and subsequent copying from their codices perpetuates the interpolation. This is, however, done through ignorance, and not through any wicked motive. Of fabrications and forgeries the Máhátmyas and local legends afford ready instances; but they are due to Pandits, and not to copyists. Corrections made by Pandits when reading are necessarily perpetuated by copyists, and to them are principally due the numerous *variæ lectiones* which are to be met with in Sanskṛit writings. This evil has been of late greatly multiplied by incompetent editors, who print texts from solitary MSS., and replace doubtful readings and fill up lacunæ by imaginary emendations. With a few praiseworthy exceptions the publications of the Bengali and Benares presses belong to this class, and they are much less trustworthy than even corrupt MSS. The plasticity of the Sanskṛit language admits of even obviously incorrect readings being explained somehow, and the authenticity of the originals is thereby irretrievably ruined. The errors of MSS. may be corrected by collation, for, though there are many faulty MSS., I have every reason to doubt that there are many falsified texts; but the fabrications in printed books issued by thousands cannot be readily detected and exposed.

With so many causes at work to injure the authenticity of ancient Sanskṛit works, and at a time when European Orientalists are so busily employed in tracing interpolations and corruptions which have already taken place, it would be futile to attempt in a report like this to enquire at length how far the charge may be sustained; but this much may be said, that the MSS. now extant do not shew any sign of dishonest fabrication; codices from three to four hundred years old, existing in different parts of India,—in Bengal, Madras, Bombay, and Kaśmír,—are so closely similar in their readings that they produce no suspicion in the mind of their having been tampered with. What happened before that time it is not necessary for me to guess; suffice it to say in the language of Isaac Taylor, that "the habitudes of eastern nations undergo so little change in the lapse of ages that probably these descriptions of things as they are now would differ little from a similarly graphic account of the same operations dated a thousand years back. Where the arts of life remain in their rude state, all those operations which depend upon them continue nearly the same."

18. *Age of MSS.*—The oldest palm-leaf manuscript I have seen bears date Saṃvat 1189 = A.C. 1132, and the oldest paper manuscript, as aforesaid, is Saṃvat 1367 = A.C. 1310; but such records are exceedingly rare, and the general run is from 150 to 250 years. Among old MSS. taken to Europe, Dr. Weber in his invaluable catalogue of the Berlin Collection notices several codices ranging from four to six hundred years. Seeing that *Charta bombycina* has lasted in Europe for eight to twelve hundred years, this age, for works which claim to be from two thousand to three thousand five hundred years old, is very unsatisfactory; but the climate of Bengal, and the manner of keeping MSS. here, as above described, are highly unfavourable to their preservation for a long time,—not to advert to the wholesale destruction of MSS. in large Maṭhs and richly endowed temples, which must have resulted from the ravages of those whose co-religionists burnt the Alexandrine Library. Indeed, it is not remarkable that old MSS. are so rare, but that, notwithstanding such potent influences constantly at work, there should still exist in the country so many and such old MSS. as have been from time to time met with. A new influence is now at work for the destruction of MSS. The halo of sanctity which formerly surrounded Sanskṛit literature is fast fading away: the ancient Hindu religion is gradually losing its hold on men's minds; Sanskṛit is no longer a paying study; European literature is rapidly replacing it everywhere; the venerable old Pandits,—the repositories of traditional and book knowledge of ages, whose erudition was the profoundest, to whom no modern scholar, European or Asiatic, can for a moment be compared, and who have hitherto preserved with such unflinching zeal the oldest literary monuments of the Aryan race,—are rapidly dying out, and their places are not being supplied by the rising generation. For hundreds who formerly studied Sanskṛit we have now scores; and there being little demand, very few new MSS. are being prepared to take the place of those which are crumbling down by age. Many works of great literary value and age have already disappeared, and others are in imminent risk, and, unless timely saved, will in half a century more be irreparably lost.

19. *Accessibility of MSS.*—Generally speaking, the heads of Ṭols are the only persons who have really old and scarce works. They know the value and history of the several works on particular branches of Sanskṛit learning to which they severally devote their attention, and each tries his utmost to secure copies of all the leading and rare works bearing upon the subject of his study. It also often happens that the son takes

up the subject in which his father was most proficient, and in some families for many successive generations the same subject has been studied, and the works collected by them are generally very correct and complete. But the worthy professors, deeply learned as they are, are not open to worldly influence, and are extremely shy and suspicious. In their estimation the most valued treasures they possess are their MSS., and they evince the greatest reluctance to shew them to strangers. Ordinarily, they do not flatly refuse access to their stores, though some do so; but the passive resistance they offer is often insurmountable. The first day's visit is generally passed in conversation; on the second day a few of the commonest works are shewn; on the third the proprietor is busy with other duties and has no time to bring out MSS.; on the fourth day he is not at home; and so on. Several days are lost before a really good MS. is brought to light; and as my plan requires the copying of the initial and final lines, and an abstract of the contents, a great deal of valuable time is lost before a single collection is finally examined; and before this consummation can take place, it often happens that the owner of the MSS. is called away by a distant invitation or some other errand, and my travelling Pandit's work is brought to a stop. No possessor of a Ṭol has any catalogue or list of his MSS., and if by dint of repeating the names of a great number of rare works, the owner is made to acknowledge he has a particular work, very little advance is made towards getting access to it, for the bundles in which MSS. are kept are not numbered; and as from six to twenty different works find place in each bundle, the task of finding it out takes days, if it be forthcoming, which is not always the case.

In the houses of private gentlemen access is readily given; but when visits have to be repeated for days, the party in charge of the library offers much passive resistance, and a great deal of time is lost to meet his convenience.

If I could satisfy myself with bare names, the work could advance more expeditiously; but as a work of this kind can only be done once, I think that it is better to lose some time than to produce a result which cannot be satisfactory to scholars. It is not at all likely that an undertaking of this nature will be attempted a second time.

20. *Lists of rare works.*—With a view to help the travelling Pandit, I have printed two lists of very rare MSS., for which he makes enquiries at every Ṭol. Copies of these lists have also been sent through the Director of Public Instruction to the heads of all the schools under his control; but as yet no satisfactory return has been obtained.

21. *Compilation of a general list or inventory.*—The work under the second head of my enquiry has been conducted by me with the assistance of a Pandit and a writer. The lists procured by the travelling Pandit, and by me through friends and correspondents, are regularly entered alphabetically in a large book, writing only the names of the MSS., their subjects, and the names of their owners. This book, when completed, will be an inventory of all the Sanskṛit MSS. of value extant in Bengal. A compilation is next made from this record of all works which require to be noticed in detail, and the descriptive accounts are then written out in full.

22. *Publication of Notices.*—At first I was under an impression that separate lists of particular collections would be the best, as suggested in the orders of Government; but I soon perceived that it involved much unnecessary trouble and expense, and caused the repetition of the same names a great number of times. So it had to be given up. The nominal list referred to in the last preceding paragraph will, I think, when completed and published, supply the information fully and in a handy form.

In the meantime my attention has been devoted to detailed notices of all works not included in the catalogue of the Asiatic Society's collection. Of these "Notices," two volumes and one part have already been published, comprising altogether 861 pages royal octavo, and descriptive accounts of 1,140 separate codices. For the sake of carrying on the printing while my researches are in progress, no systematic arrangement is attempted, and manuscripts are noticed as they turn up. The inconvenience arising from this course is, however, obviated by annexing to each volume a classified table, and a full alphabetical index.

23. *Contents of the Notices.*—The number of Vedic works or portions of the Vedas in the published Notices is limited, and all of them have been seen or obtained at Benares, not a single codex having been seen in the possession of a Pandit of Bengal in the several Ṭols which have been visited. This total absence of the most important and most revered of Sanskṛit works in the libraries of those who have been the principal custodians of Sanskṛit literature is a remarkable fact, and it is usually accounted for by the Pandits by reference to a verse of the Yoginítantra which says: "Whoever keeps MSS. of the Vedas in his home soon finds his abode struck by lightning." The verse is obviously due to the sectarian zeal of the Tantra, which would admit of no rival in its neighbourhood; but the true cause, I believe, is that Bengal has never been the seat of a Vedic school, and consequently it has never been taught here, nor MSS. prepared

or preserved. It is said that when, on the overthrow of the Pála Rájás, A'disúra, the Hindu sovereign of Bengal, wanted to celebrate a great Vedic sacrifice, he could find no native Bráhman competent to officiate at it, and had to indent for five learned priests from Kanauj. These priests settled in the country, and gave new life to Hinduism everywhere; and many of their descendants have been noted as great scholars and distinguished authors; but they do not seem to have cultivated the Vedas, and there is not a single treatise on the Vedas or Vedic learning among their writings. Their special *forte* has been philosophy, and works on the subject are abundant everywhere. The Nyáya schools of Tirhút and Nadiyá have enjoyed deserved celebrity all over India, and every Pandit of any note has some work or other on the subject not common elsewhere. Works on the Vedánta are also numerous. The former class is represented in the published Notices by 98 treatises, and the latter by 67 codices. The Upanishads, as bearing on the Vedánta, are represented by 92 works. The Tantras come next to Nyáya; Bengal is particularly noted for them, and of them I have noticed 205 works, or parts of works. In my last report I have already given an account of the nature and character of this class of works. Grammar, Lexicography, Rhetoric, and other branches of Sanskrit learning are also fairly represented in my Notices, as will be evident from the following classified list:—

I. Vedaśástra—	
a. *Saṃhitá* (Hymns)	2
b. *Bráhmaṇa* (Ceremonials)	9
c. *A'raṇyaka* (Ditto appropriate for forest-life)	2
d. *Upanishad* (Theology)	92
e. *Vaidika* (Sútras, Rituals, Phonetics, &c.)	100
II. Aitihásikaśástra—	
a. *Itihása* (History)	15
b. *Puráṇa* (Ancient legends)	40
III. Kávyaśástra—	
a. *Kávya* (Poems)	68
b. *Náṭaka* (Drama)	14
c. *Champú* (Poetico-prose compositions)	8
d. *Kosha* (Miscellaneous poetical collections)	60
e. *Upákhyána* (Tales and romances)	16
IV. Abhidhánaśástra (Lexicography)	30
V. Vyákaraṇaśástra (Grammar)	29
VI. Chhandasśástra (Versification)	7
VII. Alankáraśástra (Rhetoric)	6
VIII. Jyotishaśástra (Astronomy and Astrology)	61
IX. Smṛitiśástra (Law, Civil and Canonical)	164
X. Sangítaśástra (Music)	5
XI. Śilpaśástra (Art)	3
XII. Kámaśástra (Erotics)	2
XIII. Darśanaśástra (Philosophy)—	
a. *Sáṅkhya* (Hylotheistic)	1
b. *Nyáya* (Dialectic)	98

c. Vaiśeshika (Physical) .	0	XV. Tantraśástra (Mysticism) .	205
d. Mímánsá (Ritualistic) .	3	XVI. Vaidyaka (Medical science)	44
e. Vedánta (Monotheistic) .	67	XVII. Jainaśástra (Jaina religion) .	7
f. Yoga (Theocratic) . .	13	XVIII. Bauddhaśástra (Buddhist religion)	0
g. Aparadárśanika (Minor systems of Philosophy)	2	XIX. Anirdishṭa (Miscellaneous) .	7
XIV. Bhaktiśástra (Faith) . .	21	Total . .	1,140

It should be noted that in making my selections I have been guided by a desire to exclude all works existing in the library of the Asiatic Society of Bengal, a descriptive catalogue of which is now in the press, and it is not desirable that the same works should be twice noticed. My work will, in conjunction with the catalogue of the Calcutta Sanskṛit College and of the Asiatic Society, constitute a complete record of the bulk of the Sanskṛit literature extant in Bengal; and as all the three works are being printed at the cost of Government, they may well be taken to be parts of one undertaking.

24. *Facsimiles.*—At the suggestion of Mr. Burnell of Mangalore, I have introduced in the last two fasciculi facsimiles of some of the more ancient and important MSS. noticed. When a sufficient number of these illustrations has been published, they will prove of much use in determining the age of manuscripts from the style of their writing, and as contributions to a knowledge of Indian palæography.

25. *Oudh catalogue.*—While carrying my Notices through the press, I have been also engaged in editing a catalogue of Sanskṛit MSS. existing in Oudh. Four fasciculi of this work have already been published.

26. *Purchase of MSS.*—Manuscripts are not marketable articles, as they do not readily find purchasers; the people at large look upon them as worthless, and consequently there are no shops in Bengal for the sale of MSS., while the Pandits of the province, who are the principal owners of MSS., look upon them as treasures of inestimable value, never to be parted with on any account. I have, therefore, found the greatest difficulty in buying MSS. in Bengal. The case is different at Benares. From all parts of India, Pandits at an advanced age, leaving everything behind them except their MSS., repair to that sacred place to die, and on their demise hawkers purchase their stocks for a trifle, and subsequently sell them to pilgrims and others at a considerable profit; and my purchases have been made principally from these hawkers. The total of my acquisitions on account of

Government comprises 656 codices, mostly entire works, some being fragments of larger treatises. Most of these have been purchased, a few being copied to my order. They may be thus classified :—

I. Vedaśástra—
- *a. Saṃhitá* (Hymns) . . 2
- *b. Bráhmaṇa* (Ceremonials) 5
- *c. A'raṇyaka* (Ditto appropriate for forest-life) . 1
- *d. Upanishad* (Theology) . 36
- *e. Vaidika* (Sútras, Rituals, Phonetics, &c.) . . 143

II. Aitihásikaśástra—
- *a. Itihása* (History) . . 9
- *b. Puráṇa* (Ancient legends) 7

III. Kávyaśástra—
- *a. Kávya* (Poems) . . 36
- *b. Náṭaka* (Drama) . . 2
- *c. Champú* (Poetico-prose compositions) . . 2
- *d. Kosha* (Miscellaneous poetical collections) . 3
- *e. Upákhyána* (Tales and romances) . . . 7

IV. Abhidhánaśástra (Lexicography) . . . 8

V. Vyákaraṇaśástra (Grammars) 28

VI. Chhandasśástra (Versification) 3

VII. Alaṅkáraśástra (Rhetoric) . 5

VIII. Jyotishaśástra (Astronomy and Astrology) . . 43

IX. Smṛitiśástra (Law, Civil and Canonical) . . 58

X. Saṇgítaśástra (Music) . . 1

XI. Śilpaśástra (Art) . . 0

XII. Kámaśástra (Erotics) . . 1

XIII. Darśanaśástra (Philosophy)—
- *a. Sáṅkhya* (Hylotheistic) . 3
- *b. Nyáya* (Dialectic) . . 48
- *c. Vaiśeshika* (Physical) . 1
- *d. Mímáṇsá* (Ritualistic) . 5
- *e. Vedánta* (Monotheistic) . 62
- *f. Yoga* (Theocratic) . . 10
- *g. Aparadárśanika* (Minor systems of Philosophy) 0

XIV. Bhaktiśástra (Faith) . . 17

XV. Tantraśástra (Mysticism) . 76

XVI. Vaidyaka (Medical science). 14

XVII. Jainaśástra (Jaina religion) 0

XVIII. Bauddhaśástra (Buddhist religion) . . . 0

XIX. Anirdishṭa (Miscellaneous) . 0

Total . . 656

LIST OF MANUSCRIPTS.

I.—Veda.

(a) *Saṃhitá.*

95 Śákalasaṃhitá.
430 Pavamánasúkta.

(b) *Bráhmaṇa.*

22 Aitareyabráhmaṇa.
460 Aitareyabráhmaṇa.
331 Gopathabráhmaṇa.
605 Chhándogyopanishadbráhmaṇa.
253 Rudrabháshya.

(c) *A'raṇyaka.*

100 A'raṇyakapañchaka.

(d) *Upanishad.*

364 Atharvapañchamopanishad.
357 Amṛitanádopanishad.
353 Amṛitavindúpanishad.
534 A'tharvaṇatápaníyopanishadbháshya.
616 A'tharvaṇatápaníyopanishadbháshya, with Gúḍhárthapradípiká and A'tharvaṇopanishaṭṭiká.
364 A'tharvaṇapañchamopanishad.

167 Íśvaragitopanishad.
371 Upanishatkáṇḍa.
370 Ṛishikopanishad.
441 Káṭhakopanishadbháshya.
607 Kenopanishadbháshya.
606 Kenopanishadvyákhyávivaraṇa.
359 Kaivalyopanishad.
372 Kaushitakyupanishad.
360 Gáruḍopanishad.
361 Gáruḍopanishad.
369 Golokopanishad.
358 Chhurikopanishad.
443 Taittiríyopanishad, Bhṛiguvallí.
444 Taittiríyopanishadantargatabhṛiguvallíbháshya.
366 Náráyaṇopanishad.
337 Nṛisiṇhottaratápaníyavyákhyá.
363 Paramahaṇsopanishad.
289 Paingalopanishad.
611 Bahvṛichabráhmaṇopanishad.
368 Brahmopanishad.
356 Mahopanishad.
442 Máṇḍúkyopanishadbháshya.
610 Muṇḍakádyupanishadaḥ.
365 Rámottaratápaníyopanishad.
354 Vajrasúchikopanishad.
367 Śivopanishad.
374 Śvetáśvataropanishad.
355 Sandhyopanishad.
276 Sureśvarabháshya.
362 Haṇsopanishad.

(e) *Vaidika.*

18 Agniprayoga or Baudháyanágni.
422 Agnihotraprayoga.
160 Agnihotrahoma.
260 Agnyádhána.
1 Agnyádhánapaddhati.
28 Agnyádhánabaudháyana.
3 Achchhávákaprayoga or Dvádaśáhaprayoga.
580 Anukramaṇiká.
346 Anukramaṇikávivaraṇa.
512 Antyeshṭipaddhati.
90 Antyeshṭiprayoga.
573 Apatníkádhánanirṇaya.
43 Aśvamedhapaddhati.
635 Aśvamedhasútra.
86 Ádhánaprayoga or Ádhánapaddhati.
516 Ádhánaprayoga.
448 Ádhánaprayoga.
92 Ádhánabaudháyana.
474 Ádhánabaudháyani.
447 Ádhánánvárambhaṇíyahotra.
294 Ádháneshṭi.
490 Ápastambasomaprayogasútra.
633 Ápastambasútra.
634 Ápastambasútra.
644 Ápastambasútra.
645 Ápastambasútra.
646 Ápastambasútra.
648 Ápastambasútra.
649 Ápastambasútra.
643 Ápastambasútradhúrtabháshya.
501 Ápastambíyaprúyaśchittádhyáyaṭíká.
421 Ápastamboktágnyádhánanirúpaṇa.
453 Áśvaláyanabrahmaṇyaprayoga.
88 Áśvalayanasútraprayoga.
421 Áśvaláyanasútraprayogadípiká.
423 Áśvaláyanoktágráyaṇahotraprayoga.
304 Áhitágnyanteshṭiprayoga.
43 Ukthaprayoga.
437 Upanishadbráhmaṇa.
259 Úhachchalákshara.
550 Ṛikprátiśákhyabháshya.
312 Ṛigvedanukramaṇiká.
61 Ṛishitarpaṇam Maitrágniśákhíyam, Ṛigvedaprátiśákhya.
104 Ṛigvedasaṃhitáhomavidhána.
647 Ekáhapraśna.
636 Kapardisvámibháshya.
413 Kalpavivaraṇa.
29 Kátyáyanaprayoga.
80 Kuṇḍárkamaríchimálá (Text).
45 Kuṇḍárkamaríchimálá (Commentary).

520 Gáni.
105 Gáyatríbrahmakalpaprayoga.
280 Gṛihyasútraprâyoga.
386 Chayanapaddhati.
306 Chayanapaddhati.
484 Cháturmásyaprayoga.
503 Cháturmásyaprayoga.
248 Cháturmásyaprayoga.
40 Cháturmásyaprayoga.
461 Cháturmásyasútra.
66 Cháturmásyahotra.
458 Cháturmásyahotra.
455 Cháturmásyakáriká or Vihárakáriká.
36 Chhandogáparasútra.
50 Jyotiratirátra.
581 Jyotsná (Hiraṇyakeśisútravyákhyá).
449 Darśapaurṇamása.
30 Darśapaurṇamása.
429 Darśapaurṇamásaprayoga.
486 Darśapaurṇamásaprayoga.
463 Darśapaurṇamásaprayoga.
303 Darśapaurṇamásapráyaśchittakáriká.
39 Darśapaurṇamásádhvaryavaprayoga.
180 Daivatanirṇayakáṇḍa.
431 Dvádaśáhahotraprayoga.
652 Dhúrtasvámibháshyaṭiká.
247 Nakshatreshṭiprayoga.
373 Náradíyaśikshá.
513 Nighaṇṭu.
518 Nirukta, púrvárdha.
508 Nirukta, uttarashaṭka.
293 Neshṭṛiprayoga.
35 Pañchapádiká.
54 Padagáḍha.
539 Padagáḍha.
557 Pavamána.
102 Pavamánahomavidhi.
432 Pavamánahomavidhi.
574 Paśubandha (Baudháyanasútríya).
375 Pushpasútra.
270 Prayogaratna.
299 Prayogasára.
467 Prayogadípiká.
507 Prastotṛiprayoga.
428 Prátiśákhya of the Ṛigveda.
478 Bálakhilyaśástra.
287 Bṛihatísahasraśástra.
344 Bṛihadṛigvidhána.
542 Baudháyanasútra.
97 Baudháyanacháturmásyasútraprayoga.
300 Baudháyanasomayágasútra.
499 Baudháyaníyaśulvasútra.
480 Baudháyanadarśapaurṇamásapráyaschitta.
479 Baudháyanasomaprayoga.
446 Bháradvájaparibháshásútra.
416 Bháradvájasútra.
59 Mahágniprayoga.
514 Mṛigáreshṭi (Ápastambíyá).
541 Mṛigáreshṭi.
425 Maitrávaruṇaprayoga.
481 Yajamánakṛitya.
85 Yajñapráyaśchittavivaraṇa.
258 Rahasyachchhalákshara.
63 Rudrajapa.
17 Rudrapaddhati.
41 Rudránushṭhánapaddhati.
433 Laghuvṛitti.
32 Vájapeyaprayoga.
34 Vájapeyaprayoga.
491 Vináyakaśántiprayoga.
455 Vihárakáriká or Cháturmásyakáriká.
603 Vyáḍihayagrívaprátiśákhyavivaraṇa.
106 Śántikalpadípiká.
33 Śulvasútravivaraṇa.
650 Śulvavivaraṇa.
345 Śaunakalaghvṛigvidhána.
189 Sangrahaṇeshṭi.
497 Sarvapṛishṭáptor Yámaprayoga.
632 Sámányasútra.
157 Sávitrachayana.
651 Suparṇachitipaddhati.
450 Subrahmaṇyasámaprayoga.
641 Somaprayoga.
420 Somaprayoga.
307 Subodhiní, Kalpasútraṭiká.

107 Sánkháyanasútra.
569 Svaramañjarí.
482 Ságnikáśvaláyanamṛitavidhi.
78 Sankshepaprayoga, Áśvaláyana.
38 Saptasomasaṃsthápaddhati.
438 Hiraṇyakeśisútra.
631 Hiraṇyakeśisútra.
64 Hotrakalpadruma.

II.—Aitihásikaśástra.

(a) *Itihása.*

591 Adhyátmarámáyaṇa.
483 Bháratabhávapradípa.
397 Mahábhárata.
109 Maháváṇśávalí.
393 Rámáyaṇa, Prathamakáṇḍa.
394 Rámáyaṇa, Dvitíyakáṇḍa.
395 Rámáyaṇa, Tṛitíyakáṇḍa.

(b) *Puráṇa.*

523 Ekákáraṭíká (in Mahratti).
311 Kapilasaṃhitá.
399 Kúrmapuráṇa.
406 Gaṇeśagítá from Gaṇeśapuráṇa.
507 Narasiṇhakalpa.
317 Padmapuráṇa.
7 Padmapuráṇa, Pátálakhaṇḍa.
528 Padmapuráṇa, Pátálakhaṇḍa.
84 Paráśarapuráṇa.
308 Paráśarapuráṇa.
233 Bṛihaddharmapuráṇa, Gangástava.
226 Bṛihannáradíyapuráṇa.
275 Bṛihannáradíyapuráṇa.
392 Bṛihannáradíyapuráṇa.
298 Brahmapuráṇa.
398 Brahmáṇḍapuráṇa.
396 Bhágavatapuráṇa.
400 Lingapuráṇa.
365 Lokevyavávyaślokaṭíká.
8 Vikhyátapuráṇa.
587 Vidvanmanoramá.
538 Vindhyamáhátmya.
588 Vishṇupuráṇa.
315 Vedastutivivaraṇa.
540 Vyankatagirimáhátmya.
297 Śivapuráṇa.
536 Śivaváyavíyasaṃhitá (Uttarabhága).
213 Śivasaṃhitá.
626 Saurabhasaṃhitá, Indraprasthamáhátmya.

III.—Kávyaśástra.

(a) *Kávya.*

412 Ekákáraṭíká.
77 Kavichandrodaya.
385 Kámadhenu or Kavikalpadruma.
271 Khaṇḍapraśastiṭíká.
162 Gangáshṭaka.
161 Gangástotra.
290 Gaṇeśasahasranámavyákhyá.
127 Gítagovindaṭíká.
418 Gítagovindaṭíká.
498 Gítagovindaṭíká.
70 Guṇaságara.
327 Guṇaságara.
145 Ghaṭakarpara.
140 Chandronmílana.
142 Chaurakávya.
334 Chaurakávya.
103 Jagachchandriká, a Commentary on the Raghuvaṇśa.
531 Dásabodha (in Mahratti).
506 Dvádaśastotravyákhyá.
576 Nítiśataka.
582 Naishadhacharita, with ṭíká.
194 Padyapushpáñjalistotra.
192 Pavanavijaya.
15 Manmohanavilása.
101 Mukundavijaya.
404 Meghadúta.
403 Raghuvaṇśa.
533 Rámalingavarṇana.
578 Lalitastotra.
24 Váráṇasídarpaṇa or Káśikáprakáśiká.
640 Vibudhopadeśa.
510 Viśvaguṇádarśa.
436 Śrírámachandrasyáshṭottaraśataka.
37 Satyanáthábhyudaya, with ṭíká.

525 Harimíḍestotra.
330 Harivilásakávya.

(b) *Náṭaka.*

124 Dhúrtasamágama.
340 Śákuntala.

(c) *Champú.*

283 Damayantíchampú.
570 Prahládachampú.

(d) *Kosha.*

567 Vidvadbhúshaṇa.
415 Vihárísataśayyá.
215 Śántiśataka.

(e) *Upákhyána.*

401 Kathákalpataru.
318 Daśakumáracharita.
530 Daśakumáracharita.
73 Damayantíkathá.
34 Śukasaptatiká.
48 Satyopákhyána or Rámarahasya.
53 Siṇhásanadvátriṇśatkathá.

IV.—Abhidhána.

111 Akárabheda.
410 Anekárthamañjarí.
409 Amarakosha.
146 Dvirúpakosha.
562 Pañchatattvaprakáśa.
119 Padárthakaumudí, a Commentary on the Amarakosha.
496 Páraśikaprakáśa.
125 Lingádisangrahaṭíká.

V.—Vyákaraṇa.

65 A'khyátavádaṭíká.
261 A'khyátaviveka.
343 Audáryachintámaṇi.
172 Kátantrapariśishṭa.
209 Kátantravṛittiṭippaṇi.
177 Kátantravṛittiṭíká.
281 Kárakavichára.
469 Kaiyaṭaṭíká.
517 Chidasthimálá.
263 Daśalakáraváda.
473 Prakriyákaumudí.
590 Bhásháviṛitti.
252 Madhyakaumudí.
175 Mugdhabodha.
178 Mugdhabodhaṭíká.
264 Rapratyáháramaṇḍana.
526 Laghuśabdaratna.
487 Vaiyákaraṇabhúshaṇa.
477 Vaiyákaraṇasiddhántamañjúshá.
5 Vaiyákaraṇasiddhántaratnákara.
642 Śabdakaustubha.
387 Śabdaśásanavyákaraṇa. Śabdánuśásanavṛitti.
273 Sárasvataprakriyá.
411 Sárasvataprakriyá.
262 Subodhiní.
165 Harinámámṛita.
388 Harinámámṛita.

VI.—Chhandaḥśástra.

407 Chhandomañjarí.
316 Pingalachchandovṛitti.
558 Vṛittamuktávalí.

VII.—Alankára.

555 Ekonashashtyalankáraprakáśa.
546 Kávyaprakáśaṭíká.
82 Rasataranga.
532 Rasataranginí.
383 Sárabodhiní, a Commentary on the Sáhityadarpaṇa.

VIII.—Jyotisha.

134 Adbhutasárasangraha.
74 Ketúdayaphala.
476 Keśavíṭíká.
20 Kośalágama.
157 Granthasangraha.
243 Granthasangraha.
475 Grahalághavodáharaṇa.
27 Jagachchandriká.
269 Jaiminitájikodáharaṇa.
168 Jyotiḥságarasára.
240 Jyotirbhúshaṇa.
575 Jyotisharatnamálá.

623 Tájikasáraṭiká.
151 Divyachúḍámaṇi.
52 Daivajñachintámaṇi.
620 Daivajñabándhava.
621 Pañchasvara.
378 Prichchhájñána.
189 Praśnakaumudí.
55 Praśnárṇava.
341 Praśnávalí.
268 Bádaráyaṇapraśna.
439 Bṛihajjátaka.
348 Bṛihaspatisaṃhitá.
351 Bṛihatpáráśarí.
266 Bhávachintámaṇi.
519 Makarandavivaraṇa.
524 Muhúrtagaṇapati.
339 Muhúrtachintámaṇiṭíká.
72 Yoginídaśáphala.
577 Ramalapraśna.
622 Ramalasára.
349 Rekhájátakasudhákara.
71 Lagnachandriká.
76 Laghujátakaṭíká.
62 Laghuśaunakí.
426 Vásanábháshya, a Commentary on the Siddhántaśiromaṇi.
212 Śiśubodhiní.
254 Shaṭpraśni.
604 Saṃhitávivṛiti by Bhaṭṭotpala.
249 Sámudrika.
216 Svarodaya.
350 Hastasañjíviní.

IX.—Smṛiti.

462 Antyeshṭipaddhati.
488 Antyeshṭipaddhati.
245 Antyeshṭiprayogapaddhati.
4 Aśauchakáṇḍa.
118 Aśauchamañjarí.
502 Áhnikaprayoga.
14 Utsargamayúkha.
522 Ṛituśánti.
96 Ṛishitarpaṇa.
267 Karmaprakáśa.
352 Kámarúpayátrápaddhati.
445 Kálatattvavivechana.
521 Kálanirṇaya.
11 Kṛityaprakáśá.
91 Gadádharabháshya or Smártadharmaprayoga.
624 Chaturvargachintámaṇi, Seshakáṇḍa.
329 Jírṇoddháravidhi.
500 Jívatpitṛikakartavyasañchaya.
468 Tattvakamalákara.
389 Tithitattva.
419 Daśakarmádipaddhati or Saṃskárapaddhati.
113 Durgotsavavíveka.
144 Dolárohaṇapaddhati.
19 Dharmasindhusára.
42 Nándiśráddhapaddhati.
116 Paddhatisangraha.
427 Piṇḍapitṛiyajñaprayoga.
452 Punarupanayanaprayoga.
129 Puráṇadánamáhátmya.
386 Purushottamatattva.
380 Pújápaddhati
114 Pratishṭháviveka.
417 Prayogachúḍámaṇi.
278 Prayogapaddhati.
295 Prayogaratna.
639 Prayogaratna and Aurdhvadehikapaddhati.
112 Pravásakṛitya.
302 Práyaśchittachandriká.
246 Práyaśchittapradípiká.
464 Práyaśchittamuktávalí.
451 Mangalapújáprayoga.
58 Maháśántipaddhati.
56 Yajñapráyaśchittavivaraṇa.
120 Vástutattva.
227 Vástuhoma.
637 Vidyákalpasútra.
235 Vyavasthárṇava.
9 Vratodyápanavidhi or Vratakathá.
116 Śuddhitattvakáriká.
214 Śuddhidípiká.

218 Śráddhavidhi
110 Shoḍaśapiṇḍadánaprayoga.
115 Sankrántinirṇaya.
207 Sandhyápaddhati.
435 Sannyásagṛihyapaddhati or Sannyásaprayoga.
277 Samayapratibandhavichára.
47 Súryádipañcháyatanapratishṭhápaddhati.

X.—Sangíta.

566 Nádakárikávṛitti.

XI.—Śilpa.

XII.—Káma.

313 Vátsyáyanakámáśástra.

XIII.—Darśana.

(a) *Sánkhya.*

206 Sánkhyakaumudí.
274 Sánkhyatattvakaumudí.
324 Sánkhyárthatattvapradípiká.

(b) *Nyáya.*

49 Anubhavasára.
131 Anumitirahasya.
133 Aparokshánubhútirahasya.
472 Kusumáñjalibodhiní.
44 Khaṇḍanaprakáśa.
545 Guṇasáramañjarí.
326 Chintámaṇiprameyadípiká.
225 Tarkaṭippani.
559 Tarkaprasanga.
222 Tarkarahasya.
579 Tarkámṛita with Ṭíká.
322 Dvitíyavyutpattiváda.
571 Nischayatvanirukti.
584 Nyáyatrisútrívárttika.
319 Nyáyavindu.
544 Nyáyasiddhántamañjarídípiká or Tarkaprakáśa.
99 Nyáyasiddhántamuktávalídípiká.
186 Pakshatáṭippaṇí.
189 Pakshatárahasya.
342 Pakshatárahasya.
602 Padárthakhaṇḍana.
601 Padárthakhaṇḍanaṭippaṇí.
188 Padárthadharmasangraha.
556 Parokshajñána.
595 Pramáṇaparáyaṇa.
495 Bauddhádhikáraśiromaṇi.
494 Bauddhádhikárasútra.
68 Bhavánandíyabhávaprakáśiká.
296 Bhávadípiká.
381 Bháshápárichchheda.
229 Viśeshavyáptirahasya.
230 Vyadhikaraṇadharmávachchhinabhávarahasya.
228 Vyáptigrahopáyarahasya.
382 Vyáptijñána.
231 Vyáptipañchakarahasya.
238 Vyáptyanugamaṭippaṇi.
211 Śabdhachintámaṇyáloka.
126 Śabdárthasáramañjarí.
67 Śiromaṇipúrvárdhaṭíká.
202 Sámányábhávaṭippaṇí.
200 Sámányábhávarahasya.
549 Sámányalakshaṇadídhitiṭippaṇí.
203 Sámányalakshaṇarahasya.
219 Siṇhavyághra.
589 Syádvádamañjarí.
548 Hetvábhásadídhitiṭippaṇí.

(c) *Vaiśeshika.*

Vaiśeshikadarśana.

(d) *Mímáṇsá.*

468 Nyáyasudhá.
594 Púrvamímáṇsárthasangraha.
583 Mímáṇsásárasarvasva.
434 Viháravápí.
309 Vaiyásikádhikaraṇamálá.
572 Sphoṭatattva.

(e) *Vedánta.*

325 Advaitadarpaṇabhávaprakáśiká.
286 Advaitadípiká.
338 Advaitadípiká.
25 Advaitabrahmasiddhi.
586 Advaitasiddhi
552 Advaitasiddhántavidyotana.
537 Aparokshánubhúti.

563 Amṛitavarshiṇí, a Commentary on the Brahmasútra.
613 Amṛitavarshiṇí.
560 A'káśopanyása.
310 A'tmapuráṇa.
511 A'tmavidyopadeśavidhi.
489 Upadeśarahasya.
617 Gauḍapádabháshya with Ṭiká.
529 Jívanmuktiprakaraṇa.
615 Jívanmuktiviveka.
504 Tattvadipa and Tattvanibandhaṭiká.
320 Tattvaprakáśiká.
109 Tattvamuktávalí.
305 Tattvánusandhána.
143 Darśanakaliká.
301 Dṛikdṛiśyavivekavyákhyá.
98 Dvaitanirṇayasiddhántasangraha.
585 Nareśvaraparíkshápraká́śa.
561 Nibandhatattvadípa.
630 Pañchabhútavivekádiṭíká.
332 Prakáśárthapradípiká.
128 Bálabodhiní.
292 Brahmavidyá.
592 Brahmavidyábharaṇa, a Commentary on the Vedántasútra.
593 Brahmavidyábharaṇa.
21 Brahmasiddhántapaddhati.
284 Brahmasútra.
333 Brahmámṛitavarshiṇí.
243 Bháshyachchháyávyákhyá.
547 Bháshyaṭíkávivaraṇa or Vivaraṇopanyása.
564 Mánacharitra (in Mahratti).
565 Muktáphala with Ṭíká.
335 Mumukshusarvasvasára.
596 Laghuchandriká.
492 Vákyavṛitti with Vivaraṇa.
553 Vakyasudhá with Vivaraṇa.
414 Vivekasára (in Mahratti).
471 Vivekasindhu (in Mahratti).
515 Vivekámṛita, Uttarárdha.
288 Vedántakalpalatá.
535 Vedántaparibháshárthadípiká.
614 Vedántasañjñánirúpaṇa.
291 Śástrapradípiká.
597 Sástrasiddhántaleśa.
600 Sanatsujatíya with Vivaraṇa.
456 Sarvopanishatsára.
457 Sarvaślokíṭíká with Text.
328 Siddhaparibháshá.
626 Sahasropadeśí gadyátmiká.
627 Sahasropadeśí padyátmiká.
598 Siddhántachandriká with Ṭíká.
69 Siddhántachandrodaya.

(f) *Yoga.*

160 Gorakshásh ṭaka.
94 Dattagítá.
147 Dattátreyasaṃhitá.
391 Yogavásishṭharámáyaṇa.
239 Yogavásishṭhasára.
470 Yogavásishṭhasáraṭíká.
241 Yogavivaraṇa.
255 Yogavíja.
96 Yogasárasangraha.
347 Haṭhapradípiká with Ṭíká.

(g) *Aparadárśanika.*

XIV.—Bhaktiśástra.

629 Gúḍhárthadipiká.
459 Gopálaviveka.
390 Gopálalílámṛita.
402 Dásabodha.
608 Piśáchabháshya.
137 Bhaktiratnávalí.
638 Bhagavadbhaktichandrikollása.
138 Bhagavadbhaktivilása.
257 Rangabhṛingavallí.
408 Rádhákuṇḍádinirṇaya
279 Vishṇubhaktikalpalatá.
612 Śivagítá from the Matsyapuráṇa.
466 Srímadbhagavadgítátátparyanirṇaya.
465 Srímadbhagavadgítábháshya.
525 Harimíḍestotra with Ṭíká.
525 Haristutivyákhyá or Haritattvamuktávalí.

XV.—Tantra.

130 Annadákalpa.
377 Aparájitastotra.

132 A'chárasáratantra.
166 Íśánasaṃhitá.
46 Upáṅgalalitapújana.
175 Karpúrádistavaṭíká.
244 Kámaratnatantra.
173 Kámarúpayátrápaddhati.
171 Kálikádisahasranámaṭíká.
176 Kálísahasranámastotra.
170 Kálistavarája.
174 Kaivalyatantra.
158 Gáyatrikalpa.
155 Gáyatríbrahmollásatantra.
272 Gáyatríviśvámitrakalpa.
143 Gáyatríhṛidaya.
242 Gáyatríhṛidaya.
163 Guptasádhanatantra.
156 Gurugítá.
159 Gurutantra.
164 Gurupádukápañchakastotraṭíká.
142 Gaurikaśchuliká.
141 Chakradipikáshaṭchakravivaraṇa.
169 Jñánatantra.
87 Jñánárṇava.
93 Jñánárṇavaṭíká.
220 Takárádisvarúpa.
223 Takárádisvarúpavyákhyá.
13 Tantraratna.
121 Tántrikapújápaddhati.
379 Tárábhakti.
221 Tárárahasyavṛittiká.
224 Tripurásárasamuchchayaṭíká.
148 Durgádinámastotra.
150 Durgávákyaprabodha.
149 Devikavacha.
185 Nigamatantrasára.
138 Nílatantra.
12 Nyáyarakshámaṇi.
112 Párthivaliṅgapújávidhi.
196 Píṭhanirṇaya.
187 Puraścharaṇarasollása.
193 Puraścharaṇaviveka.
159 Púrṇándachakranirúpaṇaṭíká.
123 Práṇatoshiṇí.
81 Bálatantra.
136 Brahmajñánatantra.
139 Brahmajñánatantrarája.
117 Bhagavatígítá.
135 Bhagavatígítá.
180 Matṛikákosha.
182 Mátṛikájaganmaṅgalakavacha.
181 Máyátantra.
179 Muṇḍanamálátantra.
336 Liṅgárchana or Liṅgachayana.
237 Vagalápaṭala.
236 Vagalámukhístotrakavacha.
250 Varshatantra.
376 Vámakeśvaratantra, Pichchhilatantra, Avadhútánubhúti, Bhairavatantra, Pratyaṅgirákavacha.
234 Vidyotpattiguhyátiguhyatantra.
232 Víjakosha.
323 Śaktisaṅgamatantra.
83 Śivapújápaddhati.
10 Śyámápújápaddhati.
199 Śyámástotra.
217 Śrígurusahasranámastotra.
122 Shaṭchakrabheda.
208 Shaṭchakrabhedaṭippaṇí.
210 Shaṭchakravṛittiṭiká.
31 Samayáchára ratna or Samayáchára-tantra.
204 Sarasvatítantra.
201 Sundaríśaktidánastotra.

XVI.—Vaidyakaśástra.

485 Chikitsására.
256 Jvarádichikitsá.
184 Náḍijñánadípiká.
160 Paryáyaratnamálá.
26 Bhávaprakáśa.
16 Rasáyanaprakáśa.
145 Rasendrachintámaṇi.
198 Rájavallabha.
197 Rogaviniśchaya.
554 Vidyáprakáśachikitsására.
618 Vaidyarahasyapaddhati.
619 Sañjñásamuchchaya.
51 Śárṅgadharasaṅgraha.
75 Sárasaṅgraha.

From R. SIMPSON, Esq., Secretary to the Government of the North-Western Provinces, to E. C. BAYLEY, Esq., Secretary to the Government of India, Home Department, Simla,—No. 1600, dated Allahabad, the 6th April 1869.

WITH reference to the Resolution in the Home Department, No. 4341, dated the 3rd November last, I am directed to forward, for the information of His Excellency the Viceroy and Governor-General in Council, a copy of a letter* from the Director of Public Instruction, North-Western Provinces, and of its enclosure, describing the measures which it is proposed to adopt for carrying into effect the scheme for the collection of valuable Sanskṛit manuscripts.

* No. 2616, dated 18th ultimo.

2. The Hon'ble the Lieutenant-Governor recommends that the sum of R 1,600, allotted to the North-Western Provinces for this purpose, may be allowed, as suggested in paragraph 2 of Mr. Griffith's letter, to be drawn annually, to form a fund, the unexpended balance of which will accumulate for any larger operations that may be required in one year than another.

3. The other proposals of Messrs. Griffith and Kempson are considered judicious, and have been approved.

From M. KEMPSON, Esq., M.A., Director of Public Instruction, North-Western Provinces, to R. SIMSON, Esq., Secretary to the Government of the North-Western Provinces,—No. 2616, dated Allahabad, the 18th March 1869.

WITH attention to your No. 2064A., dated 25th November last, I have the honour of submitting herewith, for His Honour's information, copy of a letter received from the Principal of the Benares Sanskṛit College, relative to the collection of Sanskṛit manuscripts.

2. I agree with Mr. Griffith in his view of the Native feeling, and am of opinion that valuable Sanskṛit works wanted in Europe may be perfectly well represented by copies, so long as the copies are prepared in the Sanskṛit College, and bear its stamp of authentication. The proposal to employ the College Librarian for the duty of collection is judicious, and, in offering his services as superintendent of the transactions, Mr. Griffith answers for the success of his plan. A half-yearly report from him of the progress of enquiry, purchase, and registration would keep the Government and the public sufficiently informed.

From R. T. H. GRIFFITH, Esq., Officiating Inspector, 3rd Circle, Department of Public Instruction, North-Western Provinces, to M. KEMPSON, Esq., M.A., Director of Public Instruction, North-Western Provinces,—No. 119, dated Benares, the 13th March 1869.

I HAVE the honour to acknowledge the receipt of your docket No. 1759, dated 30th November last, with a copy of G. O. No. 2064A., dated 25th idem, and its enclosures, and submit herewith my proposals for carrying out the object of the Government of India therein referred to; and if they meet your approval, I shall be able, I think, to submit before long my quarterly list, as ordered in paragraph 5 of Mr. Howell's letter to the address of the Secretary to the Government, North-Western Provinces, No. 4351, dated 3rd November 1868, for the first quarter of 1869.

2. The Government has sanctioned an outlay of R1,600 per annum, as noted in the margin, for the North-Western Provinces. I propose that this sum may be drawn annually and formed into a fund, which, if there be savings now, may meet future extra expenses when our operations are extended, commensurate to the information we collect and the experience we gain.

	R
Tour expense . . .	500
Purchase expense . .	500
Transcription expense . .	600
Total . .	1,600

3. For the present, I propose to employ, with the consent of the Principal of the College, Pandit Ramánáth, the Sanskṛit College Librarian, as our agent for the discovery and preservation of the records of ancient Sanskṛit literature. He was bred a librarian; his father was also a librarian. He knows Sanskṛit enough for the purpose; and his acquaintance with the people, and his experience in the way of procuring rare Sanskṛit manuscripts, make him peculiarly fitted for the work. I propose to pay him R15 per mensem as an honorarium for his extra work out of College hours, and 1½ anna per mile when travelling by rail, and 4 annas per mile when marching by stages, with R1 per diem for halts, as travelling expense: the whole will not exceed the sum (R500) allowed for tour expenses. Benares being the first city in the North-Western Provinces, and the chief seat of Sanskṛit learning in India, he will be able to collect much of his information, and do much of his work, at home, and by going out during the two and half months in the year, when the College is closed, to do the rest to meet the object in view.

4. If allowed, I am prepared to undertake to superintend the printing of the lists of Sanskṛit manuscripts in the North-Western Provinces.

5. I shall submit, from time to time, the list of those manuscripts which I have thought worth purchasing or copying.

6. But, before closing this letter, I feel myself bound to bring to your notice a matter so closely connected with the ultimate success of the noble design of the Government of India. When talking the other day on the subject with some intelligent Hindus, to engage their zealous co-operation in the matter, their invariable remark, with reference to paragraph 8 of the above-quoted letter, was, that "Pandit Rádhákrishṇa wanted to have lists of books here and in Europe, to preserve them in original, or in copies, for the use of his countrymen"; but his efforts have resulted only in hurrying on the catastrophe so emphatically predicted in the end of paragraph 10 of Mr. Whitley Stokes' note, dated 6th August 1868, where he says—'To Europe we should send everything obtained in working out this scheme—original manuscripts, copies, extracts; for in Europe alone are the true principles of criticism and philology understood and applied, and, fifty years hence, in Europe alone will any intelligent interest be felt in Sanskṛit literature. There will then, it is safe to say, be as few Sanskṛit scholars in India as there are Greek scholars in Greece.'

7. It is well known how a Hindu worships his scriptures; and, with him, almost every book which is written in the sacred Sanskṛit language is a scripture. It is well known how averse Hindus are to part with their Sanskṛit books, especially when they know they are to fall into the hands of those who are sure to use them as weapons against their religion. They do not bind their books, simply in order that they may not have to lend them all at once, even to their friends or co-religionists. Some years ago, I heard, an old Pandit had tied up and sealed all his books in bags, making a will that they were to be sunk in the Ganges as soon as his life was extinct; and leaves of books have often been seen floating in the river. Mr. Whitley Stokes is aware of this, and proposes, in the end of the 9th paragraph of his Note (above-mentioned), the conferring of titles on Śástrís who exhibit liberality in this respect; but I am afraid there are very few Śástrís, at least in this part of the country, so enlightened. It is only poverty, and extreme poverty generally speaking, which forces them to part with their books for pecuniary considerations. It was to remove this difficulty that some intelligent Hindus of this city started a project in 1851 to store the Benares College with Sanskṛit manuscripts, with a guarantee from the Government that they were never to be removed from the place. The following remarks of the late Lieutenant-Governor, Mr. Thomason,

on the prospectus, are taken from a private note:—"As to the Library at Benares, I cannot conceive that such a measure would ever be thought of as Śivaprasád seems to apprehend, nor do I see how any pledge that I can give, or that any one can give, precludes the possibility of such a measure hereafter, if any Goths or Vandals were ever to think of it. However, I will do or say what I can to prevent such a possible occurrence." His Honour's lamentable death put an end to the undertaking.

8. My thus prominently bringing the matter before you is simply to suggest whether it will not be advisable to ask the Government to put us in a position that we may be able to assure the Hindus that the books sought for are to be placed in the College Library for the benefit of the public, and to remove the apprehension that they are to be sent to the Secretariat only to be forwarded to Europe. When once the books are in the Library, there would be no difficulty in supplying copies of them for the use of scholars in Europe. By giving out that we want books to preserve them here for the benefit of the Indians, we can engage the general sympathy of the people on our side; whereas, when it is known that they are sought after only to be removed from this country, we cannot reasonably expect them to sympathize with us, if they do not oppose; though the money and individual energy will work as far as it can.

No. 2057, dated Simla, the 5th May 1869.

Copy forwarded to the Financial Department with a recommendation that the formation of a fund, as proposed by the Lieutenant-Governor, be sanctioned both in the North-Western Provinces and other Provinces.

Extract from the Proceedings of the Government of India, in the Financial Department,—No. 689, dated Simla, the 31st May 1869.

READ—

An endorsement by the Home Department, No. 2057, dated 5th May 1869, on a letter from the Government of the North-Western Provinces, proposing that the sum of ₨1,600, allotted to those Provinces for the purpose of carrying out the scheme for the collection of valuable Sanskṛit manuscripts, may be allowed to be drawn annually, to form a fund, the unexpended balance of which will accumulate for any larger operations that may be required in one year than another.

RESOLUTION.—The Governor-General in Council, being averse to the formation of petty funds of the above description, thinks it sufficient to give the saving of the annual allowance for five years, at the end of which period, any accumulated balance may be resumed at the discretion of the Government of India.

ORDER.—Ordered, that the foregoing Resolution be sent to the Home Department and the Accountant-General, North-Western Provinces.

No. 2913, dated Simla, the 25th June 1869.

Copy forwarded to the Government of the North-Western Provinces, with reference to communication thence, No. 1600, dated the 6th April last.

Nos. 2914-21.

Copy of the correspondence* forwarded to the Governments of Madras, Bombay, Bengal (General Department), and the Punjab; the Chief Commissioners of Oudh, Central Provinces, and Mysore and Coorg; and the Foreign Department, with reference to this Office Resolution Nos. 4338-48, dated 3rd November last.

* From Government, N.-W. P., No. 1600, dated 6th April 1869.
To Financial Department, No. 2057, dated 5th May 1869.
From Financial Department, No. 689, dated 31st May 1869.

From C. A. ELLIOTT, Esq., Secretary to the Government of the North-Western Provinces, to the Officiating Secretary to the Government of India, Home Department,—No. 2816A., dated Allahabad, the 1st December 1874.

WITH reference to Home Department Resolution No. 4341, dated 3rd November 1868, sanctioning a grant of R1,600 per annum to the North-Western Provinces for the cataloguing and purchase of Sanskṛit manuscripts, and Financial Resolution No. 689, dated 31st May 1869, authorising the utilization of the saving of the annual allowance for five years, I am directed to say that the period of five years expired on 31st March 1874, and to report what progress has been made.

2. Two hundred copies of Part I of the Catalogue of Manuscripts examined have been printed and distributed as directed by the Government of India, and the total expenditure up to the end of September 1874 amounts to R1,053-5-10, while liabilities have been incurred to the extent of R1,769-4-0, making a total of R2,822-9-10.

3. Mr. Griffith, to whom the supervision of the work has been entrusted, writes as follows:—"Sanskṛit scholars in Europe, for whose benefit the work has been begun under the orders of the Government of India, are anxiously expecting the completion of what they call the 'Literary Survey of India'; and I suppose the examination and cataloguing of manuscripts must be continued in the North-Western Provinces, as the work is still going on under other Governments and Administrations. I propose, however, to reduce the size and cost of future parts of the Catalogue by the omission of all details in the case of such manuscripts as are manifestly of no interest or importance."

4. Mr. Griffith's name is in itself sufficient guarantee that the work has been, and will be, done in a satisfactory manner. I am accordingly to recommend that sanction may be given to cover the expenditure and liabilities incurred in the past; and that a further sum of R2,000 be placed to Mr. Griffith's credit for the continuance of the work. When that is expended, further report can be made to the Government of India.

No. 2817A.

COPY forwarded to the Director of Public Instruction, North-Western Provinces, for information, with reference to his letter No. 857G., dated 11th November.

From A. P. HOWELL, Esq., Officiating Secretary to the Government of India, Home Department, to the Secretary to the Government of the North-Western Provinces,—No. 194, dated Fort William, the 1st February 1875.

I AM directed to acknowledge your letter No. 2816A., dated the 1st December last, reporting on the progress made in the preparation of Catalogues of Sanskṛit manuscripts, and I am to say that the Governor-General in Council sanctions the expenditure, and also the liabilities, amounting in all to R2,822-9-10, incurred for the publication of Part I of the Catalogue. The particulars of the expenditure should be communicated to this Department, and fifty copies of the Catalogue, together with a list of the distribution made, should also be forwarded.

2. A further grant of R2,000, for the continuance of the work of examination and of cataloguing the manuscripts, is also authorized. I am to

ask for a report as to the place where any manuscripts, purchased or copied, are deposited, sending a list of them.

No. 195.

COPY of the correspondence forwarded to the Financial Department for information.

From the Officiating Secretary to the Government of the North-Western Provinces, to the Secretary to the Government of India, Home Department,—No. 823A., dated Naini Tal, the 7th May 1875.

I AM directed to reply to your letter No. 194, dated 1st February 1875, regarding Catalogues of Sanskṛit manuscripts.

2. The particulars of the expenditure are contained in the Statements A and B hereto appended.

3. Fifty copies of the Catalogue were forwarded to the Home Department by Mr. Griffith on the 8th March 1875.

4. The distribution of the Catalogues has been made in accordance with the orders of the Government of India, as contained in Home Department's Nos. 662C., dated 24th October 1873, and 18-632, dated 24th February 1874.

5. The manuscripts are deposited in the Library of the Benares Sanskṛit College. A list of them, marked C, is forwarded for the information of His Excellency the Governor-General in Council.'

A

Statement showing the actual expenditure on account of Sanskrit Manuscripts, from January 1870 to September 1874 (as tested by Accountant-General).

	R a. p.
Salary of Pandit Ramánáth Sukul, Agent for collecting Sanskrit Manuscripts	765 0 0
Travelling allowance	120 10 0
Purchase of manuscripts	167 11 10
Total . . .	1,053 5 10

BENARES COLLEGE;
The 12th September 1874.

R. GRIFFITH,
Principal, Benares College.

B

Statement of charges incurred out of the balance of the grant for collection of Sanskrit Manuscripts, R1,076-1-0 (as supplied by Accountant-General).

MONTH.	1869-70.	1870-71.	1871-72.	1872-73.	1873-74.	1874-75.	TOTAL.
	R a. p.	R a. p.	R a. p.	R. a. p.	R a. p.	R a. p.	R a. p.
April . . .	...	...	15 0 0	47 14 0	43 3 4	...	
May . . .	...	130 0 0	15 0 0	15 0 0	15 0 0	...	
June . . .	...	...	15 0 0	...	89 0 0	...	
July . . .	...	14 9 0	15 0 0	30 0 0	53 8 6	60 0 0	
August . . .	...	14 9 0	15 0 0	15 0 0	25 8 0	...	
September . .	...	15 0 0	15 0 0	15 0 0	15 0 0	...	
October . .	...	15 0 0	15 0 0	15 0 0	15 0 0	...	
November . .	...	15 0 0	15 0 0	31 8 0	15 0 0	...	
December . .	...	15 0 0	15 0 0	15 0 0	15 0 0	...	
January . .	...	15 0 0	15 0 0	15 0 0	...	...	
February . .	...	15 0 0	15 0 0	15 0 0	...	...	
March . . .	117 12 0	15 0 0	15 0 0	15 0 0	...	...	
TOTAL .	117 12 0	264 2 0	180 0 0	229 6 0	286 3 10	60 0 0	1,137 7 10

C.

List of Sanskrit Manuscripts purchased.

No.	Name.	Subject.	Leaves.	Lines.		Ślokas.	Remarks.
1	Ṛigvedapada	Veda	627	9	On paper; Devanágari character.	14,000	Separates the words of the Ṛichas of the Ṛigveda. Such a copy is not procurable anywhere else, and it is not in the Library of the College; old and apparently correct.
2	Śárngadhara, with Ṭíká.	Medicine; the text by Śárngadharapaṇḍit, and commentary by Ádmalla.	373	7	Ditto	6,200	A commentary on Śárngdhara, with text. Contains medicine, &c. Recent, and little known.
3	Tantravárttika.	Mímánsá; philosophy by Kúmarilasvamin.	145	8	Ditto	3,668	A commentary on the Bháshya of the aphorisms of the Mímáṇsá philosophy. The complete copy is not procurable in Benares. The manuscript is old, and apparently correct.
4	Bhedádhikára, with Ṭíká.	Vedánta philosophy; the text by Nṛisiṇhásráma, and commentary by Rámáśrama.	78	12	Ditto	3,042	A commentary on Bhedádhikára, with text. Contains objections to difference in general. The manuscript is recent, and apparently correct.
5	Sáṅkhyáyanasútra	Veda	62	9	Ditto	1,300	Gives rules for the performance of sacrifice. The manuscript examined is very old, and differs from the modern Devanágarí.
6	Vivádabhangárṇava	Law by Jagannáthatarkapañchánana.	268	9	Ditto	7,300	On lending and borrowing money, &c. The manuscript is recent, and apparently correct.
7	Vivádaratnákara	Law by Chandeśvara	77	9	Ditto	1,800	A treatise on law, containing Dáyabhága, &c. The manuscript is recent, and apparently correct.
8	Manubháshya	Law by Medhátithi	235	9	Ditto	5,200	A large commentary on Manusmṛiti. The manuscript is recent, and apparently correct.
9	Káśiká	Grammar by Vámanajayáditya	30	19	Ditto	16,000	A commentary on the aphorisms of Páṇini. Such a copy is not procurable in Benares. It is not in the College Library. The manuscript is old and very correct.
10	Śrímadbhágavatatátparyadípiká	Puráṇa; the text, with a commentary by Śrídhara.	1,062	12	Ditto	...	A large commentary, with the text of the Bhágavata. It is also called Bhávárthadípiká. Such a copy is not easily procurable. It is not in the Library. The manuscript is old and correct.

R. GRIFFITH,

Principal, Benares College.

No. 912, dated Simla, the 29th May 1875.

Extract from a letter from the Government of the North-Western Provinces,— No. 823A., dated Naini Tal, the 7th May 1875.

PARA. 1. I am directed to reply to your letter No. 194, dated 1st February 1875, regarding catalogues of Sanskrit manuscripts.

2. The particulars of the expenditure are contained in the Statements A and B hereto appended.

A

Statement showing the actual expenditure on account of Sanskrit Manuscripts, from January 1872 to September 1874 (as tested by the Accountant-General).

	R a. p.
Salary of Pandit Ramánáth Sukul, Agent for collecting Sanskrit Manuscripts.	765 0 0
Travelling allowance	120 10 0
Purchase of manuscripts	167 11 10
TOTAL . .	1,053 5 10

BENARES COLLEGE;
The 12th September 1874.

R. GRIFFITH,
Principal, Benares College.

B

Statement of charges incurred out of the balance of the grant for collection of Sanskrit Manuscripts, Rs. 1,076-1-0 (as supplied by the Accountant-General).

MONTH.	1869-70.	1870-71.	1871-72.	1872.73.	1873-74.	1874-75.	TOTA .
	R a. p.	R a. p.	R a. p.	R a. p	R a. p.	R a. p.	R a. p.
April	...	...	15 0 0	47 14 0	43 3 4	...	
May	...	130 0 0	15 0 0	15 0 0	15 0 0	...	
June	...	...	15 0 0	...	89 0 0	...	
July	...	14 9 0	15 0 0	30 0 0	53 8 6	60 0 0	
August	...	14 9 0	15 0 0	15 0 0	25 8 0	...	
September . . .	...	15 0 0	15 0 0	15 0 0	15 0 0	...	
October . . .	...	15 0 0	15 0 0	15 0 0	15 0 0	...	
November . . .	...	15 0 0	15 0 0	31 8 0	15 0 0	...	
December . . .	...	15 0 0	15 0 0	15 0 0	15 0 0	...	
January . . .	...	15 0 0	15 0 0	15 0 0	...	...	
February . . .	...	15 0 0	15 0 0	15 0 0	...	...	
March	117 12 0	15 0 0	15 0 0	15 0 0	...	...	
TOTAL .	117 12 0	264 2 0	180 0 0	329 6 0	286 3 10	60 0 0	1,137 7 10

Forwarded to the Financial Department for information, in continuation of endorsement No. 195, dated the 1st February last.

From F. S. CHAPMAN, Esq., Chief Secretary to the Government of Bombay, to E. C. BAYLEY, Esq., Secretary to the Government of India, Home Department,—No. 1976, dated the 18th August 1869.

I AM directed by the Right Hon'ble the Governor in Council to forward herewith a copy of the Proceedings of this Government as per margin, consequent on the instructions of the Government of India, conveyed in Mr. Officiating Secretary Howell's communications Nos. 4339 and 4350, dated the 3rd November last, in regard to the conservancy and preservation of records of ancient Sanskṛit literature in this Presidency.

Government Resolution No. 2357, dated 10th December 1868.
Letter from the Director of Public Instruction, No. 1242, dated 13th July 1869, with enclosures.
Government Resolution No. 1975, dated 18th August 1869.

2. Appendix D to Dr. Kielhorn's report is being printed. Copies of it will be forwarded hereafter.

Extract from the Proceedings of the Government of Bombay in the General Department,—No. 2357, dated the 10th December 1868.

READ the following:—

Letter from the Officiating Secretary to the Government of India, No. 4350, dated 3rd November 1868, forwarding copy of a Resolution recorded by the Government of India in regard to the discovery and preservation of records of ancient Sanskṛit literature, and communicating their sentiments and instructions on the subject.

Memorandum from the Officiating Secretary to the Government of India, No. 4339, dated 3rd November 1868, forwarding an extract from the Proceedings of the Government of India in regard to a suggestion made by Pandit Rádhákṛishṇa for the compilation of a catalogue of all the Sanskṛit manuscripts preserved in the Libraries of India and Europe.

RESOLUTION.—Copies should be forwarded to the Director of Public Instruction, with a request that he will state to Government how the objects may be best attained.

2. In the meanwhile, it would be well if Professor Kielhorn were directed to proceed on a tour through Dharwar, Belgaum, and Canara, and to be absent for not more than four weeks. By including the Christmas vacation in this time, there would probably be no inconvenience to the College; and Professor Kielhorn should reserve for another season such portions of those districts as he may not be able to visit within the time.

Professor Bühler should be requested to undertake the Northern Division; it may be convenient that he should proceed on his tour somewhat later. The Director should request Professor Bühler to undertake the duty referred to in paragraph 2 of the Resolution of the Government of India No. 4350, and should call on him for suggestions as to carrying out the rest of the Resolution.

3. The Collectors should be requested to give every facility to the gentlemen who proceed on these tours.

From J. B. Peile, Esq., Director of Public Instruction, Bombay, to C. Gonne, Esq., Secretary to the Government of Bombay, Educational Department,—No. 1242, dated Poona, the 13th July 1869.

I have the honour to forward, in original, for transmission to the Government of India (as required in Resolution No. 4350 of November 3rd, 1868, paragraph 3), the reports by Drs. Bühler and Kielhorn of their proceedings in searching for Sanskṛit manuscripts in the past season. Their success has been marked and important, and their reports are, in many respects, curious and interesting. I propose to print them as appendices to my annual report. The Catalogue of Manuscripts required by the Government of India is under preparation.

From G. Bühler, Esq., Acting Educational Inspector, Northern Division, to J. B. Peile, Esq., M.A., Director of Public Instruction, Bombay,—Dated Surat, the 5th July 1869.

I have the honour to submit my report regarding the search for Sanskṛit manuscripts instituted in the Northern Division during the first five months of the year 1869.

(1) Operations.

1. After receiving charge of the office of Inspector, I addressed a circular to the Deputies of Surat, Broach, Kaira, Ahmedabad, Káttiáwár, Rewakantha and Khandeish, requesting them to name the chief towns where Sanskṛit manuscripts are to be found, and to furnish me with lists of persons possessing Sanskṛit libraries. The Deputy Inspectors were also furnished with lists of desiderata and forms for cataloguing books. On my tour, I visited a number of towns where Sanskṛit learning is cultivated, amongst which I may mention Ahmedabad, Dholka, Limdi, Rájkoṭ, Gondal,

Junágaḍh, Pálitáná, Bhaunagár, Nariad, Cambay, Broach, and Balsár. In all these places I had interviews with the Native scholars and possessors of libraries, and I explained to them the intentions of Government, and the purposes for which the present search for Sanskṛit manuscripts is instituted. I mostly met with a very friendly reception on the part of the Bráhmans and Śástrís. They came willingly to talk with me, to shew me the lists of their books, and to bring those which I wanted to inspect. At Balsár I held a regular *sabhá*, or assembly of the learned, for the purpose of learned discussions. It was well attended. I examined first the pupils of the various Śástrís, and next proposed a few questions to the teachers, which they discussed in their peculiar manner, one upholding the Púrvapaksha, the first proposition, and the other its opposite, Uttarapaksha. Finally I addressed them on the object pursued by Europeans in studying Sanskṛit; the intentions of Government in regard to the cultivation of that language; the purpose for which Sanskṛit books are collected, &c. All these topics appeared to have great interest for them, as they listened eagerly, and frequently asked questions demanding fuller explanations. The ceremony was concluded by the recitation of improvised poetry, and the orthodox distribution of *pán, supárí,* and of *dakshiṇá*. In Junágaḍh, also, the whole *posse* of Śástrís was assembled at the examination of the Sanskṛit School, and submitted to a rigorous examination in Sanskṛit grammar; and I afterwards received a curious proof how deeply the Pandits had been impressed by seeing a foreigner able to converse in their sacred language and acquainted with their Śástras. On the last evening of my stay in Junágaḍh, a deputation came to me with an address, which assured me of their friendliness, and requested me to answer some questions, amongst which the following were the most curious :—

(1) Whether in Europe, especially in Germany, the learned lived according to the Bráhmanical law.

(2) Whether they performed sacrifices, as a European had done in Poona (Dr. Haug).

(3) Whether I preferred sacrifices, or the study of the Vedánta, as the road to salvation.

(4) How, supposing that I was descended, as I had told them, from the Aryan stock, I could consider mysef entitled (*adhikṛita*) to study the Vedas and Śástras without having been initiated.

Though I hereupon disclaimed all belief in the Vedas and Śástras, I succeeded in satisfying them that I had no sinister intentions against their creed; and one of them volunteered to teach me the correct way of reading the Śatapathabráhmaṇa from Professor Weber's edition. Besides Śástrís, I saw also some Pandits of the Jainas, Yatis, who willingly talked about their creed and literature. One of them even invited me to his house and shewed me his books there. He gave me permission to take away what I wanted, and asked in exchange nothing but a railway-guide—a request which I readily granted. Finally, I appointed some paid agents for making catalogues of the libraries to which access had been gained, and for collecting books.

(2) RESULTS.

2. The results of these operations are—

(*a*) Catalogues of a number of libraries containing a little more than 7,000 numbers.
(*b*) The acquisition of a number of old books, and copies of old books.

(a) The Catalogues.

All these catalogues are made, or at least appeared to be made, according to the plan proposed by Mr. Whitley Stokes, and amended by Dr. Kielhorn and myself. Selections from them, which will comprise between one-half and two-thirds of the number mentioned, are now being prepared for publication. As these preparations, I hope, will be completed shortly, I shall confine myself here to mentioning a few of the most important works contained in the lists. A great many Vedic manuscripts have come to light. Among them are not only copies of the more common books, such as the Saṃhitás and Bráhmaṇas of the Ṛik, the Yajush and Sáman, with their commentaries; but also the rarer works, such as the Maitráyaṇí Śákhá of the Yajurveda, all the books belonging to the Atharvaveda, the Uvaṭabháshya on the Yajurveda, &c. To these may be added a few books, as the Aukhíyá Śákhá of the Yajurveda, and the Khádiragṛihyasútra of the Sámaveda, of which up to this time no copies had been obtainable. The lists are rich also in works on the various Śástras, and here likewise occur a number of rare books and novelties. Among the latter I mention a portion of the Nyása, the commentary of Jinendrabuddhi on the Kásiká, a Bhoja Vyákaraṇa with a commentary, a portion of the Kaumáravyákaraṇa, some Smṛitis, *e. g.*, that attributed to Vyághrapáda, a fragment of the Śákalyasmṛiti, and, finally, a Karaṇa of Brahmagupta, called Khaṇḍakhádyaka with the commentary of Pṛithúdakasvámin. The lists include also about 800 Jaina works, and I saw large catalogues of books belonging to this important sect. But, as the operations in this respect are still in an incipient stage, I refrain from giving any details. I hope, however, to be able to supply soon some fresh information on the Jaina literature. Besides the regular catalogues, I received a large number of lists not executed according to the prescribed plan.

(b) Purchases.

1.—Bráhmanical literature—

1. Sáṅkhyáyanábráhmaṇa, dated Saṃvat 1765.
2. Sáṅkhyáyana Áraṇyaka, dated Saṃvat 1714.
3. " " Adhyáyas I and II, dated Saṃvat 1752.
4. " Gṛihyasútra (last page, new copy).
5. Baudháyananakshatrasattra, with the commentary of Bhadradeva, dated Saṃvat 1717.
6. Baudháyanadharmasútra.
7. Káśiká vṛitti, by Vámanácharya, dated Samvat 1535 (A.D. 1479).
8. Kátantravyákaraṇa, with the Daurgasiṇhí Vṛitti (to the end of the Taddhitaprakaraṇa), dated Saṃvat 1504 (A.D. 1448).
9. Sárasvatavyákaraṇa with the Chandrakírttivṛitti, dated Saṃvat 1709.
10. Śiromaṇi (Sámányalakshaṇa), by Jagadiśá.
11. Máthuranáthí (Kevalánvaya, Pakshatárahasya, and Sámányalakshaṇarahasya).
12. Sárasangraha, by Varadarája, a commentary on the Tárkikarakshá.
13. Dravyakiraṇávalí (a fragment).
14. Padárthamálá (Dravyaparichchheda), by Jayarámapañchánana (two first leaves wanting).
15. Vágbhaṭṭálaṅkára.
16. Śálihotra (on the treatment of horses), by Bhojarája.
17. Pañchatantra.
18. Bhartṛihari's Three Centuries, with an anonymous commentary.
19. Charaṇavyúha, dated Saṃvat 1808.
20. Lingánuśásana of Vararuchi (new copy).
21. Paribháshendupradípa.

Besides these works actually obtained, I am in negotiation for more than double the number of the Jaina books bought. I shall have the honour to furnish, later, a separate list, together with a separate report on them.

3. The operations of this year have convinced me that Gujarat is exceedingly rich in Sanskṛit libraries and books, and that, with patience and care, a good many valuable works may be obtained. I am told that to catalogue the more important libraries in Ahmedabad alone would take a man a full year.

4. I finally beg to mention that Mr. Premábhái Himábhái, Ráo Bahádur Bholanáth Sárábhái, Ráo Bahádur Gopálrao Hari at Ahmedabad, and Mr.

Párvatíśankar Maṇiśankar, Head Master of the Broach Anglo-Vernacular School, very readily and kindly opened their libraries to me, and that my best thanks are due to them. I beg also particularly to mention Ráo Sáheb Gopálji Surbhái Desáis, Deputy Educational Inspector of Káttiáwár, from whom I received a large number of lists.

From F. KIELHORN, Esq., Superintendent of Sanskṛit Studies, to J. B. PEILE, Esq., M.A., Director of Public Instruction, Bombay—dated Deccan College, Poona, the 20th June 1869.

I HAVE the honour of submitting to you the following report on the work done by me from the 22nd of December 1868 to the 31st of March 1869, in carrying out the Government Resolution No. 2357, dated the 10th of December 1868.

2. I was directed, in section 2 of the Government Resolution referred to above, to proceed on a tour through Dharwar, Belgaum and Kanara, and to be absent for not more than four weeks. Accordingly, I left Poona on the 27th of December 1868, and returned on the 24th of January 1869. As I had only a few days' time given to me to prepare for my tour, and to obtain preliminary information regarding the places at which Sanskṛit manuscripts might be extant, I decided, after consultation with your predecessor, to confine my researches chiefly to those places which Dr. Bühler had visited on his tour in November and December 1866 and January 1867, and about which he was enabled to give me some general information. Dr. Bühler also placed various lists of manuscripts at my disposal, which he had procured on his tour, or which had been sent to him subsequently. During the four weeks I was absent from Poona, I visited Satara, Kurrar, Ashte, Sangli, Miruj, Kolapur, Kagul, Napani, Sankeshwar, Wattanmurri, Belgaum and Dharwar. At Miruj, at Kolapur, and at Belgaum, I stayed three days; at each of the remaining places, one or two days.

3. On the whole, I may express myself satisfied with the results of my tour. I received a great number of lists of manuscripts, and examined as many manuscripts as my very limited stay in each place would allow me to do. Yet I cannot but admit that I left some places disappointed. Many of the possessors of books are very averse to showing their libraries to strangers. Even with the assistance of the mamlatdárs, kárbárís, head-masters of schools, &c., it took me often a long time to induce the owners of libraries to communicate to me lists of the books in their possession.

I had great difficulty in convincing these gentlemen that Government, in ordering me to examine the various Sanskṛit libraries, had no other object than the preservation of Sanskṛit literature. And not seldom it happened that, when I hoped I had succeeded in convincing owners of books of the real intentions of Government, lists were brought to me which I had good reason to believe did not contain the titles of all the works which the owners really possessed. Much time was lost in this way, which more advantageously might have been bestowed on the examination of manuscripts. From the experience which I have thus gained myself, as well as from the judgment which I have formed on tours made by other scholars, and from the opinions of gentlemen who are well acquainted with this country, it would appear to me advisable that, whenever any scholar intends to proceed on a tour in search of manuscripts, he should fix at least three months beforehand on the part of the country which he wishes to visit, and that he should send a good Śástrí to make enquiries and to obtain lists of the books extant in the various libraries. By this means the scholar would be enabled to devote most of his time to the examination of the manuscripts mentioned in the lists previously prepared by his Śástrí.

4. Next to the examination of manuscripts, I considered it one of the main objects of my tour to interest Native gentlemen residing in the various places which I visited, in the plans of Government: and in this aim I venture to believe that I was successful. I explained to these gentlemen the way in which lists of manuscripts ought to be prepared to be of use, and left with them printed forms in which to catalogue all books which they might meet with. I also furnished them with printed lists of desirable manuscripts which I had previously prepared with the help of my colleague, Dr. Bühler. Several of these gentlemen have taken great interest in the work of cataloguing manuscripts. Since my return to Poona, I have received some excellent lists from Mr. Mahádev W. Barve, the Deputy Collector of Dharwar, containing the titles and descriptions of the manuscripts that are extant at Nargund, at Dharwar, and at Konnoor; also from Mr. Lakshman Y. Ashkhedkar, at Belgaum, and from Mr. Mahádev M. Kunte, the Head Master of the Kolapur High School. In some instances I appointed Śástrís to prepare, with the permission of the owners, reliable lists of the works actually existing in certain libraries. Owners of libraries generally possess lists of the works in their possession, but these lists give only very scanty information; they contain mostly only the titles of the works, and rarely, besides this, the number of ślokas in each work. Moreover, in

many cases, a great number of the manuscripts mentioned in the Native lists have disappeared from the library, so that altogether but little reliance can be placed on these lists. Mr. Bálakrishṇa M. Kalganokar, the Master of the Anglo-Vernacular School at Ashte, prepared a good list of the books contained in the great library of the Limaye family; and other lists are still in preparation.

5. I have begun to compile a classified catalogue from the lists so received, and from those which I have prepared myself; but, as much of the material for this catalogue has come only lately into my hands, and as by far the greater part of my time is taken up by other duties, I have not yet been able to catalogue more than about 600 manuscripts. The result of my labours in this direction I submit to you in Appendix D.

6. From the lists of works which I have received, and from the information which I have gathered on my tour, I may, I think, state with confidence, that only few books that are not yet known to European scholars are to be found in the Southern Mahratta Country. There are no very old libraries in this part of the Presidency, and most of the Sanskṛit learning has, so far as I am able to judge at present, been imported from the north of India within the last two centuries.

7. I cannot leave this subject without adding a few remarks on the state of Sanskṛit learning in the parts which I have visited on my tour. Though I have endeavoured to become acquainted with all those Śástrís who were mentioned to me with praise of their learning, I regret to state that I have found only few really good scholars. Most of the men with whom I conversed on various branches of their ancient literature had only a slight knowledge of the subjects which they professed to know. The race of the old profound scholars is evidently dying out fast. I will not here discuss the causes which have brought about this state of things, nor will I dwell on the advantages which this country is sure to derive eventually from the European method of studying Sanskṛit; but I venture to maintain that no unprejudiced scholar can anticipate without a feeling of deep regret, and without serious apprehension, the days when the class of the old Śástrís will be extinct. The philosophical literature of India comprises many difficult works, written on a method which requires not only that they should be read, but that their concise sentences should be explained by a full oral instruction. Many of these works, although accompanied by numbers of written commentaries, are almost unintelligible without the help of the tradition embodied in, and kept up by, the Śástrís. But this tradition being merely oral, is likely to die

with the generation. I have frequently discussed this subject with Native scholars, and have found that the remedy which they propose is the re-institution by Government of the old Sanskṛit schools in which nothing but Sanskṛit was studied. But the time of these schools has gone by; and where they still exist, they do, as far as I have observed, no longer fulfil the functions for which they were established. A careful examination of the Grammar and Logic Schools at Sangli has convinced me that Sanskṛit learning can derive only few benefits from the existence of those and similar establishments. In order to guard against its total loss, the traditional explanation of the scientific literature of India ought to be fixed in writing; otherwise, in the present neglect, it will pass away with this generation of Śástrís. To avert this, it occurs to me that part of the magnificent sum which Government has assigned to the preservation of Sanskṛit literature might be expended on encouraging young Native scholars to collect and publish as much of this traditionary learning as they can gather from the best Śástrís.

8. I have purchased during the quarter under report the following seventeen original manuscripts:—

1. Vájasaneyiprátisákhyadípiká, by Rámágnihotrin; 89 leaves.
2. Harivaṇśa, with commentary, 473 leaves.
3. Kálikápuraṇá, 239 leaves.
4. Naishadhiya commentary, by Mallinátha, 952 leaves; 150 years old.
5. Mantramahodadhi, with commentary; 190 leaves.
6. Saundaryalahari, with commentary, by Śríkaivalyáśrama; 86 leaves.
7. Paribháshárthamañjari, by Bhíma; 95 leaves.
8. Vaiyákaraṇasiddhántamañjúshá; 307 leaves.
9. Prasáda, 306 leaves; 284 years old.
10. A commentary on the Prakriyákaumudi, by Krishṇapaṇḍita; 314 leaves; 242 years old.
11. Kulárṇava; 138 leaves.
12. Setubandha; 236 leaves.
13. Nirṇayadípaka; 436 leaves.
14. Yájñavalkyasmṛiti; 58 leaves.
15. Śántiratna; 347 leaves.
16. Kálatattvavivechana; 380 leaves.
17. Rugviniśchaya, with commentary; 451 leaves.

The commentary on the Naishadhíya by Mallinátha, the Vájasaneyiprátiśákhyadípiká, and the Paribháshárthamañjarí, were, to the best of my knowledge, up to the present unknown to European scholars; some others of these manuscripts are rare. All are very well and correctly written, and part of them are, for Sanskṛit manuscripts, of considerable antiquity. Most of them, doubtless, are to be found in the libraries of Europe; but I feel convinced that European scholars will be glad to receive additional and correct copies. I cannot conceal from you the misgivings which I have at times felt regarding the purchase of manuscripts. Though I possess printed catalogues of several of the most important libraries of Europe, and although I am, from personal knowledge, tolerably familiar with the manuscripts existing in other libraries, yet I am sometimes in doubt whether manuscripts of a particular work do exist in Europe, or whether the condition of the manuscripts in European collections makes the purchase of new manuscripts of the same work advisable. In all such cases, I have, up the present, considered it best to buy the manuscripts that I could lay hold of, provided they were correct, and could be purchased for a moderate sum. The amount of money which I have expended on the above-named manuscripts will appear from Appendix A.

9. The following nine manuscripts have been copied for Government:—

1. A commentary on the Paráśaragṛihyasútra, by Agnihotrín Harihara.
2. A commentary on the Áśvaláyanagṛihyasútra, by Devasvámin.
3. Dyánitimañjarí.
4. Áśvaláyanakáriká.
5. Śákalakáriká.
6. Mṛichchhakaṭikávṛitti.
7. Bṛihachchhabdenduśekhara.
8. Siradeva's Paribháshávṛitti.
9. Gautamí Mitákshará Haradattakṛitá.

The prices paid for these copies are given in Appendix B.

10. Copies of the following works are in preparation:—

1. Maṇḍalabráhmaṇa.
2. Maṇḍalabráhmaṇavyákhyá.
3. Táṇḍyabráhmaṇabháshya.
4. Bháshikasvara.
5. Bháshikasútrabháshya.
6. Saptasvaralakshaṇa.
7. Phitsútra.
8. Gadádharakṛitagṛihyasútrabháshya.
9. Hariharabháshya.
10. Ujjvaladatta's Uṇádivṛitti.
11. Haláyudha's Amṛitasañjivaní.
12. Hemádrichintámaṇi.
13. Rapratyáharakhaṇḍana, by Vaidyanáthapáyaguṇḍa.

11. The statement contained in Appendix C shews that I have expended altogether R452-14-1, and that there remain, therefore, R647-1-11 of the sum of R1,100 entrusted to me by Government.

12. In conclusion, I feel it an agreeable duty to express my sincere thanks to the following gentlemen who have assisted me by their influence and advice, and who have taken a warm interest in the work entrusted to me by Government:—the Collectors of Satara and Dharwar; the Political Resident at Kolapur; the Educational Inspector of the Southern Division; Mr. M. W. Barve, Deputy Collector at Dharwar; Mr. Vírabhadra M. Pandit, Munsiff at Chikodi; Mr. M. M. Kunte, Head Master of the High School at Kolapur; Mr. L. Y. Ashkhedkar at Belgaum; the Mamlatdárs of Kurrar and Malwa; the Kárbárí at Kagul; Mr. G. B. Nene, Head Master of the English School at Satara; Mr. B. B. Limaye, Head Master of the English School at Miruj; and Mr. N. M. Ronghe, Head Master of the Anglo-Vernacular School at Kurrar.

APPENDIX A.

PURCHASE OF ORIGINAL MANUSCRIPTS.

	R	a.	p.
1. Vájasaneyiprátiśákhyadípiká	15	0	0
2. Harivaṇśa	25	0	0
3. Kálikápuráṇa	40	0	0
4. Naishadhiya Commentary	68	0	0
5. Mantramahodadhi	10	0	0
6. Saundaryalaharí	5	0	0
7. Paribháshárthamañjarí	6	0	0
8. Vaiyákaraṇasiddhántamañjúshá	12	0	0
9. Prasáda	12	0	0
10. Commentary on the Prakriyákaumudí	10	0	0
11. Kulárṇava	5	0	0
12. Setubandha	6	0	0
13. Nirṇayadípaka	11	0	0
14. Yájñavalkyasmṛiti	4	0	0
15. Śántiratna	11	0	0
16. Kálatattvavivechana	10	0	0
17. Rugviniśchaya	10	0	0
TOTAL	260	0	0

APPENDIX B.

COPYING OF MANUSCRIPTS.

	R	a.	p.
1. Commentary on Paráśaragṛihyasútra	17	0	0
2. Commentary on Áśvaláyanagṛihyasútra	13	5	3
3. Dyánítimañjarí	22	0	0
4. Áśvaláyanakáriká	3	13	2
5. Śákalakáriká	6	0	0
6. Mṛichchhakaṭikávṛitti	4	3	8
7. Bṛihachchhabdenduśekhara	13	9	0
8. Síradeva's Paribháshávṛitti	12	15	0
9. Gautamí Mitákshará Haradattakṛitá	16	0	0
TOTAL	108	14	1

APPENDIX C.

STATEMENTS OF ACCOUNTS.

	R	a.	p.
Purchase of original manuscripts	260	0	0
Copying of manuscripts	108	14	1
Printing of forms for cataloguing manuscripts	16	0	0
Service stamps	10	0	0
Paid to Mr. B. M. Kálgánokar, at Ashte, for preparing a catalogue of the Limmaye Library	25	0	0
Paid to a Śástrí at Miruj for cataloguing manuscripts	10	0	0
Paid to several other Śástrís	23	0	0
Balance	647	1	11
TOTAL	1,100	0	0

F. KIELHORN.

Extract from the Proceedings of the Government of Bombay, in the General Department,—No. 1975, dated the 18th August 1869.

READ the following :—

Letter from the Director of Public Instruction, No. 1242, dated 13th July 1869, submitting, with reference to Government Resolution No. 2357, dated the 10th December last, reports by Drs. Bühler and Kielhorn of their proceedings in searching for Sanskrit manuscripts in the past season, and stating that he proposes to print them as appendices to his annual report, and that the catalogue of manuscripts required by the Government of India is under preparation.

RESOLUTION.—The thanks of Government to be conveyed to Professors Bühler and Kielhorn for the care and industry they have displayed in carrying out the duty entrusted to them; and copies of their interesting reports to be forwarded for the information of the Government of India.

2. Government have read with much satisfaction their testimony to the assistance rendered to them by the several gentlemen named in their reports.

3. Copies to be furnished to the Secretary of the Bombay Branch of the Royal Asiatic Society.

From A. P. HOWELL, Esq., Under-Secretary to the Government of India, Home Department, to the Secretary to the Asiatic Society of Bengal,—No. 4111, dated Simla, the 8th September 1869.

I am directed to forward, for the information of the Asiatic Society, copies of reports* by Drs. Bühler and Kielhorn of their proceedings in searching for Sanskṛit manuscripts in the Bombay Presidency.

* Dr. Kielhorn's report, dated 20th June.
Dr. Bühler's report, dated 5th July.

2. A copy of Appendix D to Dr. Kielhorn's report will hereafter be forwarded.

From A. P. HOWELL, Esq., Under-Secretary to the Government of India, Home Department, to the Honorary Secretary to the Trustees of the Indian Museum,—No. 4112, dated Simla, the 8th September 1869.

I am directed to forward, for the information of the Trustees of the Indian Museum, copies of reports† by Drs. Bühler and Kielhorn of their proceedings in searching for Sanskṛit manuscripts in the Bombay Presidency.

† Dr. Kielhorn's report, dated 20th June.
Dr. Bühler's report, dated 5th July.

2. A copy of Appendix D to Dr. Kielhorn's report will hereafter be forwarded.

From A. P. HOWELL, Esq., Under-Secretary to the Government of India, Home Department, to WHITLEY STOKES, Esq.,—No. 4113, dated Simla, the 8th September 1869.

I am directed to forward, for your information, copies of reports‡ by Drs. Bühler and Kielhorn of their proceedings in searching for Sanskṛit manuscripts in the Bombay Presidency.

‡ Dr. Kielhorn's report, dated 20th June.
Dr. Bühler's report, dated 5th July.

2. A copy of Appendix D to Dr. Kielhorn's report will hereafter be forwarded.

REPORTED to the Right Hon'ble the Secretary of State for India, in letter No. 79 of 1869, dated the 20th September.

Extract from the Proceedings of the Government of Bombay, in the General Department,—No. 1898, dated the 11th August 1870.

READ—

Letter from the Director of Public Instruction, No. 1413, dated 30th July 1870, forwarding, for transmission to the Government of India, a report prepared by Dr. Kielhorn, in the absence of Dr. Bühler on sick leave, of his proceedings in acquiring Sanskṛit manuscripts during 1869-70.

RESOLUTION.—The report and list of manuscripts to be forwarded to the Government of India with a request that they will communicate at an early date their instructions in regard to the amendment in the compiling and printing of catalogues of Sanskṛit manuscripts suggested in paragraphs 7 and 8 of Dr. Kielhorn's report No. 122 of the 22nd March 1870, which was forwarded to the Government of India with this Government's endorsement No. 792, dated the 2nd April last.

No. 1899.

FORWARDED to the Government of India, with the report and list.

From F. KIELHORN, Esq., Superintendent of Sanskṛit Studies, Bombay, to J. B. PEILE, Esq., M.A., Director of Public Instruction, Bombay,—dated Deccan College, Poona, the 1st July 1870.

I have the honour to submit to you the following report on the progress during the last year of the search for Sanskṛit manuscripts instituted by Dr. Bühler and myself, in accordance with Government Resolution No. 2357, dated the 10th of December 1868.

2. The Bombay Presidency was, up to the beginning of December 1869, divided between Dr. Bühler and myself, as in the preceding year. Since the departure of Dr. Bühler for Europe in December last, however, the work, which was commenced by him in the Northern Division, was

carried on by myself, in addition to my own work in the Southern Division.

3. I regret that my duties in the College, which, owing to Professor Oxenham's absence during the greater portion of the year under report, were heavier than usual, and the preparation of some literary works, one of which you had desired me to undertake, have prevented me from absenting myself from Poona during the cold season for any length of time, and that I have thus been unable to make anything deserving the name of a tour in search for manuscripts. The very short time—about ten days—which I could spare for travelling, I spent, with your permission, in visiting Ratnagiri, where I combined my endeavours for the preservation of Sanskṛit manuscripts with an examination of the Sanskṛit classes of the Ratnagiri High School, as may have been reported to you by the Educational Inspector of the Central Division. Dr. Bühler, on the other hand, visited again, I understand, the greater portion of the Northern Division in the course of his work as Educational Inspector, and took, with his usual care and circumspection, efficient steps to carry out the orders of Government.

4. In the year under report, I have carried through the press the first fascicle of my "Classified Alphabetical Catalogue of Sanskṛit Manuscripts in the Southern Division of the Bombay Presidency." As copies of this work have been forwarded to you, it is needless in this place to speak of its contents and arrangement; but I may, perhaps, be permitted to remark that this specimen number of my catalogue appears to have been received with favour by European Sanskṛit scholars.

5. At present I am engaged in preparing for the press the second part of the above catalogue, from the materials which I have collected in the course of last year. Amongst the latter I may mention a catalogue of the manuscripts in the library of His Highness the Mahárája of Kolapur, prepared by order of Colonel Anderson, the Political Agent of Kolapur and the Southern Mahratta States; another catalogue of a large number of manuscripts in Poona, and a catalogue of a large library of Sanskṛit manuscripts in Satara, prepared for me under the supervision of Mr. G. B. Nene, the Head Master of the Anglo-Vernacular School in Satara. From Ráo Sáheb Bhikaji Rámchandra, the Deputy Educational Inspector at Ahmednagar, I have received a long list of manuscripts procurable in his district; and the Deputy Educational Inspector of Ratnagiri has communicated to me lists of manuscripts, as well as

other valuable information regarding the state of Sanskṛit learning in his sub-division. It would lead me too far to mention all the other smaller lists which have been forwarded to me in the course of the year.

6. I have ventured to submit to you, in paragraphs 7 and 8 of my report on a classified catalogue of Sanskṛit works in the Sarasvatíbháṇḍáram Library of His Highness the Maháràja of Mysore (letter No. 122 of 1869-70, dated March 22nd, 1870), my opinion on the practice of compiling and printing catalogues of Sanskṛit manuscripts. As further experience has tended to convince me of the correctness of my views, especially those expressed in paragraph 8 of the letter referred to, I shall be glad if you will permit me to carry them into practice in the second part of my catalogue.

7. Dr. Bühler, on his departure for Europe, handed over to me a manuscript copy of an exceedingly bulky classified catalogue of Sanskṛit manuscripts in the Northern Division of this Presidency, which had been prepared under his superintendence by different Śástrís. I regret that Dr. Bühler's illness and subsequent departure from India have prevented him from subjecting this catalogue to that final revision which it must undergo before it can be printed,—a task which I would gladly have undertaken myself had my other engagements permitted me to do so.

8. From the enormous number of works that are mentioned in the catalogue referred to in the preceding paragraph, and from the long lists of manuscripts which were sent to me by my agent in the Northern Division since Dr. Bühler's departure, it appears that Gujarat is far richer in Sanskṛit libraries than the southern part of this Presidency. Besides, Gujarat manuscripts are generally older and more correct than those procurable in the Dekhan and Konkan, south of Bombay. Any Sanskṛit scholar, therefore, who might have the good fortune to be allowed to travel in Gujarat and the adjoining districts for any length of time, would, in my opinion, have a good opportunity of collecting a great number of rare and important works.

9. The following is an alphabetical list of manuscripts bought for Government during the year under report :—

Number.	Title of Work.	Author.	Subject.	Leaves.	Lines on each page.	Number of Ślokas.	Samvat (if given).	Complete or not.
1	Anuthάthyá	Vallabhácharya	Vedánta	452	6-10	5,931	...	Complete.
2	Anekárthasangraha	Hemachandra	Kosha	43	15	1,822	...	,,
3	Alankáratilaka	Vágbhaṭa	Alankára	33	15	1,152	...	Incomplete.
4	A'bhíyádhikárasútráṇi	Páṇini	Vyákaraṇa	4	7	42	1716	Complete.
5	A'ryasiddhánta	A'ryabhaṭṭa	Jyotiḥśástra	46	10-11	380	...	,,
6	Uṇádivṛitti	Ujjvaladatta.	Vyákaraṇa	132	6-7	2,390	...	,,
7	Uttarachampú	A'treyavyankaṭa	Kávya	13	13	425	...	Incomplete.
8	Uttarádhyayanasútrárthakathá	......	Jaina work	254	15	7,620	...	Complete.
9	Upasargaharastotra	Sadvara	,,	25	15	1,000	1823	,,
10	Ṛiktantravyákaraṇa	......	Vyákaraṇa	14	6	78	...	,,
11	Ekáksharanámamálá	Viśvaśambhu	Kosha	4	15	163	...	,,
12	Katháḥ*	......	Jaina work	22	16	660	...	Incomplete.
13	Kalyáṇamandirastotravrittiḥ Saubhágyamanjarí.	......	,,	11	15	346	1627	Complete.
14	Kátiyaśráddhasútrabháshya.	Gadádhara	Dharma	61	9	1,090	1853	,,
15	Kámasamúha	Ananta.	Kávya	45	12	1,160	...	,,
16	Kálikápuráṇa	Vyása	Puráṇa.	353	11	...	...	Incomplete.
17	Kirátárjuníyaṭíká (Sarga, XV)	Pṛithunáthabhaṭṭa	......	12	14	275	...	Complete.
18	Kumárapálacharitra	......	Jaina work	57	15	3,380	1558	,,
19	,,	......	,,	85	15	3,380	...	,,
20	Kaumudíkathá	......	,,	102	11	3,145	...	,,
21	Gurvávalí	......	,, (in Mágadhí).	12	12	300	1680	,,
22	Gotrapravaranirṇaya	......	Dharma	11	7	100	...	,,
23	Gautamasútra	Gautama	,,	14	10	225	1854	Incomplete.
24	Gautamasútra A'chárakáṇḍa	......	,,	8	11	160	...	Complete.
25	Gautamasútrapanchádhyáyí	Gautama	Nyáya	14	9	255	...	,,
26	Grahagaṇitachintámaṇau Goládhyáye prathamádhikáraḥ	Chintámaṇi	Jyotiḥśástra	58	10	1,800	...	Incomplete.
27	Ghaṭakarpariká Saṭíká	Kálidása	Kávya	10	10	178	...	Complete.
28	Chamatkárachintámaṇi	......	Jaina work (Jyotiḥśástra).	9	7	187	...	,,

29	Jambúcharitra	Padmasundaragaṇi.	Jaina work (in Mágadhí).	41	7	720	1769	„
30	Jambúdvípaprajñapti	......	„ „	98	15	4,171	...	„
31	Jambúdvípaprajñaptisútram ṭíká-sahitam.	Commentary by Híravijayasúri.	Jaina work	454	15	18,398	...	„
32	Jnátádharmakathásútra	......	„ (in Sanskṛit and Prákṛit).	155	15	4,570	...	„
33	Daṇḍaka	......	Jaina work (in Mágadhí).	20	16	450	1692	„
34	Tattvachintámáṇyáloka	Jagaddevamiśra	Nyáya	122	10	3,660	1646	„
35	Teravállí	......	Jaina work (in Prákṛit).	8	12	143	...	„
36	Daśavaikálikasútra	......	Jaina work (in Mágadhí).	19	16	840	1650	„
37	Dútángadanáṭaka.	Hanumat	Náṭaka.	6	13	125	1910	„
38	Dhátutaranginí	Śríharshakírtti	Vyákaraṇa	166	14	2,020	...	„
39	Nalachampúṭíká	Śrídurgáchandreśvara.	......	25	18	1,500	...	Incomplete.
40	Navatattvárthavivaraṇa	......	Jaina work (in Mágadhí).	21	13-20	1,300	...	Complete
41	Navalingasútráṇi	......	Jaina work	6	14	150	...	„
42	Nágarájaśataka	Nágarája	Kávya	15	9	252	1926	„
43	Pañchagauḍabhedáḥ	......	Dharma	3	7	16	...	„
44	Panchatantra	Vishnuśarman	......	54	15	1,300	...	Incomplete.
45	Pañchadráviḍabhedáḥ	......	Dharma	3	8	22	...	Complete.
46	Pañchopákhyána	Vishnuśarman	......	93	18	5,525	...	„
47	Pattávali	......	Jaina work	2-7	13	140	...	Incomplete
48	Páraskaragṛihyasútravyákhyána	Agnihotriharihara	......	207	10	4,140	1791	Complete.
49	Páráśaríjátaka, Bhuktilakshaṇa and Śeshagrahaṇa.	Paráśara	Jyotiḥśástra	11	7	98	...	„
50	Páráśaríbhásháphala	......	„	13	9	234	1926	„
51	Párshadavyákhyá	......	Prátiśákhya	94	10	2,200	1626	Incomplete.
52	„	......	„	262	8	4,680	...	„
53	Prakriyákaumudí	......	Vyákaraṇa	88	9	2,200	...	„
54	Prakriyákaumudívyákhyáprasáda	Vitthala	„	659	10	11,862	1606	Complete.

* The proper title of this work is not given in the manuscript.

Number.	Title of Work.	Author.	Subject.	Leaves.	Lines on each page.	Number of Slokas.	Samvat (if given).	Complete or not.
55	Prabodhachandrodayanáṭakaṃ saṭíkam.	Kṛishṇamiśra. Commentary by Kámadása.	Náṭaka.	82	13-14	2,952	...	Complete.
56	Praśamarati	......	Jaina work	5	33	330	...	„
57	Bálachittánurañjiní Kávyaprákaśaṭiká.	Sarasvatítírthasvámin.	Alaṅkára	133	15	5,000	1585	„
58	Bṛihadvasantarája	......	Jyotiḥśástra	91	11	2,264	1599	„
59	Brahmaguptasiddhánta	Brahmagupta	„	73	11	1,260	...	„
60	Brahmaguptoktakhaṇḍakhádyakaṭíká.	......	„	105	12	3,300	...	Incomplete.
61	Brahmavaivarttapuráṇa, Brahmakhaṇḍa.	Vyása	Puráṇa.	92	10	2,000	...	„
62	Bhágavatasubodhinídaśamaskandhavyákhyá.	Vallabhadíkshita	„	116	11	3,016	...	Complete.
63	Bhuvanadípaka	Padmaprabhúsúri.	Jaina work	12	7	125	1765	„
64	Bhṛigusaṃhitá	......	Jyotiḥśástra	87	9	1,462	...	„
65	Manichchhasamjuaka	Mahídásabhaṭṭa	„	9	7	85	...	„
66	Manitha	......	Jaina work	4	14	121	...	„
67	Málatímádhavaṭíká	Jagadvara	......	18-83	13	2,953	...	Incomplete.
68	Mímáṇsárthasaṅgraha	Laugákshibhaṭṭabháskara.	Púrvamímáṇsá	27	8	328	...	Complete.
69	Mṛitasañjíviní	Haláyudha	Chhandas	31	12	1,040	...	„
70	Yogayátrá	Varáhamihira	Jyotiḥśástra	18	14	700	...	„
71	Ratnávalí	Śriharsha	Náṭaka.	46	10	810	1654	„
72	Rapratyáhárakhaṇḍana	Vaidyanáthapáyaguṇḍa.	Vyákaraṇa	20	13	798	...	„
73	Rájaníti	Devídása	Níti (in Prákrit)	27	9	450	...	„
74	Rájapraśnasútra	......	Jaina work (in Mágadhí).	42	15	2,000	..	„
75	Rádhávinodakávyaṃ saṭíkam	Rámachandrakavi	Kávya	8	15	180	...	„
76	Lílávatí.	......	Nyáya	20	10	500	...	Incomplete.
77	Vanadurgopanishad	......	Upanishad	21	12	500	...	Complete.
78	Vasishṭhasiddhánte Bhúgoládhyáyaḥ.	......	Jyotiḥśástra	12	9	160	1926	„

79	Vasudhará	......	Jaina work	9	9	80	...	,,
80	Vágbhaṭálankára	Vágbhaṭa	Alankára	10	15	325	...	,,
81	Vádaratnákarasútra	......	Jaina work	23	18	1,150	...	,,
82	Vipákasútra	......	,, (in Mágadhí).	29	13	1,080	...	,,
83	Viváhapastala	......	Jaina work	25	5	1,000	...	,,
84	Vishamaślokí ṭíká	......	Commentary on difficult verses of the Mahábhárata.	88	16	2,992	1724	,,
85	Vírasiṇhávaloka	Vírasiṇhadeva	Vaidyaśástra	2-415	8	5,810	1572	Incomplete.
86	Vṛiddhapáráśarí	......	Jyotiḥśástra	11	9	80	...	,,
87	Vetálapañchaviṇśatiká	Śivadása	......	81	10	1,600	...	Complete.
88	Vyásasútrabháshya	Ánandatírthasvámin.	Vedánta	122	10-11	2,151	...	,,
89	Vyutpattidípiká	......	Jaina work	3-164	15	3,075	...	Incomplete.
90	Śataślokí	Vopadevapaṇḍita	Vaidyaśástra	8	11	245	...	Complete.
91	Śánkhyáyanasútra	Śánkhyáyana	Sútra	192	8	2,850	...	,,
92	Śánticharita	Bhávachandrasúri	Jaina work	162	15	5,832	1535	,,
93	Śábarabháshya	Kumárilabhaṭṭa	Púrvamímáṇsá	137	10-11	6,630	1575	Incomplete.
94	,,	,,	,,	95	10	3,040	...	,,
95	Śiromaṇiṭiká	Bhavánanda	Nyáya	209	16	8,800	...	Complete.
96	Śukranítisára	......	Níti	102	7	2,500	...	,,
97	Śaunakoktavṛiddhákáriká	Śaunaka	Dharma	188	11	4,700	1553	,,
98	Śrígurvávaliváitti	Dharmasáragaṇi	Jaina work	21	15	600	...	,,
99	Śrípálarásah	......	,, (in Mágadhí	27	15	978	...	Incomplete.
100	Śrímadviṭṭhala Ṛigmantrasárabháshya.	Káśináthopádhyáya.	Dharma	39	13	1,404	1731	Complete.
101	Śríhariguṇákhya	Keśava	Vaidyaśástra	12	11	440	...	,,
102	Shaḍdarśanasamuchchayaṭiká	Haribhadra	Jaina work	19	18	1,252	1714	,,
103	Shaḍbháshástotra	......	,,	3	13	96	1851	,,
104	Shoḍaśakaprakaraṇa, with commentary.	......	,,	38	16	1,850	1896	,,
105	Sangrahaṇávashúrṇi	......	,,	15	23	1,320	1530	,,
106	Sangrahaṇivṛitti	......	,,	72	15	3,500	...	,,
107	Sangrahaṇisútra	......	,, (in Mágadhí)	24	9	390	...	,,

Number.	Title of Work.	Author.	Subject.	Leaves.	Lines on each page.	Number of Ślokas.	Samvat (if given).	Complete or not.
108	Sadácháráchandriká . . .	......	Dharma . .	77	10-11	1,500	1787	Complete.
109	Sanatkumárarása	......	Jaina work (in Mágadhí).	19	16	630	1765	"
110	Samaváyasútra	......	Jaina work . .	46	13	1,667	1626	"
111	Sarasvatíhridayálankárabharatabháshya.	Śrimannányapati .	Alankára . .	221	11	7,920	...	Incomplete.
112	Sarvamangalá*	Śeshaśarman. .	Vyákaraṇa . .	102	10	3,550	...	"
113	Sarvánukramaṇivṛitti . . .	......	Anukramaṇi. .	178	9	4,450	1449	Complete.
114	Sárasangraha	Bhaṭṭamahádeva .	Jyotiḥśástra . .	27	15	1,080	...	"
115	Siṇhásanadvátriṇśattiká . .	......	Kathá . . .	23	11	550	...	Incomplete.
116	Síradevabṛihatparibhásháv̤ṛittiṭippaní.	Śrímánaśarman .	Vyákaraṇa . .	16	10	500	1825	"
117	Sugamángasútra	......	Jaina work (gadhí). .	31	11	1,000	...	Complete.
118	Smṛitichandriká	Bhaṭṭopádhyáya .	Dharma . .	210	10	6,300	...	Incomplete.
119	Tleiciavyákaraṇadípiká . .	Jinaságarasúri .	Vyákaraṇa . .	63	17	6,750	...	"
120	Tlaimavyákaraṇa	......	" Jaina work (in Prakṛit).	16	12	620	...	Complete.

* A commentary on Nágojabhaṭṭa's Paribháshenduśekhara.

Besides, there are fifteen manuscripts which have not been forwarded to me by the Librarian of Elphinstone College together with the other manuscripts collected by Dr. Bühler; these I am obliged to quote from the list of manuscripts that accompanied your letter No. 3992 of 1869-70.

	Title of work.	*Author.*	*Number of leaves.*
No. 121.	Pradyumnacharitra	Ratnachandrasúri	92
122.	Háritasmṛiti	Hárita	110
123.	Praśnavyákaraṇaṃ vivṛitisahitam	Abhayadevasúri	111
124.	Karmagranthavṛitti	Devachandrasúri	54
125.	Siddhántasundara	......	49
126.	Ávaśyavṛitti	......	152
127.	Bṛihatkathá	Somadeva	44
128.	Áchárángavṛitti	Ácháraśílanka	291
129.	Kávyánuśásanaviveka	Hemachandra	150
130.	Amarakoshasya saṭíkasya káṇḍam.	Amarasiṇha	131
131.	Amarakoshaḥ Sudhákhyaṭíká-sahitaḥ.	,,	412
132.	Párśvanáthacharitra	....	152
133.	Sadvṛittidharmasangraha	Mahávíra	341
134.	Chintámaṇyanumánabhakta	Ruchidatta	115
135.	Pratyakshaparichchheda	Vijayadeva	122

10. The following is a statement shewing the money received and expended by *myself* on account of cataloguing and buying manuscripts :—

(A) Received.	R *a. p.*
Balance of last year	647 1 11
Received from Dr. Bühler	914 8 1
TOTAL	1,561 10 0

(B) Expended.	R *a. p.*	R *a. p.*
1. To the Manager of the *Indu Prakash* Press for printing my Catalogue	......	325 0 0
2. *(a)* Tour of Ratnagiri (railway and steamer fare, R 109-15; travelling allowance for 7 days, R 70)	179 15 0	
(b) Railway fare of Mr. Joshi from Ahmedabad to Poona and back	16 0 0	
(c) Paid to a peon of Elphinstone College for bringing Dr. Bühler's MSS. to Poona	7 0 0	
Carried over	......	202 15 0

	Rs a. p.	Rs a. p.
Brought forward .	......	202 15 0
3. *(a)* To Mr. Joshi for copying, preparing lists, &c., from October 5th, 1869, to April 5th, 1870	180 0 0	
(b) To Mr. G. B. Nene in Satara, on account of the same .	50 0 0	
(c) To Govind Śástrí for the same	25 0 0	
(d) To Mr. Sane for arranging lists	15 0 0	
	———	270 0 0
4. Paid for MSS.—		
(a) In Poona and Ratnagiri	55 11 0	
(b) " Gujarat	196 4 0	
(c) " Káttiáwár	15 10 0	
(d) " Kolapur and Kagul	19 10 0	
(e) " Dharwar	9 15 7	
	———	297 2 7
5. *(a)* Printing new forms	18 0 0	
(b) Service stamps	10 0 0	
(c) To Mr. G. Paut for copying letters, &c.	30 0 0	
(d) For cloth for wrapping up MSS.	5 0 0	
	———	63 0 0
6. Balance remaining	......	403 8 5
Total .		1,561 10 5

11. As regards the expenditure in the Northern Division up to December 1869, I beg to refer you to Dr. Bühler's own accounts, forwarded in Appendix A.

APPENDIX A.

Account of money drawn for Sanskrit Manuscripts.

Receipts.	Amount. R	a.	p.	Expenditure.	Amount. R	a.	p.	Total. R	a.	p.
				Copying Fund.						
Balance as per last account	875	3	6	Amount paid to Uttamarám Durlabharám Joshi for copying Sanskṛit manuscripts	196	9	0			
Amount drawn as per bill dated 22nd September 1869—				,, Mr. Prabhákar Rámachandra, for copying Sanskṛit manuscripts	30	0	0			
For transcription of Sanskṛit manuscripts	600	0	0	,, Ráo Sáheb Gopálji Surbhai, to be given to certain persons	27	9	0			
For buying Sanskṛit manuscripts	500	0	0	,, Mártanḍ Śástrí, for copying Sanskṛit manuscripts	15	0	0			
For travelling allowance	500	0	0	,, Deputy Educational Inspector, Khandesh, for copying Sanskṛit manuscripts	30	0	0			
				,, the Rev. Mr. J. Wallace, for printing two tabular forms in English and Sanskṛit, 1,000 copies	29	2	0			
				,, Náráyan Śaṅkar Śástrí, for copying Sanskṛit manuscripts	30	0	0	358	4	0
Carried over	2,475	3	6	Carried over	......			358	4	0

Account of Money drawn for Sanskrit Manuscripts—continued.

Receipts.	Amount.	Expenditure.	Amount.	Total.
	R a. p.		R a. p.	R a. p.
Brought forward .	2,475 3 6	Brought forward .	......	358 4 0
		Amount paid to Girija Śankar Śástri, for copying Sanskṛit manuscripts	7 8 0	
		„ Viśvanáth V. Śástri, for copying out lists . .	40 0 0	47 8 0
		Buying Fund.		
		Amount paid to Purushottam Bhikhári, for Kálikápuráṇa . .	45 0 0	
		„ Mártaṇḍ Śástri, for several Sanskṛit manuscripts .	146 0 0	
		„ Gorji Gaṇpatságar, for several Sanskṛit manuscripts	20 0 0	
		„ Gorji Gangárám, for several Sanskṛit manuscripts,	3 0 0	
		„ Rámachandra Haribhái for several Sanskṛit manuscripts . . .	48 8 0	
		„ Uttamarám Durlabharám Joshi for several Sanskṛit manuscripts . .	183 4 0	
		„ Rámachandra Dínanáth for several Sanskṛit manuscripts . . .	189 11 2	
		„ Rámakrishṇa Mairál, for several Sanskṛit manuscripts	136 0 0	
		„ Girijáśankar Hariśankar		

Receipts	Rs. a. p.	Expenditure	Rs. a. p.	Rs. a. p.
		for several Sanskrit manuscripts . . .	42 0 0	818 7 2
		Travelling Fund.		
		Amount paid to Prabhákar Rámachandra, for salary, railway fare, and contingencies .	63 9 0	
		,, Rámachandra Haribhái, for railway fare, &c. .	7 12 0	
		,, the Assistant Deputy Educational Inspector, Rewa Kanta, S. D., for contingencies . . .	0 4 0	
		,, Mártaṇḍ Śástrí, for pay and contingencies .	72 0 0	
		,, Uttamarám Durlabhrám Joshi, for contingencies.	1 6 0	
		,, Rámchandra Dinanath Śástri	30 0 0	
		,, Bhíma Śástrí, for arranging Sanskṛit manuscripts	30 0 0	
		,, Náráyaṇaśaṅkar Śástrí, for arranging Sanskṛit manuscripts . . .	27 0 0	
		,, Mártaṇḍ Śástrí, for arranging Sanskṛit manuscripts	27 0 0	
		,, Girijáśaṅkar Hariśaṅkar, for arranging Sanskṛit manuscripts . . .	13 0 0	
		,, Bábáji Śákhárám, for arranging Sanskṛit manuscripts . . .	20 0 0	
				291 15 0
Carried over .	2,475 3 6	Carried over .	......	291 15 0

Account of Money drawn for Sanskrit Manuscripts—concluded.

Receipts.	Amount.	Expenditure.	Amount.	Total.
	R a. p.		R a. p.	R a. p.
Brought forward	2,475 3 6	Brought forward	......	291 15 0
		Amount paid to Vishṇu Govind, for arranging Sanskṛit manuscripts	11 0 0	
		" Edalji for six blank books	12 0 0	
		Country thick paper	1 13 0	
		Receipt stamps	0 10 0	
		Needles and thread	0 2 3	
		Gum and paste	0 12 6	
		Scissors	0 1 0	
		2 Brushes	0 5 0	
		Service postage stamps as per receipt	16 0 0	
		3rd class railway fare of one peon from Surat to Bombay and back	6 13 6	
		Total Expenditure	......	1,560 11 5
		Balance	......	914 8 1
Total	2,475 3 6	Total	......	2,475 3 6

J. BÜHLER,
Acting Educational Inspector, N. D.

Extract from the Proceedings of the Government of Bombay, in the General Department,—No. 2816, dated the 2nd October 1871.

TRANSFER from the Educational Department of the Secretariat, No. 749, dated 20th September 1871, of a letter from the Director of Public Instruction, with which he forwards nine copies of the reports by the Sanskṛit Professors of their proceedings in acquiring Sanskṛit manuscripts during 1870-71,—five for transmission to the Government of India, Home Department, and four for His Excellency the Governor and the Members of his Council; and adds that the report forms part of the Appendix of his Report on Public Instruction for 1870-71, now in the press.

RESOLUTION.—The report of Drs. Bühler and Kielhorn is most satisfactory, and should be submitted to the Government of India. Government desire to express their acknowledgments to these gentlemen for their pains-taking efforts in their search for these manuscripts.

No. 2817.

FORWARDED to the Government of India, with a copy of the printed report.

No. 4796, dated Simla, the 18th October 1871.

Endorsed by the Government of India, Home Department.

FORWARDED to the Director General of the Archæological Survey of India for perusal and return.

From G. BÜHLER, Esq., Acting Educational Inspector, Northern Division, to J. B. PEILE, Esq., M.A., Director of Public Instruction, Bombay,—dated Surat, the 13th July 1871.

I have the honour to submit my report on the search for Sanskṛit manuscripts during the period from 1st July 1870 to 10th July 1871.

2. As I was on leave up to 6th November 1870, Dr. Kielhorn was in charge of the operations in the whole Presidency during the first four months of that period. From 6th November, we again divided the work according to the order of Government. In January 1871, Dr. Kielhorn obtained sick leave, and the whole charge, at his request, was made over to me.

3. The number of manuscripts bought by Dr. Kielhorn amounts to seven, among which there is the very rare and important Śriharshacharitra, a poetical account of the great king who, under the name Śiláditya, is mentioned by Hiouen Thsang, the famous Chinese Buddhist pilgrim of the seventh century A.D. The work was first discovered by Mr. Fitz-Edward Hall, and he possesses the only known copies of the book. Our copy, like his, breaks off in the middle of the eighth Uchchhvása.

4. As regards my own operations, I am happy to state that I have been very fortunate, though the pressure of official work, which had accumulated before my arrival, and the interruption of my former connections with my agents, did not allow me to proceed during the travelling season as vigorously as I should have liked to do. Still, the total number of manuscripts bought amounts to fifty-seven, among which forty-four are Bráhmanical and the rest Jaina books. Nearly all these manuscripts are very old—some as old as four hundred years,—and only two or three are modern transcripts made to order. The most important acquisition is that of a collection of books belonging to the Atharvaveda, enumerated under Nos. 1 to 16 of the accompanying list. Professor Haug saw these books on his tour in Gujarat in 1864, and gave an enthusiastic account of them in his report. They were shewn to me in 1869; but it was only last January that I succeeded in obtaining them. Amongst them, three numbers are, as far as I know, new discoveries, *viz.*, the Padapáṭha of the XIXth book of the Atharvasaṃhitá, a small Prátiśákhya, and a Paddhati on the Kauśikasútra. Two other works—the Sarvánukrama and the Śáunakíyá Chaturadhyáyiká—were hitherto known through a single copy each. The news of this purchase seems to have considerably interested my European and American colleagues. Professor Weber published a short notice of these works in the *Transactions of the Royal Academy of Berlin;* and Professor Whitney, of Yale College, Newhaven (United States), wrote to me for copies of the new Prátiśákhya, and of the Śáunakíyá Chaturadhyáyiká, which have been since furnished to him. The Secretary of the Bengal Branch of the Asiatic Society has asked you for a loan of the Gopathabráhmaṇa, to be use din the edition of this work which is in progress in the *Bibliotheca Indica.*

5. Among the other books, I mention as particularly interesting the Gaṇitaskandha of the Vásishṭhasiddhánta, the very old copies of the Mághakávya, and of the Smṛityarthasára, the newly-discovered commentary on that work by Vallabha, the piece of Ekanátha' s commentary

on the Kirátárjuníya, and the fine old manuscript of the Mahábháshya, which, however, is unfortunately not complete.

6. Since I have been in Surat, I have received almost daily offers of manuscripts, and I feel confident that during this year I shall be able to make both large and important additions to our collection.

7. Since the end of the travelling season, I have begun to print a portion of the large catalogue of Sanskṛit manuscripts obtainable in Gujarat, which had been prepared under my superintendence in 1869. The first fascicle, of which 140 pages have been printed, and which contains a list of the Vedic manuscripts (about 1,500 in number), will appear at the end of the current, or in the beginning of the next, month. As the catalogue comprises about twelve to fifteen thousand manuscripts, I doubt whether it will be advisable to print the whole. I should prefer to give selections only from the manuscripts of the common Sanskṛit works.

8. A good many of the minor and more remote towns in Gujarat, which are known to contain large Sanskṛit libraries, have not yet been explored, and it will be my care during this year to procure catalogues of the chief collections there extant.

9. I beg to annex my accounts and the list of books bought. Dr. Kielhorn has sent his accounts and list direct.

Number.	Name of Manuscript in Roman character.	Author.	Subject-matter.	No. of pages.	No. of lines of each page.	Saṃvat.	Where bought.	Remarks.
1	Atharvaveda, Saṃhitá text, K. I—X.	...	Vedic Mantras	199	9	...	Broach	Complete.
2	Ditto Káṇḍas, XI—XVIII	...	„	191	8	...	„	XIV, 2, 71a—75a; & XVIII, 4, 54a;—89a wanting.
3	Ditto Káṇḍa, XIX	...	„	33	9	...	„	Complete.
4	Ditto Káṇḍa, XX	...	„	66	8	...	„	„
5	Pada text, Káṇḍas, I—XX	...	„	435	8	1741	„	„
6	Gopathabráhmaṇa, Púrvárdha	...	Vedic sacrifices	75	9	152, *i.e.*, 1552 or 1522.	„	„
7	Gopathabráhmaṇa, Uttarárdha	...	„	59	10	1795	„	„
8	Vaitánasútra	...	„	48	8	...	„	„
9	Kauśikagṛihyasútra	...	Gṛihya sacrifices	44	12	1740	„	„
10	Saṃhitávidhivivaraṇa	...	Commentary on the preceding.	48	8	1614	„	„
11	Śaunakíyá Chaturadhyáyiká	Śaunaka	On phonetics	13	9	1718	„	„
12	Prátisákhyamúlasútra	...	„	6	10	2718	„	„
13	Máṇḍúkí Síkshá	Maṇḍúkya	„	13	11	...	„	Incomplete.
14	Bṛihatsarvánukrama, Paṭalas I—V.	...	Index to metres and distiches.	48	9	1647	„	Complete.
15	Ditto, Paṭalas VI—X, and 2 leaves of Paṭala XI.	...	„	50	8	1767	„	Incomplete.
16	Jyotisha	...	Astronomy	14	10	1718	„	Complete.
17	Ápastambíyá Mantrapáṭháḥ	...	Mantras for Gṛihya sacrifices.	17	9	1826	Surat	„
18	Ṛigvedasaṃhitábháshya, Ashṭaka I, 1, 2; Ashṭ. II, 1, 2.	Sáyaṇa	Commentary on Ṛigveda.	529	11	1609	„	„
19	Aitareyabráhmaṇabháshya, Pañchiká, 1—2.	„	Commentary on Ait. Br.	14	14	...	„	„
20	Karaṇakamalamártaṇḍa	Daśabala	Astronomy	11	12	...	„	„
21	Kirátárjuníyaṭíká, Sargas 17, 18	Ekanátha	Commentary on an epic poem.	33	18	...	„	„

22	Kaivalyadípiká	Hemádri	Commentary on Vopadeva's Muktáphala.	69	14	...	„	Incomplete.
23	Gotrapravaramañjarí	Purushottama	On the Bráhman races.	87	7	...	„	Complete.
24	Charaṇavyúha	...	On the redactions of the Veda.	6	10	...	„	„
25	Chintámaṇi, Śabdakhaṇḍa	Jayadeva	Nyáya	118	10	1619	„	„
26	Táṇḍyabráhmaṇa	...	On Vedic sacrifices.	280	13	...	„	„
27	Nṛisiṇhachampú	Keśava	Poetry	13	12	...	„	„
28	Páraskaragṛihyasútra and Karkabháshya, I, 1—11, 14.	Páraskara, Karka	On Gṛihya sacrifices.	26	14	...	„	Incomplete.
29	Pushpasútra	...	Sáma singing	63	9	1574	Ahmedabad.	Complete.
30	Bṛihannáradíyapuráṇa	...	Puráṇa	158	9	...	„	Last leaf wanting.
31	Mághakávya	Mágha	Kávya	73	12	1545	Surat	Complete.
32	Mághavallabha, Sargas VI—XX.	Vallabha	Commentary on the preceding.	317	12	...	„	„
33	Málatímádhavachchháyá	...	Translation of Prákṛit passages in the Malatí-mádhaa.	19	11	...	„	„
34	Romakasiddhánta	...	Astronomy	28	10	New copy	Mahudhá	„
35	Vásishṭhasiddhánta, Gaṇitaskandha.	Vasishṭha	Mathematics	36	10	„	„	„
36	Vásisṭhasiddhánta, Goládhyáya.	Vasishṭha	Geography	8	9	New copy	„	„
37	Vyákaraṇamahábháshya, I, 1; II—IV; VI, 3, 4; VII; VIII.	Patañjali	Grammar	639	12	1697	„	Incomplete.
38	Śatapathabráhmaṇabháshya, Káṇḍa I.	Sáyaṇa	Commentary on Bráhmaṇa.	250	8	...	„	Complete.
39	Śástrasiddhántalavasangraha	Appayadíkshita.	Vedánta	135	9	...	„	„
40	Sámavidhánabráhmaṇa	...	Vedic rites	29	10	...	Kapadvanj.	„
41	Shaḍviṇśabráhmaṇabháshya, I, 1; III, 1; and V, 6.	Sáyaṇa	„	32	11	...	„	Incomplete.
42	Siddhasárasvatastotra, with commentary.	Padmanábha	Devotional poetry	13	14	...	Surat	Complete.

Number.	Name of Manuscript in Roman character.	Author.	Subject-matter.	No. of pages.	No. of lines in each page.	Saṃvat.	Where bought.	Remarks.
43	Somayágaśastráṇi	...	Mantras	42	8	New copy	Surat	Complete.
44	Smṛityarthasára	Lakshmídhara	Dharma	67	13	1496	,,	,,
	Jaina Books.							
45	Arádhanasútra (Mágadhí and Gujarati Tabá).	...	,,	7	16	...	,,	,,
46	Indriyaparájayastotra (Mágadhí with Gujarati Tabá).	...	Devotional poetry	9	11	...	,,	,,
47	Kalpasútradípiká	A pupil of Vimalaharshagaṇi	Dharma	152	12	1660	,,	,,
48	Kalyáṇamandirastotra	...	Devotional poetry	3	9	...	,,	,,
49	Kriyáratnasamuchchaya	Śríguṇaratna	Grammar	74	19	1510	,,	,,
50	Gautamaprichchhávṛitti (Mágadhí and Sanskṛit).	Śrítilaka	Dharma	154	15	...	,,	,,
51	Nárachandrajyotisha	Nárachandra	Astronomy	13	9	...	,,	,,
52	Pratyákhyánabháshya (Mágadhí.	...	......	11	10	...	,,	,,
53	Vipákasútravṛitti	Abhayácharya	Dharma	20	13	...	,,	,,
54	Vítarágastotra	Hemachandra	Devotional poetry	9	11	...	,,	,,
55	Upásakadaśáṅgasútra	...	Dharma	...	...	...	,,	,,
56	Sríbhagavatísútra, (Mágadhí)	...	,,	371	15	1620	Kapadvanj.	,,
57	Samarasaraṇa	...	,,	2	23	...	Surat	,,

From F. KIELHORN, Esq, Superintendent of Sanskṛit Studies, to J. B. PEILE, Esq., M.A., Director of Public Instruction, Bombay,—dated Poona, the 1st February 1871.

I have the honour to forward to you herewith an account of the money spent on the purchase of Sanskṛit manuscripts, &c., since July last, and a remittance transfer receipt for the sum of R177-7-5, being the balance of the sum of R403-8-5 of which I had charge on July 1st, 1870 (see Report of the Director of Public Instruction for 1869-70, Appendix H, page 376).

2. The manuscripts which were purchased by me have been deposited in the Library of the Dekhan College, and Mr. Joshi, the Senior Dakshiṇá Fellow, has charge of them. Their small number is accounted for by the fact that only very few manuscripts are to be met with in this part of the Bombay Presidency of which copies have not yet been taken either by Dr. Bühler or myself. For rare and important works we now must look to Gujarat; and I am glad to hear from Dr. Bühler that, since his return from Europe, he has been able to procure many old and hitherto unknown works. All the manuscripts which my agent in Gujarat has been able to purchase since August have been handed over to, and been paid for, by Dr. Bühler.

3. The catalogues which have been prepared by me and my assistants are deposited in the Dekhan College, and I should be glad to work them up into one general catalogue on my return to India.

4. I would humbly suggest that the sum of R177-7-5, as well as the undrawn portion which is yearly allowed by Government for the Southern Division of this Presidency, should be made over to Dr. Bühler, to be expended by him in the Northern Division.

From MAJOR-GENERAL A. CUNNINGHAM, Director-General, Archæological Survey of India, to E. C. BAYLEY, Esq., C.S.I., Secretary to the Government of India, Home Department,—No. 15, dated Simla, the 17th April 1872.

I have the honour to return copy of the report of Drs. Bühler and Kielhorn of their proceedings in acquiring Sanskṛit manuscripts during 1870-71.

Should these gentlemen be induced to extend their researches beyond the limits of the Bombay Presidency, I would recommend their visiting Jesalmir and Bikanir. In the former place, Colonel Tod mentions the existence of numerous manuscripts. In the latter country, in the great fortress of Bhatner, I have myself seen a room ten or twelve feet long, and about six feet broad, half filled with manuscripts, fastened up in the Native way in red cloth, and piled one on another to a height of about four feet. From amongst the top ones I selected a palm-leaf manuscript bearing the date of Saṃvat 1200.

No. 2143, dated the 3rd May 1871.

Endorsed by the Government of India, Home Department.

COPY forwarded to the Government of Bombay, with reference to its endorsement No. 2817, dated the 2nd October last.

From C. GONNE, Esq., Secretary to the Government of Bombay, Educational Department, to H. L. DAMPIER, Esq., Officiating Secretary to the Government of India, Home Department,—No. 1344, dated the 28th November 1872.

I am directed to forward to you herewith, for submission to the Government of India, five copies of a report by Dr. Bühler, Bombay Educational Department, on the result of his search for Sanskṛit manuscripts in Gujarat during the year 1871-72.

From G. BÜHLER, Esq., Educational Inspector, Northern Division, to J. B. PEILE, Esq., M.A., Director of Public Instruction, Bombay,—dated Surat, the 30th August 1872.

I have the honour to submit my report on the results of the search for Sanskṛit manuscripts in Gujarat during the year 1871-72.

2. The work done may be divided under three heads: the publication of the lists of 1869, the collection of fresh lists of manuscripts, and the acquisition of manuscripts.

3. During the last year, two fascicles of the catalogue of Sanskṛit manuscripts from Gujarat, comprising a little more than three thousand manuscripts of Vedic books, Purāṇas, and poetical works, have been published. The third fascicle, which contains works on grammar, glossaries, works on rhetoric, metrics, and law, is ready for issue; and the fourth number, which gives the remaining Śástras, is in the press. With the publication of the fourth fascicle, all the materials collected in 1869, as far as they refer to Bráhmanical literature, will be exhausted; but as,

since 1870, I have received a large number of new lists, a supplementary fascicle will have to be prepared, which should also contain an alphabetical index to the preceding parts. Besides, the lists of Jaina books remain unpublished. I have, however, made preparations for the publication of a fascicle containing Jaina works, and hope to bring it out early in 1873. I am happy to state that my catalogue, as well as Dr. Kielhorn's of 1870, has been favourably noticed by our European colleagues in the *Oriental Record*, the *Academy*, the *Literarische Centralblatt*, and the *Revue Critique*. Applications for copies of manuscripts from old Pandits of our Presidency, who now begin to appreciate the value of an inventory of their riches, from Calcutta, England, France, and Germany, shew likewise that Government has not spent its money in vain.

4. A number of fresh lists, comprising uncatalogued Bráhmanical libraries in Lunwara, Olpar, Baroda, &c., have been prepared. Considerable progress has been made in cataloguing the Jaina libraries at Randir, Surat, Lindi, and Cambay. Several large Bháṇḍáras at Ahmedadad, Wadwan, and the largest collection of all at Patan, have, as yet, not been touched. Something in this direction will, I hope, be done during 1872-73; but I am persuaded that the work cannot be finished before the end of 1874-75.

5. The number of manuscripts purchased during the year (up to June 30th, 1872) amounts to 421. Amongst these, 150 belong to the Bráhmanical literature, the remainder to that of the Jainas; in the former class, poetical and philosophical books are most numerously represented. Particularly valuable are the complete old manuscript of Patañjali's Mahábháshya with Kaiyaṭa's Commentary, the Chandrikáśataka of Váṇabhaṭṭa, the two manuscripts of the Ápastambagṛihyasútra, the Ádityapuráṇa, the fragment of the Sarasvatípuráṇa, the Jaina Commentary on the Meghadúta, the Commentary on the Pushpasútra, &c. Our collection of Jaina books is now larger than any other public collection of which I have ever heard. We have copies of nearly all the sacred works, and commentaries, both old and new, on most of them, so that there would be no difficulty in editing the more important ones. There are also fresh materials for the history of the Jaina religion, of the political history of Gujarat, and above all for the history of the Gujarati language. I have bought a large number of Ras, and other legendary works, simply in order to obtain specimens of the ancient Gujarati. The oldest pieces in that language are some verses preserved in Ratnaśekhara's Prabandhakosha, written A.D. 1347; one of which is ascribed to a Charan belonging to Rájavíradhavala's camp.

A.D. 1235. As I hope to give in my catalogue of Jaina manuscripts an account of the most interesting works bought, I omit here the enumeration of important acquisitions.

6. As regards the utilisation of the acquired manuscripts, I may state that our copies of the Gopathabráhmaṇa (bought in 1870-71) have formed the basis of the edition of that work published in the *Bibliotheca Indica.* Babu Rájendralála Mitra states in his preface that the "Bombay copies are the best." A manuscript of the Málatímádhavaṭíká, bought in 1869, is used by Professor Bhandarkar for his edition of that drama. I find our Daśakumáracharitra very useful for my edition now in the press. Dr. Eggeling, of London, has asked for a loan of the Dhátuparáyaṇa (bought in 1872), and of the Gaṇaratnamahodadhi (bought in 1866); and Professor Weber, of Berlin, wishes to have our manuscript of Hala's "Seven Centuries." I have published articles on the Prabandhakosha and Chandikáśataka.

7. My operations since July have had even more important results than those of last year. I have already acquired several manuscripts which are fully 600 years old, and have full confidence that I shall obtain others which exceed that age by 200 years. The more I become acquainted with Gujarat, the more offers of old and valuable books I get; and I trust that Government will see fit to allow the grant for Sanskṛit manuscripts also for next year.

No.	Title.	Author.	Page.	Lines.	Age of Manuscripts.	Remarks.
	I.—BRÁHMANICAL WORKS.					
	(A) Vedas.					
1	Atharvavedasaṃhitá	......	144	9	......	Incomplete.
2	Ársheyabráhmaṇa	......	16	10	......	Complete.
3	Upanishads of the Black Yajurveda	......	63	7	......	,,
4	Ṛigvedamantrasaṃhitá, *i. e.*, the mantras used for Gṛihya rites	......	133	13	......	,,
5	Ṛigvedáraṇyakabháshya	Sáyaṇa	...	...	......	,,
6	Kálágnirudropanishad	......	5	15	......	,,
7	Garuḍopanishad	......	9	5	1756	,,
8	Bhṛiguvalli	......	2	9	......	,,
9	Commentary on the Bhṛiguvallí	Śaṅkaráchárya	19	12	......	,,
	(B) Vedángas.					
10	Ápastambagṛihyasútra	Ápastamba	19	9	New copy	,,
11	(Another copy)	Do.	19	7	1927	,,
12	Ápastambágnihotrapráyaśchittadípiká	Somapa	89	9	......	,,
13	Ápastambotsarjana	Ápastamba	28	15	......	,,
14	Ápastambíyadvádaśasaṇskára	Do.	23	12	......	,,
15	Ásvaláyanagṛihyakáriká vivaraṇa	......	168	13	......	,,
16	Áhnika of the Ṛigvedins	Śiromaṇi	25	13	1697	,,
17	Upalekhavṛitti	......	20	9	1598	,,
18	Ṛigvedasandhyábháshya	Vidyáraṇya	44	9	1764	,,
19	Charaṇavyúhabháshya	......	16	7	......	,,
20	Chhattrijńánam, on the Pada text of the Ṛigveda.	......	17	16	......	,,
21	Taittiríyasandhyábháshya	......	13	15	......	,,
22	Trikáṇḍamaṇḍana on the Somayága	Kumárasvámisuta	23	12	......	,,
23	Piṇḍapitṛiyajńa	......	2	9	......	,,

No.	Title.	Author.	Page.	Lines.	Age of Manuscripts.	Remarks.
	I.—BRÁHMANICAL WORKS—*contd.*					
	(*B*) *Vedángas*—concld.					
24	Pushpasútrabháshya, Adhyáyas I—VI, 10	Ajátaśatru	157	8	......	Incomplete.
25	Yájñavalkyaśikshá	Yájñavalkya	13	9	1820	Complete.
26	Sánkhyáyangṛihyasútra	......	25	9	1655	"
	(*C*) *Puráṇas.*					
27	Ádityapuráṇa, Adhyáyas 2 XVI	......	235	8	1741	Incomplete.
28	Matsyapuráṇa	......	498	14	1776	Complete.
29	Sarasvatípuráṇa; Description of Tírthas on the Sarasvatí near Patan.	......	94	8	New copy	Incomplete.
	(*D*) *Máhátmyas.*					
30	Girijámáhátmya	......	24	11	1752	Complete.
31	Tápimáhátmya, from the Skandapuráṇa	......	132	15	1721	"
32	Do.	......	37	15	1701	Incomplete.
33	Tryambakamáhátmya	......	61	11	......	Complete.
34	Dvárakámáhátmya, from the Váyupuráṇa	......	99	11	1715	"
35	Pushkaramáhátmya, from the Padmapuráṇa	......	54	10	......	"
36	Mallárimáhátmya, from the Brahmáṇḍapuráṇa	......	50	12	1747	"
37	Śrímálamáhátmya, from the Skandapuráṇa	......	266	7	1764	"
	(*E*) *Poetry and Fiction.*					
38	Amaruśataka	Amaru	17	10	1860	"
39	Karuṇámṛitaprapásubháshitávali	Someśvaradeva	25	11	1550	"
40	Kádambarípúrvárdhavishamapadavivṛiti	Bálakṛishṇa	23	8	......	"
41	Kirátaṭiká	Ekanátha	...	...	......	Incomplete.

42	Kumárasambhavaṭíká	Mallinátha	61	15	1844	Complete.
43	Gítágovindaṭíká	Kamalákara	54	17	......	,,
44	Do.	......	37	16	1557	,,
45	Gítágovindabháshya	Pítámbara	158	12	......	,,
46	Ghaṭakarparakávyaṭíká	Kamalákara	19	9	1792	,,
47	Chaṇḍíśataka	Váṇabhaṭṭa	9	17	......	,,
48	Damayantíkathá	Trivikrama	43	13	1699	,,
49	Daśakumáracharitra	Daṇḍin	100	10	1816	,,
50	Durghaṭakávya	Kálidása	11	10	New copy	,,
51	Nítisára, with commentary	Kamandaka	106	12	......	,,
52	Nṛisiṇhachampú	Keśava	31	9	1851	,,
53	Nṛisiṇhamahataścharitra	......	27	10	......	Incomplete.
54	Pañchatantra	Vishṇuśarman.	102	17	......	Complete.
55	Do.	Do.	103	14	......	Incomplete.
56	Púrvapañcháśiká	......	12	9	......	Complete.
57	Bálabhárata	Amarachandra	233	10	......	,,
58	Bhojaprabandha	......	51	14	......	,,
59	Bhramaráshṭakádipraśastayaḥ, half Brahmanical, half Jaina.	Śrípála	54	15	1603	,,
60	Mahánáṭaka	Hanumat	24	18	......	,,
61	Mahábhárata, Parvan I	......	330	13	1717	,,
62	Mághaṭíká	Mallinátha	177	19	1822	,,
63	Mínaketúdayakávya	Devanátha	38	8	1775	,,
64	Meghadútakávya, with Jaina Avachúri	Kálidása	13	20	......	,,
65	Raghuvaṇśasútra—Jaina MS. of the R. V.	Do.	...	...	......	Incomplete.
66	Rághavollásakávya	Pújyapádadevatánanda	57	9	......	Complete.
67	Rájnám pratibodhaḥ	Madhusúdanasarasvatí	49	10	......	,,
68	Rádhávinodaṭíká	Rámachandra	16	9	......	,,
69	Rámakathá	......	112	8	......	,,
70	Viráṭaparvavishamapadavivaraṇa.	......	31	12	......	,,
71	Veṇisaṃháranáṭaka	......	...	...	......	,,
72	Vairágyaśatakaṃ saṭíkam	Bhartṛihari	17	15	......	,,
73	Śringáravairágyavṛitti	Rámarshi	51	19	......	,,
74	Sabhyábharaṇakávya	Rámachandra	5	11	......	,,
75	Subháshitamuktávali	......	45	10	1780	,,
76	Súryastuti	Śámba	7	8	......	,,
77	Harivaṇsakávya	......	230	15	......	Incomplete.
78	Harivilásakávya	Lolimbarája	14	12	......	Complete.

No.	Title.	Author.	Page.	Lines.	Age of Manuscripts.	Remarks.
	I.—Bráhmanical Works—*contd.*					
	(*G*) *Grammar.*					
79	Kátantravivṛitivyákhyá	Trilochanadása	153	10	......	Incomplete.
80	Prakriyákaumudívyákhyá, Subanta	Nṛisiṇha	321	10	......	Complete.
81	Phitsútráṇi	Śántanava	3	15	......	,,
82	Bhojavyákaraṇa	Vinayaságara	68	10	New copy	,,
83	Manoramá, Subanta	Bhaṭṭoji	155	14	1863	,,
84	Mahabháshyam pradípasahitam	Patañjali, Kaiyaṭa	...	...	......	,,
85	Do. do.	Do. do.	...	...	......	Incomplete.
86	Sárasvataṭíká	Puñjarája	102	13	1677	Complete.
	(*G*) *Glossaries.*					
87	Abhidhánaratnamálá	Haláyudha	18	8	......	,,
88	Amarakoshaṭíká	Kshírasvámin	236	10	1678	Incomplete.
89	Amarakoshavṛitti, Káṇḍa I and II	Bhánudatta	293	19	......	Complete.
90	Nighaṇṭusamaya, Parichchheda II	Dhanañjaya	9	12	1841	,,
91	Viśvakosha	Maheśvara	88	15	......	,,
	(*H*) *Rhetoric.*					
92	Kávyapradípa	Govinda	156	12	......	,,
93	Do.	Do.	181	9	......	,,
94	Ratirahasyadípiká	Káñchinátha	82	10	New copy	,,
95	Śárngadharapaddhatyuddhṛitasubháshita	......	37	13	...	,,
	(*I*) *Dharma.*					
96	Ásvaláyanasmṛiti	Ásvaláyana	68	10	1750	,,
97	Karmatattvapradípiká	Kṛishṇambhaṭṭa	128	13	...	,,
98	Karmavipáka	Maulugi	145	16	...	Incomplete.

99	Kálanirṇayadípikávivaraṇa	Rámachandrátmaja	170	8	...	Complete.
100	Pallipatanavichára	......	4	17	...	”
101	Páráśarasmṛitivyákhyá	Mádhava	430	8	...	”
102	Prayogamuktávali	Nábhisúri	87	9	...	”
103	Saṇskáranirṇaya	Chandrachúḍa	106	10	...	”
104	Śántividhi	Vasishṭha	13	10	1655	”
	(J) Yoga.					
105	Gorakshaśataka	Goraksha	13	22	...	”
106	Śivasaṃhitá	......	74	7	...	”
	(K) Sánkhya.					
107	Vyásaprabhákara	Kapila	76	9	1457	”
	(L) Vedánta.					
108	Gítábháshya	Śankaráchárya	145	14	1750	”
109	Chaturvedatátparyaprakáśa	Haradatta	19	8	New copy	”
110	Drigdrisyaṭíká	Rámachandra	15	11	1661	”
111	Nirodhalakshaṇavivṛiti	Haridása	21	12	...	”
112	Prahastaváda	Purushottama	146	12	...	”
113	Premámṛitabháshya	Viṭṭhaleśa	74	7	...	”
114	Brahmamímáṇsábháshya	Śríkanṭha	207	9	...	”
115	Brahmasútravṛittir brahmámṛitavarshiṇi	Rámakinkara	171	18	1845	”
116	Bhaktiratnávalí (Hindi)	Vishṅupúri	54	14	1891	”
117	Bhagavatbhaktirasáyaṇa	Madhusúdanasarasvati	62	10	1699	”
118	Bhágavatatattvadípiká, Skandha IV	Vallabháchárya	26	14	...	”
119	Do., do. V	Viṭṭhala	24	25	1733	”
120	Do., Sarvanirdhára	Vallabháchárya	103	15	...	”
121	Do., Skandha XII	Do.	76	15	1733	”
122	Do., do. III	Do.	41	15	...	”
123	Bhágavatatattvadípaṭiká, Prakaraṇa IV	Do.	50	15	1733	”
124	Vidvanmaṇḍana	Viṭṭhaleśa	69	15	1735	”
125	Vishṇubhaktichandrodaya	......	26	9	...	Incomplete.
126	Vedántádhikaraṇamálá	Bháratitírtha	79	14	1782	Complete.

No.	Title.	Author.	Page.	Lines.	Age of Manuscripts.	Remarks.
	I.—BRÁHMANICAL WORKS—*concld.*					
	(*L*) *Vedánta*—concld.					
127	Vedántádhikaraṇamálá	Bháratítírtha	126	11	1688	Complete.
128	Śatasútríbhásya	Svapneśvara	63	7	1706	"
129	Sanatsujátabháshya	Śankaráchárya	43	12	...	"
130	Subodhiní	Vallabháchárya	408	7	1705	"
	(*M*) *Nyáya and Vaiśeshika.*					
131	Kiraṇávalibháskara	Padmanábha	97	11	1687	"
132	Komalaṭíká	Viśvanátha	60	8	...	Incomplete.
133	Tarkaparibháshá	Keśavamiśra	22	15	...	Complete.
134	Do.	Do.	30	11	...	"
135	Tarkaparibhásháṭíká	......	54	12	...	Incomplete.
136	Tarkaprakáśiká	Śríkaṇṭha	136	13	1819	Complete.
137	Tarkabhásháṭíká	Muráríbhaṭṭa	26	3	1680	"
138	Nyáyachandriká	Keśavabhaṭṭa	13	17	1706	"
139	Padárthadípiká	Kaundabhaṭṭa	27	16	1768	"
140	Mitabháshiṇiṭíká	Mádhavasarasvatí	39	12	1662	"
141	Saptapadárthí	Śiváditya	5	13	...	"
	(*N*) *Mímáṇsá.*					
142	Nyáyakosha	Apadeva	60	12	...	"
143	Vidhirasáyaṇamimáṇsáṭíká	......	82	10	...	"
	(*O*) *Astronomy and Arithmetic.*					
144	Jyotiḥsára	Śríharshakírtti	48	16	1731	"
145	Lílávatiṭíká Gaṇitámṛitaságarí	Gangádhara	48	15	1743	"
146	Śakunávali (Sanskrit and Gujaráti)	......	4	13	...	"

No.	Title	Author				Remarks
	(P) Medicine.					
147	Yogapradípa	......	5	25	...	,,
	(Q) Miscellaneous.					
148	Kedárakalpa	......	172	7	1797	,,
149	Vaṇśávali of Vallabhácárya	......	96	bound	in cloth.	
150	Sámudrika	......	15	13	1602	,,
	II.—JAINA WORKS.					
	(A) Dharma.					
151	Ashṭakákhyaprakaraṇa (Sanskṛit)	Haribhadra	9	15	...	,,
152	Áchárángasútra (Mágadhi)	......	150	10	...	,,
153	Do. (do.)	......	54	13	1597	,,
154	Áchárángadípiká (Sanskṛit and Mágadhi)	Jinahaṇsa	196	15	...	,,
155	Árádhanasútra (Gujaráti)	Somasundara	9	11	...	,,
156	Álokanaratnákarapañchami (Sanskṛit)	Vijayagaṇi	4	4	...	,,
157	Ávasyakasútra (Mágadhi)	......	36	15	1532	,,
158	Amvilapachhakkhan (Mág. and Gujaráti)	......	23	5	1873	,,
159	Uttarádhyáyanasútra (Mág.)	......	73	11	1651	,,
160	Do. (Sanskṛit and Gujaráti)	......	236	4	1695	,,
161	Uttarádhyayanakathá (Mágadhi)	......	36	15	1761	,,
162	Uttarádhyayanaṭíká, 13 Adhy. (Mág. and S.)	......	13	12	...	,,
163	Uttarádhyayanakathásaṅkshepa	......	19	15	...	,,
164	Uttarádhyayanaṭíká (S.)	......	285	15	...	,,
165	Uttarádhyayanávachúri (S.)	......	21	18	...	,,
166	Upadeśaprasáda (S.)	......	31	12	...	,,
167	Upadeśaprasádavṛitti (S.)	Lakshmívijaya	1,060	5	...	Stambhas VII-XXIV.
168	Do. (do.)	......	109	7	...	Incomplete.
169	Upadeśamálá with Ṭiká (M. G.)	......	94	8	1790	Complete.
170	Do. (do.)	Dadhivijaya and Dharmadása.	165	15	...	,,
171	Upadeśamálávivaraṇa (S.)	......	89	15	...	,,

No.	Title.	Author.	Page.	Lines.	Age of Manuscripts.	Remarks.
	II.—Jaina Works—*contd.*					
	(*A*) *Dharma*—contd.					
172	Upadeśaratnákara (M. S.)	Sundarasúri	252	13	...	Complete.
173	Upásakapatha (M.)	......	23	13	...	"
174	Upásakasútraṃ saṭikam (M. S.)	......	62	11	1756	"
175	Uvaisútraṃ savṛittikam (M. S.)	Abhayadeva	83	13	...	"
176	Ṛishimaṇḍalaprakaraṇa (M.)	......	27	21	...	"
177	Ekvisathánámnusamása (M. G.)	......	10	5	...	"
178	Ekvisathánam (M. G.)	......	5	6	...	"
179	Karmagrantha (G.)	......	9	13	...	"
180	Karmagranthaḥ pañchamaḥ (M. G.)	......	41	6	...	"
181	Karmagranthaṭíká (S.)	Devendra	181	17	...	"
182	Kalpakiraṇávali (M. S.)	Dharmaságara	217	13	1628	"
183	Kalpasútra (M.)	......	63	7	...	"
184	Do. (do.)	......	112	7	...	"
185	Kálasitterí saṭiká (M. S.)	......	16	9	1829	"
186	Kupakshakauśikáditya (M. S.)	Dharmaságara	241	19	...	"
187	Cháturmásikamadhyáhnavyákhyá (S. and G.)	......	13	15	1792	"
188	Chatussaraṇasútra (M. S.)	......	11	18	1686	"
189	Chandraprajñaptisútra (M.)	......	68	12	...	"
190	Jambudvípaprajñapti (M.)	......	158	11	...	"
191	Jambúpáyano and Taba (M. G.)	......	48	5	...	"
192	Jñátasútra (M.)	......	221	11	...	Incomplete.
193	Do. (do.)	......	103	15	1625	Complete.
194	Jñánadipiká and Taba (M. G.)	Jñánavijaya	183	12	1763	"
195	Jívábhigamasútra and Taba (G. M.)	......	258	7	1702	"
196	Daśavidhayatidharma (G.)	......	7	10	...	"
197	Daśavaikálikasútra and Taba (M. G.)	......	44	5	...	"
198	Daśavaikálikavṛitti (M. S.)	......	71	14	1780	"
199	Daśaśrutaskandha Avachúri	Bhadrabáhu	68	9	...	"
200	Dánakalpadruma (S.)	Jinakírtti	29	17	...	"

201	Díválikalpa (S.)	Jinasundara . . .	15	13	...	,,
202	Desanoddhárasútra and Taba (M. G.) . .	......	12	4	1735	,,
203	Nandisútra (M.)	......	29	11	...	,,
204	Do. (do.)	......	14	16	...	,,
205	Navatattvasútra (M. G.)	......	16	13	...	,,
206	Navapadakalasapújá (G.)	......	8	10	...	,,
207	Niśíthasútra (M.)	......	37	10	...	,,
208	Pachhakkhananiyukti (M.)	Bhadrabáhu . . .	64	15	...	,,
209	Pañchakasútravyákhyá (S.)	Haribhadra . . .	25	14	...	,,
210	Pañchanirgranthi (M. S.)	Yaśovijaya . . .	16	4	...	,,
211	Pañchasaptatyadhikára (S.)	......	46	21	...	,,
212	Paryushaṇavichára (M. S.)	Munichandra . . .	30	15	...	,,
213	Paryushaṇavṛitti (M. S.)	......	71	13	...	,,
214	Pákshikasútrávachúri (S.)	Yaśobhadra . . .	6	23	...	,,
215	Pudgalabhangavivṛiti	Nayavijaya . . .	6	19	...	,,
216	Prajñápannasútra (M.)	......	315	11	1771	,,
217	Pratyákhyánabháshya (M. G.)	......	13	16	...	,,
218	Pratyuttarachandriká (G.)	......	7	15	798	,,
219	Pravachanaparikshá (S.)	......	13	13	...	Incomplete.
220	Pravachanasároddhára (M.)	......	62	14	...	Complete.
221	Pravachanasároddháravṛitti (M. S.) . . .	Siddhasena . . .	316	15	...	Incomplete.
222	Praśnavyákaraṇa (M. G.)	......	95	5	...	Complete.
223	Praśnottara (S.)	Víravijaya . . .	6	17	...	,,
224	Bodhashaṭtriṇśiká (S.)	......	6	24	1483	,,
225	Bálávabodha (S. G.)	Somasundara . . .	77	16	1506	,,
226	Bhagavatísútra (M.)	......	806	9	...	,,
227	Bhagavatívṛitti (M. S.)	Abhayadeva . . .	383	14	1663	,,
228	Mahániśíthasútra (M.)	......	75	15	1536	,,
229	Maunaikádaśí (S.)	Raviságara . . .	8	13	...	,,
230	Ráyapasenivrittiá (M. S.)	......	73	16	...	Incomplete.
231	Lokanálikáprakaraṇa (S.)	......	5	16	1871	Complete.
232	Várivichára (S.)	......	4	15	...	,,
233	Vasupújyajinapuṇyaprakáśa (G.)	......	35	8	...	,,
234	Viṇśasthánakavichárámṛitasangraha (S.) . .	Jayachandra . . .	84	14	...	,,
235	Vivekavilása (S. G.)	Jinadatta . . .	122	10	1717	,,
236	Do. (do.)	Do. . . .	123	25	...	,,
237	Vishamapadárthabodha (Bháshya of the Pravachana).	......	45	21	...	,,

No.	Title.	Author.	Page.	Lines.	Age of Manuscripts.	Remarks.
	II.—JAINA WORKS—*contd.*					
	(*A*) *Dharma*—concld.					
238	Śráddhavidhi (S.)	Ratnaśekhara	44	20	1506	Complete.
239	Śrávakaprabodha (M. G.)	Śubhavardhana	366	5	...	"
240	Śripújápañcháśiká (S.)	......	9	18	1867	"
241	Shaṭtriṇśakavṛitti (M. S.)	......	19	15	...	"
242	Shaḍávaśyakasútra (M.)	......	6	14	...	"
243	Shaḍdarśanasamuchchayaṭíká (S.)	Guṇaratna	73	17	...	"
244	Sattarasayo (M.)	......	15	13	...	"
245	Do. (do.)	......	9	18	1612	"
246	Santharaporisisútra (M. G.)	......	39	6	...	"
247	Santharo (M.)	......	7	20	1480	"
248	Saptatikáṭíká (S.)	Malayagiri	63	17	...	"
249	The same (S.)	Do.	74	17	...	"
250	Saptatikávyákhyá (S. G.)	Somaguru	96	18	...	"
251	Samánasútra (M.)	......	6	6	...	"
252	Samyaktvakaumudíkathá (S.)	......	44	13	1665	"
253	Samyaktvaparíkshá (M. G.)	Vimalasúri	314	18	1814	"
254	Saṇsárádivastu, &c. (G. S.)	......	64	15	...	"
255	Sukhabodhiká (M.)	......	21	15	...	"
256	Subhodhakakarmavipáka (M. S.)	Devendra	38	18	...	Incomplete.
257	Suyadángasútra (M. G.)	......	116	11	...	Complete.
258	Do. (M.)	......	47	15	...	"
259	Sthánángasútra (M. G.)	......	273	6	1791	"
260	Do. (M.)	......	150	11	...	"
261	Sthánángavivaraṇa (M. S.)	Abhayadeva	281	17	...	"
262	Do. (do.)	Do.	289	15	...	"
263	Snánavidhi (G.)	......	3	12	...	"
264	Holíparvan (S.)	Máṇikyavijaya	18	12	1888	"

(B) Poetry.

265	Ajitaśánti (M. G.)	......	3	21	...	,,
266	Ajitastavaṭiká (S.)	......	13	10	...	,,
267	Aticháraghaṭáshṭaka (M. G.)	......	3	3	...	,,
268	Arahadasani chopai (G.)	......	33	15	...	,,
269	Indriyaśatakam (M. G.)	......	11	6	...	,,
270	Uttamaṛishisanghasmaraṇachatushpadyaḥ (G.)	......	3	15	...	,,
271	Upadeśaśataka (S.)	Merutunga	26	24	...	,,
272	Upasargaharastotraṃ saṭíkam (M. S.)	Bhadrabáhu	5	11	...	,,
273	Ṛishimaṇḍalastava (S.)	Gautama	4	12	1901	,,
274	Karpúrábhidhasubháshitakosha (S.)	Hari	4	23	...	,,
275	Kavipriya (Hindí)	......	53	16	1826	,,
276	Kámaghaṭa (M. G.)	......	28	9	...	,,
277	Káyasthitistotraṃ saṭíkam (M. S.)	......	2	17	...	,,
278	Gajasiṇharája chopai (G.)	......	15	15	1733	,,
279	Guṇávali (G.)	......	26	14	1890	,,
280	Chaturviṇśatijinastuti (S.)	Jinaprabha	2	13	...	,,
281	Cháṇakya (S. G.)	......	14	15	1840	,,
282	Chopat (G.)	Sítaráma	84	14	...	,,
283	Chovisi (G.)	Jnánaságara	10	12	...	,,
284	Jagadgurucharitrakávya (S.)	Suvarṇánanda	13	16	...	,,
285	Jayatihunastotra (M.)	......	3	11	...	,,
286	Jinasahasranáma, &c. (M.)	......	190	14	...	,,
287	Jinasahasranámavṛitti (S.)	......	75	11	1585	,,
288	Jñánachaturviṇśatiká (S.)	......	2	15	...	,,
289	Dhalaságara (Hindí)	......	157	15	...	,,
290	Daśadṛishṭíntagitá (M. G.)	Somavimala	4	13	...	,,
291	Dṛishṭántaśataka (S. G.)	Tejaḥsiṇha	25	19	1746	,,
292	Nakhaśikhavarṇan (Hindí)	Keśavamiśra	6	17	1785	,,
293	Namaskárastavana (S.)	Jinakírtti	9	17	1494	,,
294	Naláyana (G.)	Jnánaságara	147	11	1723	,,
295	Praśnaśatakaṃ saṭíkam	Jinavallabha	14	14	...	,,
296	Buddhiságara (S.)	Sangrámasiṇha	15	11	...	,,
297	Bṛihachchaityavandanaṃ saṭíkam (S.)	Hemachandra	4	22	1827	,,
298	Bhayaharastavaḥ saṭíkaḥ (M. S.)	{ Sthúlabhadra { Do.	} 2	18	...	,,
299	Bhayaharastotraṃ saṭíkam (M. S.)	Jinasiṇha	4	21	...	,,

No.	Title.	Author.	Page.	Lines.	Age of Manuscripts.	Remarks.
	II.—Jaina Works—*contd.*					
	(*B*) *Poetry*—concld.					
300	Bhaktamayastotra with Taba (S. G.)	Mánatunga	10	5	1821	Complete.
301	Bhaktamayastotram saṭíkam (S.)	Do.	23	14	...	"
302	Bhaktamayastotravṛitti (S.)	......	25	18	1677	"
303	Bhavanakulaka and Taba (M. G.)	......	4	6	...	"
304	Múrkhaśataka and Taba (S. G.)	......	2	6	...	"
305	Yogadṛishṭisajjhái (G.)	Yaśovijaya	22	13	1819	"
306	Ratnachúḍámaṇi chopái (G.)	Haṇsagaṇi	23	15	...	"
307	Rájaníti and Taba (S. G.)	......	19	5	1807	"
308	Rámacharitra (S.)	Vijayasena	148	13	1695	"
309	Do. (Hindí)	......	100	18	1920	"
310	Vasudháráidháraṇastotra (S.)	......	5	14	...	"
311	Do. (do.)	......	11	10	1863	"
312	Vidvanśataka (?) (S. G.)	......	2	5	1768	"
313	Vírastavanaṃ saṭíkam (M. S.)	......	3	21	1609	"
314	Śatruñjayamáhátmya, Sargas XIV	Dhaneśvara	195	15	1651	"
315	Śáśvatajinotsavana (M. G.)	......	2	9	...	"
316	Śiladútakávya (S.)	Sundaragaṇi	9	15	1701	"
317	Śobhanastutiḥ sávachúriḥ (S.)	Śobhana	15	16	...	"
318	Śrikumáraviháraśataka (S.)	......	5	17	...	"
319	Śṛíśuktimálá (G.)	......	9	15	1875	"
320	Samayasáranáṭaka (S. Hindí)	......	48	15	1755	"
321	Sambaprajana chopái (G.)	Jinachandra	32	11	1690	"
322	Sambodhasitteri (G.)	......	26	11	1714	"
323	Siddhapañcháśiká (M. G.)	Vidyáságara	15	14	1771	"
324	Sundaraśṛingára (Hindí)	Kavirája	41	10	1832	"
325	Suktávali (M. G.)	......	14	8	...	"
326	Svarṇasiddhiḥ saṭíká (M. S.)	Pádalipta	2	16	...	"
327	Haribhadrakṛitastutivyákhyá (G.)	......	1	16	...	"

	(C) *Biography, History, and Legends.*					
328	Agadattacharitra (G.)	Kalyáṇaságara	28	16	...	"
329	Añjanaras (G.)	......	13	16	1840	"
330	Añjanasundarí (G.)	Puṇyaságara	24	15	1762	"
331	Árdrakumáraras (G.)	Jñánaságara	21	16	...	"
332	Ánandasrávakacharitra (G.)	Kesavají	9	19	1711	"
333	Kathákosha, Adhikára II (S.)	Subhásíla	249	13	...	"
334	Kathákosha (G.)	Merusundara	88	20	...	"
335	Kathásangraha (S.)	......	87	16	...	"
336	Kanakávatícharitra (M. S.)	Jinasúri	35	12	...	"
337	Kálíkácháryakathá, illustrated (S.)	......	9	7	...	"
338	Kumáravaṇśávali (G.)	......	15	14	...	Incomplete.
339	Kumáraputracharitra (M.)	......	6	18	...	Complete.
340	Kembanoras (G.)	......	24	15	1796	"
341	Kshamaráśiprabandha (S.)	......	2	16	1714	"
342	Gaṇadharadevavandanavidhi (G.)	......	5	16	...	"
343	Gautamakula (M. G.)	Amaravijaya	77	13	1871	"
344	Chandacharitra (G.)	......	103	12	...	"
345	Chandanendracharitra (G.)	......	46	13	1837	"
346	Chandrakevalíras (G.)	......	181	15	1790	"
347	Chandraprabhasvámicharitra (M. S.)	......	214	12	...	Incomplete.
348	Champakacharitra (S.)	......	17	14	...	Complete.
349	Chitrasenapadmávatícharitra (S. G.)	Nayavijaya	136	5	...	"
350	Jambucharitra (M.)	Padmasundara	54	14	1782	"
351	Jalapújákathanaka (M.)	......	25	18	1475	"
352	Trishashṭiśalákápurushacharitra (S.)	Hemachandra	103	18	...	Incomplete.
353	Do., Parvan VIII	Do.	103	17	1704	"
354	Do., Pariśishṭaparvan (S.)	Do.	121	3	...	"
355	Dvádaśavratakathá (S.)	......	14	16	1833	Complete.
356	Nalakathanaka (S.)	......	11	20	...	"
357	Naladamayantícharitra (G.)	......	136	15	...	"
358	Naladamayantíras (G.)	Samayasundara	36	15	1800	"
359	Pañchákhyánoddhára (S.)	......	72	9	1660	"
360	Padmávatícharitra (M.)	......	144	19	...	"
361	Paradeśíra (G.)	Jñánaságara	38	11	...	"
362	Pushpamálá (M. S.)	......	14	17	...	"
363	Prabandhakosha (S.)	Chandraśekhara	50	20	...	"

Number.	Title.	Author.	Page.	Lines.	Age of Manuscripts.	Remarks.
	II.—JAINA WORKS—*concld.*					
	(*C*) *Biography, History, and Legends*—concld.					
364	Priyankarakathá (S.)	......	31	13	...	Complete.
365	Buddharas (M.)	......	3	13	...	"
366	Bhuvanabhánukevalicharitra (S.)	......	53	13	...	Incomplete.
367	Mangalakalaśacharitra (G.)	......	13	13	1663	Complete.
368	Mándhárasvámistavanahattrisi (G.)	......	3	11	...	"
369	Mahípálacharitra (G.)	......	22	9	...	"
370	Mahimávaliras (G.)	......	28	14	1776	"
371	Mánavatíras (G.)	Rúpavidya	35	16	1862	"
372	Munipaticharitra (M.)	......	19	15	1847	"
373	Yamalakaras (G.)	Samayasundara	18	13	1832	"
374	Ratnapálaras (G.)	......	32	19	1823	"
375	Rúpasenarájakathá (M.)	......	45	18	...	"
376	Dílávatíras (G.)	Premji	38	16	...	"
377	Lokaprakáśa (S.)	...	102	15	...	Incomplete.
378	Vichároaśreṇi (S.)	Merutunga	7	12	New copy	Complete.
379	Śántijinaras (G.)	Hirasúri	174	15	..	"
380	Śálicharitra (S.)	......	21	17	...	"
381	Śálibhadradhanadaras (G.)	......	10	18	1771	"
382	Śrípálacharitra (S.)	......	105	9	1725	"
383	Shaṭpurushavichára (S.)	Kshemankara	18	11	...	"
384	Sadayavatsádicharitráṇi (S. G.)	......	87	18	...	Incomplete.
385	Sáraras (G.)	......	20	18	1613	Complete.
386	Susadhacharitra (M.)	......	41	21	1908	"
387	Saubhágyapanchamikathá (S.)	Kanakakuśala.	11	13	...	"
388	Sthavirávali (S.)	......	7	15	...	"
389	Do. (M. G.)	......	42	10	1415	"
390	Do. (M. S.)	......	3	9	...	"
391	Do. (S.)	Munisundara	13	17	1508	"
392	Do. (M. S.)	......	21	13	1660	"

393	Haricharidaras (G.)	Labdhivijaya	38	15	1711	,,
394	Hutáśaníkathá (S. G.)	......	8	5	1799	,,
	(D) Miscellaneous Śástras.					
395	Abhidhánchintámaṇi (S.)	Hemachandra	58	23	1691	,,
396	Abhidhánachintámaṇiṭíká (S.)	Do.	206	15	1624	,,
397	Alankára (S.)	Lesabhatilaka	53	19	...	Incomplete.
398	Alankárachúḍámaṇivṛitti (S.)	Hemachandra	112	10	New copy	,,
399	Árambhasiddhi (S.)	Hemahaṇsa	70	21	...	,,
400	Uktipadáni (S.)	......	7	17	...	,,
401	Kávyakalpalatá (S.)	......	17	13	...	,,
402	Kshetrasamásaḥ satíkaḥ (M. S.)	Kritadeva Ratnaśekhara	67	15	1844	,,
403	Guṇaratnákara (G.)	Sahajasundara	18	15	...	,,
404	Chaturviṇśatijinávápti (S.)	......	2	9	1532	,,
405	Trailokyadípiká (M. G.)	Chandrasúri	68	4	1851	,,
406	Nayachakra (S.)	Devasena	4	18	...	,,
407	Navagrahaṇáyanakoshṭhakáni (S.)	......	5	18	...	,,
408	Nyáyamañjúshá (S.)	Hemahaṇsa	74	13	1639	,,
409	Nyáyánekárthabháshya (S.)	......	40	20	...	,,
410	Pañchavimarśa (S.)	Udayaprabha	19	13	...	,,
411	Bṛihadvṛittinámabalábalasútravṛitti	Hemachandra	14	17	...	,,
412	Rúpadípak bháshá (Hindí)	......	9	6	...	,,
413	Laghuyogaratnávaliḥ saṭíká (S.)	Nágárjuna	34	15	...	,,
414	Laghuvṛitti on the Śabdánuśásana (S.)	Hemachandra	32	17	1536	Adhyayas I—IV.
415	Vákyaprakáśa with Taba (S. G.)	Udayadharma	6	11	1507	Complete.
416	Śabdabháskara (S.)	Tarkatilaka	47	16	1781	,,
417	Sangrahanyáyávachúri (S.)	......	12	26	1491	,,
418	Sindhurapraharaṇam satikam (S.)	Somaprabha	80	15	...	,,
419	Three scrap-books by Gorjis containing various information.					
420	Maps of India and of the World according to Jaina notions.					
	III.—GUJARATI POETRY.					
421	Garabávali	Vallabhácharya	...	...	...	Incomplete.

G. BÜHLER,
Educational Inspector, N. D.

From H. Wellesley, Esq., Officiating Under-Secretary to the Government of India, Home Department, to the Secretary to the Government of Bombay,—No. 4770, dated Fort William, the 23rd December 1872.

I am directed to acknowledge the receipt of your letter No. 1344, dated the 28th ultimo, forwarding a report by Dr. Bühler on the results of his search for Sanskṛit manuscripts in Gujarat during the year 1871-72.

2. Dr. Bühler's success is most satisfactory, and the Governor-General in Council hopes that that gentleman will be able to visit Bikanir and Jesalmir, where valuable Sanskṛit manuscripts are probably to be found.

From Professor G. Bühler, Educational Inspector, Northern Division, to the Director of Public Instruction, Bombay,—dated Surat, the 20th August 1873.

I have the honour to submit my report on the results of my search for Sanskṛit manuscripts during the period from July lst, 1872, to May 15th, 1873.

2. Following the same order which I observed last year, I first render account of my operations connected with the printing of the catalogue of Bráhmanical manuscripts from Gujarat. Two new fascicles, Nos. III and IV, of this work have been published during the past year. The materials collected in 1868-69 have now been exhausted. The issue of a supplementary number, giving addenda, indices, &c., is still required. This part, as well as a fascicle of the catalogue of Jaina works, is still in preparation.

3. Several large collections of Jaina books in Cambay, Limdi, and Ahmedabad have been partly catalogued. The extent and the condition of these libraries prevent me, however, from causing complete lists of their contents to be made. Several of them contain upwards of 10,000 manuscripts, and sometimes hundreds of copies of one and the same work are found in one library. Thus a library at Ahmedabad contains, according to the statement of the cataloguing Śástrí, 400 copies of the Ávaśyakasútra. This assertion will appear neither astonishing nor incredible, if it is borne in mind that devout Jainas frequently give, or bequeath, large sums of money to the superintendents of monasteries for copying books, and that the multiplication of the sacred writings is held to be highly meritorious. To make complete catalogues of such libraries is out of the question.

In the course of 1873-74 I hope to finish the exploration of two out of the three large Jaina libraries at Ahmedabad and of those at Vadhvan, and to begin with the Bháṇḍárs at Siddhapur Pathan. But I despair of finishing my task during either the current or the next following year.

4. During the period under report, I have bought or procured copies of 200 manuscripts, of which number 75 belong to Bráhmanical literature, and 123 to the Jainas, while 2 contain Gujaráti prose-works. Among the Bráhmanical works there are several novelties and rare works, to which I beg to call special attention. Thus, No. 2, the Bháshya on the Mantras quoted in the Páraskaragṛihyasútra (I-II, 3) of the White Yajurveda, attempts a task which is usually neglected by the writers on Vedic ceremonies, and it is, at all events, highly interesting to see what meaning a Bráhmanical writer attributed to the prayers which the Bháṭṭas generally mutter without understanding, or caring to understand, them.

Among the Puráṇas, the Vahnipuráṇa is new to me. It is not identical with the Agnipuráṇa.

The Sarasvatípuráṇa is a complete copy of the fragment noticed in last year's report.

The list of manuscripts of poetical works contains several original compositions and commentaries which are seldom met with. The most important among them are the Vṛihatkathá of Kshemendra and the Párthaparákrama. The honour of the first discovery of the former work belongs to A. Burnell, Esq., M.C.S., not to myself, as stated in the *Indian Antiquary*. But the copy in my list appears to be the only other known manuscript besides that of Mr. Burnell, and, though incomplete, it contains very important portions of the original, which are wanting in that gentleman's manuscript. In an article in the *Indian Antiquary* I have pointed out how great the importance of the Vṛihatkathá is for the history of the Indian collections of apologues. I may add that further researches have convinced me that it settles the question, which of the many versions of the Pañchatantra is the original one, and that it allows us to ascertain the form of that work as it stood in the fifth century A.D. The Pañchatantra, at that period, closely resembled the so-called Southern redaction.

The second work mentioned above, the Párthaparákrama, is a drama of the class called Vyáyoga, a military piece, celebrating the deeds of Arjuna. Its author, the Yuvarája, or heir-apparent, Prahládana, who lived under a king of the name of Dhárávarsha, is quoted by Śárngadhara, the author of a large collection of elegant extracts made in the fourteenth century. King Dhárávarsha, from whose capital (Chandrávatí) the mountain Nandivardhana (Ábú) could be seen, lived probably in the tenth century. Prahládana was his brother, and founded Pálanpur.* The play is important, as only one other Vyáyoga was hitherto known. The manuscript was found in a Jaina library.

Among the works pertaining to the Śástras, the Agniveśasaṃhitá, one of the oldest works on medicine, written in the Sútra style, and the Viśrántavidyávinoda, a work on veterinary surgery, attributed to King Bhoja, deserve to be noted specially. The latter work is different from the short popular treatise usually called Śálihotra, which, likewise, is attributed to the famous king of Málava.

5. As regards the Jaina books, I have stated already, in last year's report, that the purchases of 1872-73 promise to become highly important. My hopes in this respect have been completely fulfilled. I have obtained some palm-leaf manuscripts, Nos. 78-80, 113, 114, 128-132, which all are between five and six hundred years old. The oldest, containing the Vṛihatkalpaṣútra, with its commentaries, is dated 1334 Vikrama, or 1278 A.D. It was written in Cambay, where it was preserved until it came into my hands. The other manuscripts likewise come from that town.

All these manuscripts are remarkable, not only for their age, but also for the form, the writing, and the material on which they are written.

The Achárángasútra, with its commentaries (Nos. 78-80), forms one large *pothí,* the leaves (1—411 and 1—18) of which are two feet and eleven and three-quarter inches in length, and three inches broad. Each line is broken up into three divisions, nine and one-quarter inches in length, between which, as well as on the margin at either end, usually a broad red *tilak* has been placed. Two substantial boards protect the outside of the *pothí.*

The Niśíthasútra, with its commentaries, is written on 238 leaves, numbered 105-343. It measures two feet nine inches by three inches. The lines are divided into three parts, each nine inches by three inches. Two strings pass through the centres of the red marks adorning the margin as the ends of each leaf. The outside is protected by boards.

The Vṛihatkalpasútra (Nos. 128-130), with its commentaries, and the Vyavahárasútra (Nos. 131 and 132), resemble the Niśíthasútra in appearance. They measure two feet nine inches by three inches, and two feet eleven inches by three inches, respectively.

* I owe this information to Major J. Watson, Acting Political Superintendent of Pálanpur.

All these manuscripts are distinguished from the palm-leaf manuscripts, which are so common in Southern India, by their size, by the quality of the leaves, and by the manner of writing. For, while the leaves of the Madras manuscripts are usually thick, and possess a certain degree of stiffness, those of the Cambay copies are very thin, almost flabby. While the letters of the Madras manuscripts are scratched with a stylus and blackened afterwards, the writing on those from Cambay has been executed with a very broad reed pen, or with a fine brush.

The form of the letters resembles the peculiar cramped hand of the more modern Jaina manuscripts, but the letters are very large, similar in size to those found in the inscriptions of the eleventh, twelfth, and thirteenth centuries. One very striking feature is the form of the initial *i*, which frequently consists of two dots and a stroke beneath, and resembles that of the Shah and Gupta inscriptions. The *gh*, too, has an archaic form; it consists of three vertical strokes, joined above and below by horizontal ones.

The preservation of the four manuscripts is, in spite of their great age, tolerably good. A few pages have become nearly illegible, the ink having been rubbed off; pieces of some leaves have been damaged by insects and have been broken off.

Palm-leaf manuscripts of this description, which are held in great esteem by the Jainas, are said to be found in larger numbers in Cambay and Páthan only. But one is said to exist in Surat, a few in Limdi and Vadhvan, and three are stated to be in the possession of the Jaina High Priest at Ahmedabad. One of the Limdi manuscripts, which contains the Ávaśyakasútra, and is dated Saṃvat 1189, or 1133 A.D., has been sent to me by the owner as a loan. I shall publish photographs of some pages of this manuscript in the *Indian Antiquary*.

6. Copies of all the forty-five sacred works of the Jainas, with the exception of three very small treatises, have now been obtained, and Sanskṛit commentaries on most of them. Among this year's purchases the complete collection of Païnnas or Prakírṇakas (No. 141), the Pannávaná with a commentary, the Nándyadhyayana with two commentaries, the commentary on the Jñátadharmakathá, deserve to be noted. These commentaries, as well as several others, are particularly valuable, as their authors belong to the oldest and most esteemed exponents of Jaina doctrines. Haribhadra, the son of Yákiná (*vide* Nos. 104, 110, 114, and 150), is stated to have lived in the first half of the sixth century A. D. Abhayadeva (*vide*

Nos. 91, 103, 121) wrote, according to his own statement, in the eleventh century, at Páthan, the Naváṅgivṛitti, *i. e.*, commentaries on nine Aṅgas (copies of five have been acquired for Government). Malayagiri, the most voluminous of all Jaina commentators, lived in the beginning of the thirteenth century. Special notice deserve, also, the copies of the Niryuktis, the oldest expositions of the Aṅgas, which are attributed to Bhadrabáhu, the author of the Kalpasútra, and reputed contemporary of the Nandas. The Sanskṛit commentary on the large collection called Oghaniryukti by Droṇáchárya goes back considerably beyond the time of Hemachandra. Mágadhí Bháshyas and Avachúrṇis (Nos. 105, 114, 129, 130), which are much older than the Sanskṛit glosses, are important for the history of the sacred books.

7. Of more general interest and higher importance than any of the acquisitions already enumerated, are the Deśiśabdasaṅgraha of Hemachandra (No. 184) and the Páïalachhínámamálá (No. 185). These two works are dictionaries of the ancient Prákṛit language, and contain upwards of 11,000 hitherto unknown words, many of which, in more or less modified forms, occur in the modern Prákṛits. They are indispensable for the correct interpretation of the Jaina scriptures and all other true Prákṛit works, and promise important results for the history of the living A'ryan languages of India. I may add that I have now succeeded in obtaining a loan of a second copy of the Deśiśabdasaṅgraha, and that it will be possible to prepare an edition of it.

8. As regards the utilisation of the acquired manuscripts, Professor Whitney, of Newhaven, has asked for copies of some of our Atharvaveda manuscripts bought in 1870-71, and will apply to Government for a loan of another part of that collection. Professor Foucaux, of Paris, has asked for a copy of the Meghadútávachúri, bought last year. I have furnished copies of the Agni and Váyupuráṇas for collation to the Asiatic Society of Bengal. Articles on the Vṛihatkathá, the Deśiśabdasaṅgraha, the Mayúraśatakaṭíká, and the Páïalachhí have appeared in the *Indian Antiquary.* I regret that my official duties prevent me from doing more, especially for the Jaina literature, which can only be studied in Gujarat.

No.	Title.	Author.	Page.	Lines.	Age* of Manuscripts.	Remarks.
	A.—BRAHMANICAL LITERATURE.					
	(*A*) *Vedic Works.*					
1	Bháshya of the Káṇvaśákhá of the White Yajurveda.	Ánandabhaṭṭa Chaturvedin.	181	16	...	Incomplete.
2	Bháshya on the Mantras in Páraskara's Gṛihyasútra.	Murárimiśra . . .	92	9	...	,,
3	Śrísúktabháshya	......	6	12	...	Complete.
4	Śulvasútravṛitti	Rámachandra . . .	22	12	1593	,,
	(*B*) *Puráṇas.*					
5	Náradapuráṇa	......	71	15	...	Incomplete.
6	Revakhaṇḍa (said to belong to the Váyupuráṇa) .	......	933	11	1716	67 1st leaf wanting.
7	Vahnipuráṇa	......	103	12	New copy	Complete.
8	Sarasvatípuráṇa	......	79	12	Do.	,,
	(*C*) *Máhátmyas.*					
9	Kaśímáhátmya from the Padmapuráṇa . .	......	62	8	...	,,
10	Tolakamáhátmya	......	3	12	...	,,
11	Tryambakamáhátmya from the Varáhapuráṇa .	......	17	16	1775	,,
12	Sábhramatímáhátmya	......	97	10	...	,,
	(*D*) *Poetry.*					
13	Anyopadeśaśataka	Madhusúdana Dujanti .	5	13	1836	,,
14	Itihásasamuchchaya	......	68	16	1744	,,
15	Uttararámacharita	Bhavabhúti . . .	33	15	...	,,

* The figures under this heading refer invariably to the era of Vikrama, which begins 57 B.C.

No.	Title.	Author.	Page.	Lines.	Age* of Manuscripts.	Remarks.
	A.—BRÁHMANICAL LITERATURE—*contd.*					
	(*D*) *Poetry*—concld.					
16	Kaṇsavadhanáṭaka	Dámodara	34	10	1721	Complete.
17	Kirátárjuníyaṭiká, Sargas VI and VII	Ekanátha	22	18	...	„
18	Daśakumáracharitaṭíká	......	14	11	New copy	„
19	Dhanañjayavijaya	Káñchana	10	10	...	„
20	Párthaparákrama, a Vyáyoga	Yuvarája Prahládana	12	12	Tracing from a MS. of 1426.	„
21	Prahasananáṭaka	Śaṅkhadhara	12	10	...	„
22	Mathuráchampú	Paraśurámamiśra	266	6	...	„
23	Mayúraśatakaṃ saṭíkam	Mayúra; Madhusúdana Paṇchanada.	55	15	New copy	„
24	Mayúraśatakaṭíká	......	23	11	Do.	Incomplete.
25	Meghadútakávyaṃ sávachúri	Kálidása	22	9	...	Complete.
26	Raghuvaṇśadarpaṇa, Sargas VIII-X	Hemádri	68	8	...	Incomplete.
27	Rasavatíśataka	Dharaṇidhara	7	14	...	Complete.
28	Rághavapáṇḍavíyaṃ saṭíkam	Kavirája; Śaśidhara	209	10	New copy	„
29	Rámaśatakaṃ saṭíkam	Somadeva Ekanátha	32	14	1717	„
30	Rámáyaṇasára	Agniveśamuni	12	9	1351	„
31	Vivekachandrodayanáṭiká	Śiva	31	6	1819	„
32	Víracharitanáṭaka	Bhavabhúti	31	12	...	„
33	Vṛihatkathá	Kshemendra	350	8	1742	Incomplete.
34	Vetálapañchaviṇśatí	Śivadása	46	10	1525	Complete.
35	Sundarílaharívyákhyá	Vaidyamádhava	106	6	1709	„
	(*E*) *Grammar and Glossaries.*					
36	Kátantravibhramasútra	Charitrasiṇha	5	28	1710	„
37	Bháshyapradípavivaraṇa	Íśvaránanda	80	10	...	Incomplete.
38	Anekárthatilaka	Somabhava	11	18	1490	Complete.

	(F) Rhetoric.					
39	Kávyaprakáśaṭíká	Nṛisiṇhaṭhákhura	109	14	...	Incomplete.
40	Ditto	Vatsaláñchana	95	15	1825	Complete.
41	Kávyavilása	......	36	12	1822	"
42	Kávyádarśaṭíká	Vijayánanda	90	7	1683	"
43	Rasamañjaríparimala	Śeshachintámaṇi	24	27	...	"
44	Śárngadharapaddhati	Śárngadhara	35	10	...	Incomplete.
45	(Another copy)	Do.	61	11	...	"
46	Sárasangraha	Śambhudása	30	16	...	Complete.
	(G) Dharma.					
47	Chaturvarṇadharmasangraha	......	45	10	...	Incomplete.
48	Pratápamártaṇḍa	Pratáparudra	207	9	1744	Complete.
49	Śántyudukaprayoga	......	22	11	...	"
50	Śúdrácháraśiromaṇi	Śeshakṛishṇa	62	14	1647	"
51	Smṛitikaumudí	Madanapála	121	10	1615	Three leaves wanting.
	(H) Vedánta.					
52	Átmavilása	Śambhuráma	12	23	...	Complete.
53	Ánandalaharíbháshya	Gaurikánta	82	10	...	"
54	Dattagítá	Dattátreya	22	10	1775	"
55	Pañchíkaraṇa	Śankaráchárya	18	9	...	"
56	Bhaktisámányanirúpaṇa	Madhusúdana	44	8	...	"
57	Bhagavadgítápaiśáchabháshya	......	67	10	1902	"
58	Ratnaparíkshá	Appayadíkshita	74	10	1712	"
59	Vishṇusahasranámabháshya	Śankaráchárya	105	8	1585	"
60	(Another copy)	Do.	78	10	1712	"
61	Śivagítá saṭíká	Vyankaṭádri	147	10	...	"
62	Svátmánubhava	......	42	9	...	"

* The figures under this heading refer invariably to the era of Vikrama, which begins 57 B.C.

No.	Title.	Author.	Page.	Lines.	Age* of Manuscripts.	Remarks.
	A.—BRÁHMANICAL LITERATURE—*concld.*					
	(*I*) *Nyáya.*					
63	Nyáyakusumáñjali	Udayanáchárya	49	7	...	Complete.
64	Nyáyakaustubha	......	117	15	...	"
65	Nyáyaratnamálávyákhyána	Rámánuja	87	12	1651	"
	(*K*) *Medicine.*					
66	Agniveśasaṃhitá sabháshyá	......	117	11	...	Incomplete.
67	Átreyasaṃhitá sabháshyá	......	209	17	...	Complete.
68	Vidvadvallabha	......	70	8	...	Incomplete.
69	Viśrántavidyávinoda	Bhojadeva	67	12	New copy	Complete.
70	Vaidyaratnákarabháshya	Rámakṛishṇa	71	10	1715	"
71	Śataślokíṭíká	......	71	9	...	"
	(*L*) *Miscellaueous Works.*					
72	Bhairavapaddhati	......	12	13	...	"
73	Lakshahomapaddhati	......	7	10	...	"
74	Śáradatilaka	......	78	12	...	Incomplete.
75	Sámudrika	......	18	12	...	Complete.
	B.—JAINA LITERATURE.					
	(*A*) *Dharma.*					
76	Aürapachchhakhanapaïnna (M.)	......	1	21	...	"

77	Antarváchya (S. M. G.)	......	118	16	...	„
78	Áchárángasútra (M.)	......	1—656			
79	Áchárángasútravṛitti (S.)	Śílanka	65—411	5	1348	„ written on palm-leaves.
80	Ácháránganíryuktí (M.)	Bhádrabáhu	18			
81	Áchárángasútrabálávabodha (M. G.)	......	158	12	...	„
82	Ágamasároddhar (G.)	Devachand	79	10	...	„
83	Ávaśyakasútra (M.)	......	44	15	...	„
84	(Another copy)	......	24	19	...	Incomplete.
85	Ávaśyakasútra (M.)	......	71	13	...	Complete.
86	Uttarádhyayanasútra (M.)	......	28	20	...	„
87	Uttáradhyayanaṭíká (S.)	Nemichandra	272	15	...	„
88	(Another copy)	Do.	214	15	...	„
89	Uttarádhyayanadípiká (S.)	Sudharmagaṇi	190	15	...	„
90	Upadeśakarṇiká (S.)	Udayaprabhadeva	241	14	1681	„
91	Úvaisútravṛitti (S.)	Abhayadeva	75	13	...	„
92	Ṛishimaṇḍalaprakaraṇa (M.)	......	15	10	1693	„
93	(Another copy)	......	15	10	...	„
94	Oghaniryukti (M.)	Bhadrabáhu	20	17	...	„
95	Oghaniryuktiṭíká (M. S.)	Droṇáchárya	155	15	...	„
96	Kalpasútra (M.)	Bhadrabáhu	81	9	1818	„
97	Kalpapradípa (M. S.)	......	85	15	...	„
98	Kalpasútraṭíká (M. S.)	......	21	17	1513	„
99	(Another copy)	......	84	21	...	Incomplete.
100	Kalpasútrasubodhiká (M. S.)	Vinayavijaya	75	15	1669	Complete.
101	Kusumamálá (M.)	......	25	11	...	Incomplete.
102	Jambudipápannatti with Taba (M. G.)	......	11	12	...	„
103	Jñátadharmakathávṛitti (S.)	Abhayadeva	71	17	1661	Complete.
104	Daśavaikálikasútraṭíká (S.)	Haribhadra	62	15	1745	„
105	Daśaśrutaskandhachúrṇi (M.)	......	47	15	1590	„
106	Dravyasangrahaṭíká (M. G.)	Nemichandra	25	15	...	„
107	Dvádaśángívṛitti (M. S.)	Pradyumnasúri	117	14	1474	„
108	Dharmaratnamañjúshá (S).	Devavijaya	816	9	1814	„
109	Nándyadhyayanaṭiká (M. S.)	Malayagiri	170	14	1474	„
110	Nándyadhyayanavivaraṇa (S.)	Haribhadra	88	14	1650	First leaf wanting.
111	Navatattvasútrabálávabodha (G.)	Súndarasúri	24	13	1517	Complete.
112	Nirayávalisútra (M.)	......	40	11	...	„

* The figures under this heading refer invariably to the era of Vikrama, which begins 57 B.C.

No.	Title.	Author.	Page.	Lines.	Age* of Manuscripts.	Remarks.
	B.—Jaina Literature—*contd.*					
	(*A*) *Dharma*—concld.					
113	Niśíthasútra (M.), Uddeśas I-X.	......	105—115	5—6	...	Complete: written on palm-leaves.
114	Niśíthasútrávachúrṇi (M.), Udd. I-X	Pupil of Pajjunna, *i.e.*, Pradyumna.	116—343			
115	Pañchavastuṭíká (M. S.)	Haribhadra	202	13	1662	,,
116	Pannavanasútraṃ saṭíkam (M. S.)	Śyámárya; Malayagiri	835	13	1401	,,
117	Paramátmaprakáśa (S.)	Yogendradeva.	124	13	1821	,,
118	Piṇḍaviśuddhidipiká (M. S.)	Jinavallabha; Udayasiṇha.	14	17	...	,,
119	Pratishṭhákalpa (S.)	Sahalachandra	33	15	1887	,,
120	Praśnavyákaraṇa and Vipákasútra (M.)	......	27	17	...	2nd Śútra incomplete.
121	Praśnavyákaraṇavivṛiti (S.)	Abhayadeva	86	15	...	Complete.
122	Bhagavatyavachúrṇí (S.)	......	55	15	...	,,
123	Bhavabhavana (M.)	Hemachandra.	10	18	...	,,
124	Maraṇavidhipainna (M.)	......	17	13	1589	,,
125	Rájapraśnísútraṃ savṛittikam (M. S.)	Malayagiri	88	15	1573	,,
126	Vichárasattarikávachúri (M. S.)	......	14	13	...	,,
127	Vṛiddhaśánti (M. S.)	......	34	19	...	Incomplete.
128	Vṛihatkalpasútra (M.)	......	1—9	5—7	1334	Complete: written on palm-leaves.
129	Vṛihatkalpasútrabháshya (M.)	......	10—158			
130	Vṛihatkalpasútrávachúrṇi (M.)	Pralambasúri	159—466			
131	Vyavahárasútra (M.), Uddeśa I-X	......	1—9	4—6	1412	Complete } written on palm-leaves.
132	Vyavahárasútravṛitti (S.), Uddeśa IV-X	Malayagiri	1—439			Incomplete } written on palm-leaves.
133	Śatakasútraṃ sávachúri (M. S.).	Devendra	27	17	...	,,
134	Śatapádiká (S.)	Mahendrasúri.	85	19	1646	,,
135	(Another copy)	Do.	109	15	...	,,
136	Śráddhapratikramaṇasútravṛitti (S.)	Tilakácharya	18	16	...	,,

137	Śráddhaprakaraṇavṛitti (S.)	Ratnaśekhara	187	13	...	,,
138	Santharapaïnna (M.)	......	6	11	...	Complete.
139	Samaváyángam (M.)	......	65	11	...	,,
140	Saṃyaktvasaptatibálávabodha (G.)	Ratnachandra	172	15	1829	,,
141	Sarayávalipaïnna (M.)	......	95	13	...	,,
142	Susamakathá from Chhedagrantha (M.)	Devendra	11	17	...	,,
143	Sútrakṛitángávachúrni (M.)	......	159	15	...	,,
144	Sútrakṛitángadípiká (M. S.)	Ratnaśekhara	74	24	...	,,
145	(Another copy)	Do.	101	19	1583	,,
146	Sútrakṛitángavṛitti (M. S.)	......	75	20	...	Incomplete.
147	Sthánángatabá (G.)	Dhanapati	287	17	1647	Complete.
	(B) Poetry.					
148	Rishabhapañcháśiká sávachúriḥ (S. G.)	Dharmaśekhara	7	14	...	,,
149	Kalyáṇamandirastavaḥ savachúriḥ (S.)	Siddhasenaguṇaratna	6	15	...	,,
150	Guruguṇaratnákarakávya (S.)	Somacharita	12	19	...	,,
151	Chaityavandanavritti (S.)	Haribhadra	24	15	1473	,,
152	Jainakumárasambhava (S.)	Jayaśekhara	20	19	...	,,
153	Tribhuvanadípak (G.)	Do.	24	12	...	1st leaf wanting.
154	Rághavapáṇḍavíya (S.)	Nemichandra	136	11	...	Incomplete.
155	Vikramádityachopái (G.)	Karṇavijaya	29	15	1752	Complete.
156	Vijayadevamáhátmya (S.)	Vallabhadeva	68	12	...	1st leaf wanting.
	(C) Legends and History.					
157	Kumárapálras (G.)	......	88	19	1742	Complete.
158	Chandraprabhasvámicharitra (S.)	Devendra	106	16	...	,,
159	Trishashṭiśalákápurushacharita (S.)	Hemachandra	108	15	...	,,
160	Dharmadattakathanaka (S.)	Máṇikyasundara	17	13	1681	,,
161	Pariśishṭaparvan (S.)	Hemachandra	117	13	1648	,,
162	Puṇyapálarájakathá	......	18	14	1676	,,
163	Pethadacharitra (S. G.)	Reṇuratnamaṇḍana	146	5	1876	,,
164	Pratyekabuddhakathá (M.)	......	16	13	...	,,
165	Bappabhattikathá (M.)	......	9	15	...	,,
166	Madanarekhámahásaticharitra (G.)	......	14	15	...	,,

* The figures under this heading refer invariably to the era of Vikrama, which begins 57 B.C.

No.	Title.	Author.	Page.	Lines.	Age* of Manuscripts.	Remarks.
	B.—JAINA LITERATURE—*concld.*					
	(*C*) *Legends and History*—concld.					
167	Yaśodharacharita (S.)	Somakírtti	35	14	...	Complete.
168	Ratnachúḍáras (G.)	Ratnaśekhara	13	15	...	„
169	Bohiníras (G.)	Vimala	33	17	...	„
170	Vajráyudhádikathá (S.)	......	19	21	...	Incomplete.
171	Vastupálacharitra (S.)	Harshagaṇi	80	18	1550	Complete.
172	Vikramaprabhandha (S.)	......	13	18	...	„
173	Vinayachataśreshṭhiputrakathá (G.)	......	72	15	1875	„
174	Śántináthacharitra (S.)	Munisundara	121	15	...	„
175	Do. (S.)	Bhavachandra	262	10	1743	„
176	Sáraras (G.)	......	...	...	...	„
177	Sítácharitra (M.)	......	61	16	1600	Incomplete.
178	Sollakaprabandhádi	......	18	18	...	„
179	Hariśchandrakathanaka (M.)	......	27	17	...	Complete.
	(*D*) *Miscellaneous Śástras.*					
180	Abhidhánachintámaṇiḥ satíkaḥ (S.)	Hemachandra	193	18	...	„
181	Kriyásamuchchaya (S.)	Jinadeva	55	19	1485	„
182	Chhandánuśásana (S.)	Hemachandra	46	13	...	Incomplete.
183	Daṇḍaka (M. G.)	......	40	12	1763	Complete.
184	Deśiśabdasangraha (M. S.)	Hemachandra	315	15	...	„ New copy.
185	Páialachhínámamálá (M.)	......	7	15	...	„
186	Yogaśástra (S.)	Hemachandra	16	13	...	„
187	Śabdaratnákara (S.)	Sundaragaṇi	25	15	...	„
188	Śabdánuśásanalaghuvṛitti III, 1—3 (S.)	Hemachandra	37	16	...	„
189	Do. Adhyáya IV	Do.	33	18	1510	„
190	Do. Adhyáya IV with Avachúri (S.)	Nandasundara	40	12	...	„

191	Śeshasangrahanámamálá saṭíká . .	Hemachandra; Vallabhagaṇi.	39	15	...	,,
192	Sárasvatayantrapújá (S.)	......	12	16	...	,,
193	Sároddháraśákunaparikshá (S.). . .	......	18	18	...	,,
194	Siddhavíjachakra (S.)	......	12	14	...	,,
195	Syádvádamañjari (S.)	Hemachandra . .	46	17	1502	,,
196	Syádvádamañjarivṛitti (S.). . . .	Mallisheṇa . . .	43	22	1496	,,
197	Haimalaghuprakriyávṛitti (S.) . . .	Vijayagaṇi . . .	41	12	...	,,
198	Scrapbook containing small Jaina works (S. G.).	......	38	18	...	,,
	C.—Gujaráti Literatuee.					
199	Vetálapañchaviṇśati	Jambhalabhaṭṭa . .	145	12	...	,,
200	Siṇhásanadvátriṇśati	Do. . . .	57	7	...	,,

* The figures under this heading refer invariably to the era of Vikrama, which begins 57 B.C.

From C. GONNE, Esq., Secretary to the Government of Bombay, to A. P. HOWELL, Esq., Officiating Secretary to the Government of India, Home Department,—No. 479, dated 4th May 1875.

I am directed to forward to you, for submission to the Government of India, the accompanying copy of a letter* from Dr. Bühler, Educational Inspector, Northern Division of this Presidency, giving a brief account of his operations in connection with the search for Sanskṛit manuscripts from August 1873 to 31st December 1874, together with copy of a further letter from the same officer, dated the 19th ultimo, and to request that his proposals may be sanctioned by the Government of India at an early date.

* Dated 4th February 1875.

2. Dr. Bühler, it will be observed, considers it necessary that he should start for Kaśmír about the middle or towards the end of June next, and asks for a grant of R5,000 on account of purchase of books, and R1,000 on account of travelling allowance.

3. Towards the sum of R6,000 thus asked for by Dr. Bühler, R3,200 will be available for the current year, if this Presidency budget is sanctioned; and I am to request that His Excellency the Viceroy and Governor-General in Council may be pleased to accord his sanction to an additional grant of R2,800, the balance which has to be supplied.

4. I am to add that the interest which the Government of India has already expressed in Dr. Bühler's operations, leads His Excellency the Governor in Council to hope for an early and favourable reply to the above proposal, especially as the allotment of R3,200, sanctioned for 1874-75 for the purpose of Sanskṛit manuscripts, was a saving.

From K. M. CHATFIELD, Esq., Director of Public Instruction, Bombay, to C. GONNE, Esq., Secretary to the Government of Bombay,—No. 5936, dated Poona, the 15th February 1875.

I have the honour to submit a letter† from Dr. Bühler, explaining why his detailed report on his tour in Rajputana is delayed, and submitting a short report for the information of Government.

† No. 4810 of the 4th instant.

2. Dr. Bühler appears to be desirous that this short report may be forwarded to the Government of India at an early date, with the view of securing a renewal of the grant for 1875-76; and I trust that the Government of Bombay will be pleased to recommend this renewal to the Government of India.

3. Dr. Bühler has submitted to me his accounts, and I beg to enquire whether the detail of the expenditure should be forwarded to the Accountant-General.

I may mention that I have examined the accounts, and find them complete.

From G. BÜHLER, Esq., Educational Inspector, Northern Division, to K. M. CHATFIELD, Esq., Director of Public Instruction, Bombay,—No. 4810, dated Surat, the 4th February 1875.

I have the honour to submit herewith a short report on my operations in connexion with the search for Sanskṛit manuscripts, during the period of August 1873 to December 31st, 1874; together with an account of the expenditure for the same period.

2. I regret that the non-receipt of nearly thirty copies of manuscripts from Jesalmir—without a description of which my full report would lose a great part of its interest—prevents me, even now, from submitting the detailed account of my tour through Rajputana. I have several times written to the Jesalmir Durbar to transmit these books, which were given to the copyists a year ago; but I have received no answer. I have also written, officially and demi-officially, to the Political Agent of Marwar on the same subject. The only result of his exertions has been a promise to send the manuscripts soon. As this answer was given in November last, I have now despatched my agent to Jesalmir with orders to bring the manuscripts; and they will, no doubt, arrive about the end of March. If I submit a short report now, my object is to bring officially to the notice of the Government of India the success which has attended my operations, and to solicit a further grant for the purchase of manuscripts for the year 1875-76.

3. The account of the sums entrusted to me for the purchase of books shows a balance of R420; but R106 have to be deducted from this sum for certain manuscripts which I have agreed to purchase from Bhúj in Kach, and the journey of my agent to Jesalmir will cost about R150. The real balance is, therefore, only R164, for which it will hardly be possible to print my detailed report.

4. The account of the expenditure of my travelling allowance is not furnished with vouchers, as a great part of the items is of such a nature that I cannot furnish vouchers for them. It shews that the allowance has not covered my expenses, and the deficit is, in reality, much larger than

what the paper shews; as I have had to pay also 3rd class railway fare for one servant from Okarra, on the Sind and Punjab Railway, and a not inconsiderable amount for personal luggage. I am not able to ascertain the exact amount for the last two items. I do not wish to raise a claim on account of any excess of my actual expenses over the sum granted by Government.

Abstract Report for the year 1873-74.

THE operations connected with the search for Sanskṛit manuscripts from August 1873 to December 31st, 1874, may be divided according to three periods—

I.—Operations in Gujarat, from August to 14th December 1873.

2.—Operations during my tour in Rajputana, from 15th December 1873 to 15th March 1874.

3.—Operations from 15th March to 31st December 1874.

2. The chief result during the first period was the acquisition of 45 manuscripts, partly Bráhmanical and partly Jaina. Among the former is one exceedingly important work, the Pañchasiddhántiká of Varáhamihira. This work belongs to the Tantra branch of astronomy, and is strictly scientific. It has the greatest interest for the student of Indian astronomy, as it contains the date of its author, and gives extracts from five older astronomical books which are no longer accessible. The manuscript, of which I was allowed to have a copy taken, is not very correct; but the general sense can usually be made out. The owner of the original informed me that he had copied it in Benares, where formerly Mr. Colebrooke, Dr. Kern, and others have sought it in vain; and that a commentary on the work exists. Among the Jaina books are some valuable commentaries on Sútras, which I had been unable to obtain in former years, and several historical legends.

Another success was the opening of a famous Bháṇḍár or Jaina library at Tharád, to which I gained access in the beginning of December 1873, with the kind assistance of Major Y. Watson, then Acting Political Agent of Pahlanpur. The Bháṇḍár contains a nearly complete set of the sacred and legendary works of the Jaina sect, and I was able thence to obtain copies of a few books bearing on the history of the sect and of Northern

Gujarat. Among the latter I may mention a Kaṇhadadevacharitra, a Gujarátí-Marwárí poem on the history of a Chohan prince, called Kaṇhada, who valiantly defended his country against the Musalmans.

3. During the second period, on my tour through Rajputana, I visited, among towns famous for their libraries and religious establishments, Ábú, Nandol, Palli, Jodhpur, Jesalmir, Bikanir, and Bhatner or Hanumangaoh. Ábú and Nandol furnished no books; but I obtained fresh copies of a number of inscriptions which, though already published by others, required revision. The new copies of the Nandol copperplates, of which an abstract translation was published by Colonel Tod, gave very curious and unexpected results.

In Palli, only a few not very important books were obtained. In Jodhpur, the Mahárája most liberally allowed me access to his extensive library, which contains about 1,800 Sanskṛit manuscripts, a large collection of printed Sanskṛit books, and several hundred manuscripts in the modern vernaculars, chiefly in Hindí and Marwárí. The library, though rich in rare Puráṇas, Máhátmyas, and Tantras, did not furnish much for my purposes, as most of the manuscripts were modern and incorrect. I ordered copies of two works only. I purchased in Jodhpur eleven manuscripts, several of which were of importance, *e. g.*, a complete grammar of Hemachandra, and a copy of the dictionary of *deśí* or local words by the same author. Copies of the catalogues of the Mahárája's and some private persons' libraries were procured.

In Jesalmir, the next stage on my journey, I gained, after considerable trouble, a sight of all the manuscripts preserved in the famous Bháṇḍár under the temple of Parisnath. Though this library proved to be smaller in extent than was formerly supposed, its contents are of so great importance that I should have been satisfied with the results of my journey if I had found nothing else. It contains a not inconsiderable number of very ancient manuscripts of classical Sanskṛit poems, and of books on Bráhmanical Śástras, as well as some rare Jaina works. More than 50 of the Bráhmanical manuscripts are written on palm-leaves, and date from the twelfth, thirteenth, and fourteenth centuries. The oldest of these bears the date Saṃvat 1160, or A.D. 1103-4. It is, therefore, 29 years older than the old Limdi manuscript which I noticed in my report for 1873-74.

The poetical manuscripts contain some well-known dramas, epic poems and stories, the texts of which it will now be possible to restore with a greater degree of certainty than formerly, when Sanskṛitists had to rely on manuscripts and commentaries written in the fifteenth and sixteenth centuries, or even later. They contain, also, three larger and five smaller hitherto unknown poems. Two among the former are historical,—one, entitled the Life of Vikramáṅka, gives the history of the Chálukya king Vikramáditya or Tribhuvanamalla of Kalyáṇa, A.D. 1078-1127. It was composed by his chief Pandit, Bilhaṇa, a Kaśmírian, about the year 1085. The second, written in ancient Prákṛit, and composed by Upendraharshapálita of Jálandhara (Jullunder), celebrates the victory of a king Yaśovarman over a king of Gauḍa. The remaining Bráhmanical manuscripts contain chiefly works on logic, rhetoric, and Sáṅkhya philosophy. Many of these were hitherto unknown.

With the assistance of Dr. Jacobi, a young German Sanskṛitist, who accompanied me on my journey, I looked over every manuscript in the Bháṇḍár, copied the whole of Bilhaṇa's Life of Vikramáṅkadeva, and collated a portion of the Raghuvaṇśa. I made arrangements to have prepared copies of 28 manuscripts. Unfortunately, up to this time, only four out of these have been received,—a circumstance which has prevented the submission of my detailed report.

Besides the great Bháṇḍár, Jesalmir is rich in private Jaina libraries. I secured catalogues of four, as well as that of the Rával's private collection. I acquired also 23 old manuscripts referring both to Bráhmanical and Jaina literature.

In Bikanir, the most important library which I saw belongs to the Mahárája, and contains about 1,400 manuscripts. With the assistance of my companion, I looked over every single book in it. No catalogue of the collection exists. I took only notes of the more important works, as a pandit has been engaged for several years in making a detailed catalogue, with copious extracts, of the most valuable manuscripts, 30 in number. Copies have been procured for Government. Among them are the missing portions of the commentary on the Śatapathabráhmaṇa, the old work of Bharata on Theatricals, a work on the amusements of kings, composed in the first half of the twelfth century by King Someśvara of Kalyáṇí, a rare commentary on the Mitákshárá by Aparárka. I secured also from another source a copy of the Yugapuraṇá, a piece of an ancient astrological book which contains notices on the history of India. A very large number of old manuscripts was offered for sale. I acquired 120 for Government, and my purchases were only limited by the extent of my resources. Had I had time and money, a good many more important books could have been purchased.

In Bhatner, the last town of Rajputana which I visited, I did not find the collection of old palm-leaf manuscripts, which General Cunningham saw there about twenty-five years ago. But I was shewn a large library, containing about 800 paper manuscripts, of which I borrowed five, in order to get them copied.

4. On the 16th of March I went on a month's privilege leave, and visited, during this time, Lahore, Delhi, Benares, and other towns of Northern and Eastern India. In Delhi I was fortunate enough to become acquainted with Viśveśvar Śástrí Naval Gosvámí, who not only shewed me many of his valuable manuscripts, but presented me with copies of the rare work of Yámana on Rhetoric, and of the important commentary of Aparárka on the Mitákshárá, which I have accepted for Government and added to the collection in my hands.

From Benares I obtained a loan of a collection of 38 political manuscripts, many of which are new or rare.

From Bundi I received a unique commentary on a part of the law-book of Nárada, through the kindness of the Political Agent of Haraoti.

Since my return to Gujarat I have bought about a dozen manuscripts, and received one as a present.

One of these manuscripts contains a second copy of the Prákṛit dictionary called Ṗáialachhí, which I discovered in 1872. As it is very carefully written, I have been able to discover by its means the name of the author of the work, which is hidden in a riddle, given in one of the concluding verses. Another manuscript contains a panegyric on the famous Ahmedabad Sultan, Muhammad Begada, by a Pandit, whom he seems to have protected. A still more important acquisition is a Life of Mahávíra, the founder of the Jaina religion, by Hemachandra.

5. The following steps have been taken in order to make the Government collection known and useful. The report, and classified list of purchases made in 1872-73 have been printed and issued. The Life of Vikramáṅkadeva, alluded to above, has been edited by myself, and will form part of the Bombay Sanskṛit series. Articles on the Jesalmir Bháṇḍár, and on the new manuscript of the Páialachhí, have been published in the *Indian Antiquary*.

Eight of the old palm-leaf manuscripts acquired in 1872-73 have been sent to England at the request of the Government of Bombay, and have been exhibited at the Oriental Congress. According to a notice in the Academy, they were considered the most valuable among the manuscripts exhibited.

Professor Kielhorn, in Poona, has received a loan of the Máṇḍúkí Ápiśalí and Náradíyá Śikshás acquired in Rajputana and in Gujarat.

Dr. S. Goldschmidt, in Strassburg, has received a copy of Kálidása's Setubandha; Mr. Griffith, in Benares, a copy of Jinendra's commentary on the Káśiká; and Mr. Śankar P. Pandit, a number of commentaries on the Raghuvaṇśa.

Besides, I have been able to procure loans of manuscripts from private libraries to several colleagues in Europe and in India.

I have also prepared a detailed report on the results of the year's operations, which, when it will have been completed after the receipt of the missing manuscripts copied in Jesalmir, I trust I shall be allowed to print and publish, instead of the abstract now submitted.

6. I am happy to state that the generous efforts of Government for the preservation and exploration of the remains of Sanskṛit literature are fully acknowledged by my colleagues in Europe. In order to shew how deeply interested they are in the work, I will only quote the words of Mr. J. Mohl in a notice, No. III, of my catalogue of Sanskṛit manuscripts (*Journal Asiatique*, April 1873, p. 416): "C'est" (the search for manuscripts) "une veritable œuvre de civilisation que le Gouvernement de l'Inde a entreprise et qu'il a poursuivi avec une persévérance trés-louable."

7. I have to express the sense of my deep obligations to Sir Lewis Pelly, Agent to the Governor-General, Rajputana; Major Walter, Political Agent, Marwár; and Captain Barton, Political Agent, Bikanir. I have also to bring to the notice of Government the readiness with which the Maháraja of Jodhpur, the Mahárával of Jesalmir, and the Mahárája of Bikanir have opened to me their own libraries, and have exerted themselves to prevail on their subjects to do the same. I beg respectfully to recommend that their readiness in this respect may be acknowledged by the presentation of valuable Sanskṛit works published or patronised by Government, such as Professor Max Müller's edition of the Ṛigveda.

8. In conclusion, I beg to express the hope that Government will be pleased to give me an opportunity and funds to continue the search. Besides the great library at Siádhpur Pattan, Gujarat, there are the royal and private libraries of Kaśmír, Jammu, Jaypur, Udaypur, Ujjain, and Dhar, which, if explored, no doubt will yield the solutions of many problems of Sanskṛit philology.

From G. BÜHLER, Esq., Educational Inspector, Northern Division, to the Director of Public Instruction, Bombay,—dated Camp Vijalpur, the 19th April 1875.

WITH reference to Government Resolution No. 912, dated the 27th March 1875, General Department, and No. 368, dated the 6th April 1875, Educational Department, forwarded with your memorandum No. 134, dated 9th April 1875, I have the honour to repeat my respectful request that, for 1875-76, R5,000 may be allotted for the purchase of Sanskṛit manuscripts, and R1,000 for travelling allowance; and that I may be allowed to visit Kaśmír and Jammu as well, in returning to Bombay, Jaypur and Ujjain.

2. The motives which appear to make it particularly desirable to extend the search for Sanskṛit manuscripts to Kaśmír are the following:—

Firstly, Kaśmír has been for many centuries one of the chief seats of Hindu learning and literature. Even to this day, our Pandits maintain that Sarasvatí, the Goddess of Poetry, holds her court in Kaśmír, and this fable can be traced back for more than six centuries. The Rájatarangiṇí mentions also numerous Kaśmírian poets whose works have not yet been recovered. Besides poetry, several Śástras, notably grammar and poetics, were largely cultivated in Kaśmír. We owe the preservation of the Mahábháshya, the great commentary on Páṇini, of the second century B.C., entirely to the Kaśmírian Pandits, who, twice, at the command of the kings of the country, rescued it from oblivion, and settled its text by commentaries. Of all these commentaries, only one is accessible; but the importance of the Mahábháshya as the oldest landmark in Indian literary history, makes it highly desirable to secure the remainder, in order to more fully elucidate the history of the text of the original. Several other grammatical works, among which are the grammar of Chandra, composed A.D. 50, and the commentaries on a syntactical work, the Vákyapadíya—all written by Kaśmírians—have hitherto been found in fragments only. Rhetoric and poetics, also, were cultivated in Kaśmír from an early date. In Bikanir I found the oldest work on this subject, the Náṭyaśástra, in a Kaśmírian copy; in Jesalmir, I recovered two other books on this subject, written by Kaśmírians in the eighth century A.D.; many others which we know from quotations, *e.g.*, the commentary on the Náṭyaśástra by Abhinavaguptácharya, are still to be recovered. The works on poetics are of the utmost importance for the history of Indian poetry; for it is customary with the authors on this subject to give, in illustration of their rules, verses from famous poems. Thus, each work furnishes more or less numerous data for the history of the classical poems, the origin of which is mostly enveloped in obscurity. Lately it has also become known that Kaśmír has been, and probably still is, one of the chief seats of those Bráhmans who study the Atharvaveda, which now numbers very few adherents in India proper. Professor Roth, of Tübingen, who is now engaged with the second volume of his work on that Veda, has lately published a pamphlet in which he points out the great importance of enquiries being made in Kaśmír for the Atharvan. He has also, I understand, addressed the Government of India on the subject.

Results of the greatest interest may be finally expected from an exploration of the Kaśmír libraries for the political history of India. Kaśmír has furnished the Rájataraṅgiṇí, the only larger historical work in the Sanskṛit language which hitherto has become known. The book has been twice edited, in Calcutta and in Paris; but, unfortunately, from very insufficient materials, many passages are mutilated or hopelessly corrupt; and the utter want of manuscripts of the Taraṅgiṇí in the public libraries of India, leaves the Sanskṛitist helpless in doubtful cases. I have had personal experience of this inconvenience when, last year, I searched the Calcutta libraries in vain for a manuscript of the Rájataraṅgiṇí, in order to establish the identity of one of the authors whose works I found in Jesalmir with an individual named in the history of Kaśmír. It would, therefore, be of the greatest importance for Sanskṛitists if either manuscript materials were secured, or good collations of the work were made. I think it also highly probable that some, at least, of the numerous hostorical works from which Kalhaṇa compiled the Taraṅgiṇí, such as the Nílapuráṇa, the Rájávali of Kshemendra, &c., will be found in Kaśmír. In calculating the chances of the success of a tour in Kaśmír, it must be taken into account that the country has suffered a great deal from the Musalmans, and that, for some centuries, Hinduism and Hindu learning have been almost extinct. But the fact that forty years ago copies of the Taraṅgiṇí were found in the country, and that, in recent times, rare works have occasionally been brought from Kaśmír (*e.g.*, the commentary or Báṇa's History of Harshavardhana recovered by Dr. Bhau Dájí's pandit), shews that some of the old books must have been saved. Besides, it must not be forgotten that the present and late Rájás have been, and are doing, all they can to foster Hindu learning. A large number of pandits are now entertained at the courts, and Sanskṛit manuscripts are being collected from the chief towns of Northern and Central India. In Benares, I have been told over and over again, that the Rájá of Kaśmír constantly keeps there some agents, who buy up any manuscript that may offer in the market; and this story has been confirmed by a very trustworthy pandit of mine, who passed twice, in 1872 and 1874, several months in that town.

This latter fact makes it desirable that the second capital of the Rájá of Kaśmír, Jammu, should also be visited, as a part of the Rájá's collection is said to be preserved there.

3. A journey to Kaśmír can be undertaken during the summer months only. The time required for going and returning is about six weeks. A stay of three months in the valley would be absolutely necessary in order to obtain any appreciable results. If Jammu were included in the tour, another fortnight or three weeks would have to be added.

I would, however, urge that I might be allowed another six weeks in order to visit Jaypur and Ujjain. The former town is the chief seat of the Digambara Jainas in Northern India; and according to information received from Digambaras who visited me at Bikanir, it would be easy to procure there a set of the sacred books of this sect. The writings of the Śvetámbaras have been collected; but I find that, for the complete elucidation of the history of their creed, the writings of their brethren, the Digambaras, are indispensable. As regards Ujjain, it is the old seat of the Hindu astronomers, and it is clear that the missing Saṃhitás and Siddhántas are to be had there. The reasons which prove this conclusively are the following: About sixty years ago, Dr. William Hunter made enquiries about the older Hindu astronomers at Ujjain. The Jyotishís gave him the dates of ten persons, without explaining the grounds on which they based their statements. The works of five of these old astronomers have since been recovered, and the dates given by the Ujjain Pandits occur at the head of the Karaṇas composed by these authors. The inference is, therefore, that Dr. Hunter's informants actually possessed the works of the persons of whose times they gave an account.

Ujjain is also very likely to furnish further information regarding the works and time of Kálidása, as it is asserted that descendants of his live in the neighbourhood.

4. If these proposals are approved of, the whole tour would extend over seven months, and it ought to be begun by the end of June; else, there would be difficulties, on account of the monsoon, in reaching Kaś-

mír. As regards the funds, I think that R 5,000 for the purchase of books, and R1,000 for travelling allowance, would enable me to carry out the plan. Last year's grant for Sanskṛit manuscripts, R 3,200, has not been drawn. If the Government of India would sanction the money again for this year in addition to the grant for 1875-76, there would be ample funds to carry out the proposal—at least, as far as the question of purchase-money for manuscripts and travelling allowance is concerned.

From A. P. HOWELL, Esq., Officiating Secretary to the Government of India, Home Department, to the Secretary to the Government of Bombay,—No. 906, dated Simla, the 29th May 1875.

IN reply to your letter No. 499, dated 4th instant, and enclosures, I am directed to convey sanction to an additional grant of R2,800 towards defraying the cost of Dr. Bühler's proposed tour in search of Sanskṛit manuscripts.

No. 907.

COPY of the correspondence forwarded to the Financial Department for information and further orders.

Office memorandum from A. P. HOWELL, Esq., Officiating Secretary to the Government of India, Home Department, to the Foreign Department,—No. 1060, dated Simla, the 26th June 1875.

IN continuation of office memorandum No. 3238, dated the 20th October 1873, the undersigned is directed to forward the accompanying correspondence* with the Government of Bombay, regarding the deputation of Dr. Bühler to Kaśmír, Jaypur, and Ujjain, for collecting old Sanskṛit manuscripts, and to request the issue of the necessary orders in view to securing Dr. Bühler all the assistance that he may require in furtherance of his enquiries.

* From Bombay, No. 499, dated 4th May 1875.
To Bombay, No. 906, dated 29th May 1875.

2. The undersigned is to express regret that, by an oversight, this communication was not made simultaneously with the orders issued to the Bombay Government.

From G. BÜHLER, Esq., Educational Inspector, Northern Division, to the Director of Public Instruction, Bombay,—dated Bombay, the 23rd June 1875.

I have the honour to submit my report on the search for Sanskṛit manuscripts during the year 1874–75.

2. On returning from my tour through Rajputana in April 1874, I had at my command only a very small balance of about R600 from the allotment for 1873–74, which I had reserved for the printing of the report. As I received no intimation that Government had again sanctioned R3,200, I carried on the work very leisurely for a long time. Only towards the end of the official year, when the long delay in the arrival of the manuscripts which had been ordered to be copied in Jesalmir convinced me that I should be unable to bring out soon the detailed Report for 1873–74, and when I heard that the Government were willing to devote further sums to the search for Sanskṛit manuscripts, I resolved to spend the balance in my hands and to renew my efforts to obtain access to the yet unexplored libraries of Gujarat. These remarks will explain why the number of the purchases made during the year is very small.

2. Only one publication appeared during the year, the Report for 1872–73. By your permission, copies of a photograph of the last page of the Limdi manuscript of the Ávaśyakaśútra, dated Saṃvat 1189, which Mr. A. East, C.S., had been good enough to take, were prefixed to it.

3. Important catalogues of libraries have been obtained from Nariád, Ahmedabad, Bhúj, and Páthan.

The Nariád collection, which belongs to a Bráhman of that town, is not very large. But it contains some rare books, such as commentaries on the Náṭakas and several important grammatical works, among which there is a copy of the Gaṇaratnamahodadhi by Vardhamána.

The chief list from Ahmedabad is that of the Bháṇḍár of the Jainas belonging to the Tapágachha. During my usual autumn stay in Ahmedabad, I obtained this catalogue through Seṭh Maganbhái Háthisiṇh, who takes a warm interest in the researches regarding the history and literature of his sect. The collection contains 887 manuscripts in 26 dábadás, or cardboard boxes. The manuscripts are all written on paper, and are copies of the usual stock works of Jaina libraries—the Angas with their commentaries (always excepting the Pañchakalpa and Piṇḍaniryukti), the numerous Charitras, Rásas, Sejjháis, and Chopáis, descriptive of the lives, or composed in honour, of Jaina saints, and a small number of Bráhmanical works referring to the Alankárasástra and poetry. A few rare books, however, occur also, as, for instance, the Mágadhí Sítácharitra and the Prabhávakacharitra. The latter is a continuation of Hemachandra's Pariśishtaparvan of the Trishashṭiśalákápurushacharitra. It is of great importance, as it contains the lives of the Jaina teachers and theological writers, who lived after Vajrasvámin, down to the twelfth century.

A Bhúj collection, which belongs to Bhaṭṭárakjí Jívankul, is nearly as large as the Ahmedabad Bháṇḍár, and much of the same character. The number of manuscripts is 614, which are divided among 41 *pothís*. Among the Jaina books there is a very rare copy of the Mahániśíthasútra with a Tabá or interlinear Gujaráti version. Hitherto no other copy of this Sútra has become known, which contains anything but the bare text. The library contains also numerous works on Alankára, some of which are little known; and a large amount of Kachhí-Gujaráti poetry. During my stay in Bhúj, His Highness the Ráo also was good enough to allow me to inspect his library, which contains a few rare works, of which copies were obtained some years ago.

The most important results are, however, furnished by the opening of the Bháṇḍárs at Páthan in the Gaikváḍ's territory, the ancient Anhilvád. This town is still, as in the eleventh and twelfth centuries of our era, the true centre of Jainism in Gujarat. It is inhabited by a larger number of Śrávakas than Ahmedabad, Vadhván, or Cambay. Its religious institutions, especially the Upáorayas or Upáśrayas, which are the places of residence for the Yatis, are likewise very numerous. It is a general rule that every Upáśraya contains, at least, some books, and that the older the establishment, the larger and the more valuable the library. As Páthan possesses more than a dozen Upáśrayas, and some of these date from the times of the Chálukya kings, it may easily be imagined how great the quantity of the manuscripts amassed is. Among all these libraries, the so-called Bháṇḍár of Hemácharya, which was first discovered by Colonel Tod, and which is usually called *the* Páthan Bháṇḍár, surpasses all the rest in importance and extent. Colonel Tod* has given a graphic description of the manner in which the Yati in his service obtained admission to it. Since his time, only one other European, Mr. Kinloch Forbes, has obtained books from it. He saw its list, and his assistant, Kavi Dalpatrám Dháyábháí, who is now employed in the Educational Department, was allowed to

* *Travels in Western India, p. 232 seq.*

take out Hemachandra's Dvyáśrayakosha. My own attempts to enter the Páthan Bháṇḍárs were begun in November 1873, when the shortness of my stay of thirty-six hours in the town prevented my effecting anything, though Colonel Phayre had kindly procured for me letters to the Gaikváḍí officials. In March last, when returning from a tour to Ídar, Pálanpur, and Dísa, I resolved to make another attempt. Sir Lewis Pelly was good enough to give me another letter to the Súbá of the Uttar Mahals. On my arrival in Páthan, the Sir Súbá was absent on duty in Baroda. But I found in the Sir Faujdár (now Náib Súbá), Mr. Múlchand Makandás, a most efficient helper. After endless conferences with the Nagarseṭh and the Panch, under whose control all the libraries are, he prevailed upon them to admit me to some of the Bháṇḍárs. The first which I saw was the Pophliápádáno Bháṇḍár,* established by Rúpavijayasúri of Ahmedabad. It contains four large boxes, three of which are filled with paper manuscripts, while the fourth contains also some palm-leaf manuscripts. The number of manuscripts is between four to five hundred. There is no general catalogue, but in each dábadá a list of the contents is found. Among the paper manuscript I found only one novelty, the Titthogaliu Sútra. The palm-leaf manuscripts, part of which, to judge from their shape, seem to have come from Cambay, contain :—

(a) Religious works; Uttarádhyayana with Śánti's vṛitti, fols. 428; Ávaśyakasútra with a Píṭhiká for the use of Harshakírttigaṇi, dated Saṃvat 1391, fols. 63; Pachchákkhánaniryukti, fols. 136; Pravachanasároddhára, fols. 253; Jítakalpachúrṇi, fols. 108; Upamitibhávaprapañcha, dated Saṃvat 1261; Sárdhaśatakavṛitti, fols. 208;

(b) A collection of legends in Mágadhí, fols. 208, dated Saṃvat 1398;

(c) Two manuscripts of the Taddhitaprakaraṇa of Hemachandra's Śabdánuśásana, fols. 151 and fols. 365, the latter dated Saṃvat 1297;

A copy of the same author's Alaṅkárachúḍámaṇi, fols. 252, dated Saṃvat 1393.

The second library which I visited was that called Bhábhánápádáno Bháṇḍár, which is preserved in the Upáśraya of the Vimalagachchha. It consists of 27 dábadás, containing upwards of 300 paper manuscripts, and has a general catalogue. Its contents are not very important. I noted, however, a new Sútra called the Jamáli, of which a copy has been made,

* Most Bháṇḍárs are called according to the Pádo in which they are situated. A Pádo is what in Ahmedabad and elsewhere is called a Pol, a street, or a net-work of lanes which can be closed by gates, *i. e.*, a ward.

and a copy of a portion of the Nyáyakandalí,* and the commentary on the latter work (fols. 124). The first copy of this ancient book on Nyáya was found in Jesalmir.

A third collection, called the Sanghavinápádáno Bháṇḍár, was so far opened that the list was sent to me for inspection, as well as such books as I selected for copying. This library is much more important than the two preceding ones. It contains three boxes with nearly five hundred manuscripts, all of which are written on palm-leaves. Its catalogue is, unfortunately, not accurate, and it is necessary to make a new one, in order to obtain a full knowledge of its contents. Among the books which were sent to me for inspection was a copy of the Naishadhíya (called in the catalogue, erroneously, Śaśánkakírtana), dated Saṃvat 1304; a copy of a new play by Rámachandra, a pupil of Hemachandra, entitled Raghuvilápa; and large pieces of a Prakriyá based on Jinendra's grammar, a work which is also procurable in Southern India. The old catalogue enumerates, besides a complete collection of the Jaina Ágamas, their Bháshyas, Chúrṇis, and Vṛittis, several of the rare works first discovered in Jesalmir. Among these are the Nyáyakandalí and the Gauḍavadha, the historical Prákṛit poem on the defeat of the king of Gauḍa by Yaśovarman of Kánoj. A trained Śástrí is now engaged in making a new catalogue of the library, and several of its rare works are being copied. The Seṭh, in whose possession it is, has expressed and proved his willingness to allow the books to be used for copying or collating in Páthan.

These were all the results which I obtained on my visit in March. As the Śrípúj of the Khartaragachha, who, together with the Panch, is the keeper of Hemachandra's Bháṇḍár, was absent on a tour in Rajputana, it was necessary to defer the attempts to open this library until later. In May, I received letters from the Sir Súbá, and from my agent, stating that the Śrípúj had come back and had agreed to shew me his books. I accordingly made, on May 16th, a second journey to Páthan, which a sand-storm and several thunder-storms that surprised me in the open field made anything but a pleasure trip. On my arrival, the Śrípúj seemed to have changed his mind. He at first tried to put me off by shewing me one kothalí, or bagful, of dilapidated paper manuscripts. On being pressed further, he produced, one after another, six more such kothalís, which contained altogether between 600 and 700 manuscripts. He then solemnly

* Guṇapadártha, fols. 3.

assured me that this was all he had—an asseveration which I refused to accept as true.

As my annual report was nearly due, I had, though with great reluctance, to return a second time *re infectá.* My disappointment was not much moderated by the discovery of a few rare works in the collection which the Śrípúj shewed me, and by my admission to a fourth minor Bháṇḍár. The former were a volume of elegant extracts from Prákṛit poems, with a Sanskṛit translation by Jayavallabha, entitled Prákṛitasubháshitávali ; the life of a king who favoured the Jainas, Maṇipatimahásámantacharita ; a new commentary on the Paribháshás ; the portion of Hemachandra's supplementary dictionary giving the names of various kinds of grain, Nighaṇṭuśeshadhányakáṇḍa ; * and a new Prakírṇaka, or detached treatise on Gachháchára, with a Sanskṛit commentary.

Hardly, however, had I come back to Surat, when the incessant exertions of the Gaikváḍí officials, combined with those of my agent and of a few friendly members of the Panch, caused another change in the Śrípúj's disposition. He suddenly wrote to me stating that he would shew me the old Bháṇḍár, and took the Vahivatdár and my agent to see it. According to the report of the latter, it contains forty boxes filled with manuscripts, while the Śrípúj mentions twenty-five in his letter. It is still asserted that there is no catalogue, though in Tod's and Forbes' time there was one. This circumstance is suspicious. The season, and my proposed tour to the North of India, made it impossible for me to personally follow up the success gained. I have despatched another Śástrí, together with two writers, to Páthan, in order to make new catalogues of Hemácharya's and of the Sanghavinápáda Bháṇḍárs, and to copy such manuscripts as I have already selected, and may still select.

Together with the last news regarding Hemácharya's Bháṇḍár, I received the catalogue of that belonging to the Tapágachha of Páthan. This collection also is very extensive and important. It contains 80 dábadás with upwards of 1,200 manuscripts, among which there are a goodly number of novelties, and apparently some new historical works.

I belive that, though a good deal is still to be done, the battle is won, and I trust that in my next report I shall be able to complete the account of the Páthan Bháṇḍárs.

* Hemachandra wrote, besides the Abhidhánachintámaṇi and Anekárthasangraha, a number of Śeshas, one of which, giving the names of trees (Vanaspati), I found in Satara in 1866. The late Dr. Bháu Dájí mentioned to me another, enumerating the precious stones.

3. Several among the Bráhmanical manuscripts purchased deserve special notice. No. 6, the *Bháratamañjarí*, is a poetical epitome of the Mahábhárata. It closely follows the divisions of its original, and is divided into the same number of Parvans. Its metre is the Anushṭubh śloka. The author, Kshemendra, appears to be the poet who wrote the epitome of the Vṛihatkathá of Guṇáḍhya, as his surname, Vyásapáda, shews that he was a Bhágavata. The manuscript was acquired in Bhúj. It is about three hundred years old, and tolerably correct.

No. 16, the *Naishadhíyadípiká*, is one of the oldest commentaries on Śríharsha's epic which has become known. Its author, Chándúpaṇḍita, the son of A'liga, was a Nágara Bráhman of Dholká near Ahmedabad. He states that he composed poetry, officiated as priest at many great sacrifices, studied Sáṅkhya philosophy, and wrote a commentary on the Ṛigveda. His teachers were Vaidyanátha and Narasiṃha. The Naishadha he learned from one Munideva, apparently a Jaina Yati. He asserts that before his time only one commentary on the Naishadha existed, composed by Vidyádhara (*alias* Sáhityavidyádhara, *alias* Cháritravardhanamuni), of which I have found fragments in Ahmedabad and in Jesalmir. He partly confirms the story of the Jaina author, Rájaśekhara, who places Śríharsha under Jayantachandra, or Jayachandra, of Kánoj, in the end of the twelfth century. He also calls the Naishadhíya "*navaṃ kávyam*" a modern poem. Chándúpaṇḍita gives as the date of his own work the 15th day of Śuklapaksha Bhádrapada of the year 1513, according to Vikrama's era, or 1456 A.D. When he wrote, Sáṅga was chief of Dholká, and Mádhava his minister. Chándú's younger brother, Tálhana, revised and corrected the book. The manuscript bears two dates, 1473 (at the end of canto XXII) and 1476 (at the end of canto II), and consists of four pieces, which, however, have been written by the same writer, a Vaidya called Náráyaṇa, the son of Bhábhala. The dates refer, no doubt, to the Śáka era. I received the manuscript from Gandeví in the Gaikváḍ's territory.

No. 17, the *Yudhishṭhiravijaya*, or "Victory of Yudhishṭhira," is another novelty. It belongs to the numerous compositions which are based on legends taken from the Mahábhárata. It contains eight A'śvásas. The end of the first canto is gone. The second contains "the sports of Krishṇa and Arjuna" (Kṛishṇárjunaviháravarṇana); the third, "the departure to the forest" (vanavásagamana); the fourth, "the battle between the Kiráta and Arjuna" (kirátarjunayuddhavarṇana); the fifth, "the death of Kíchaka" (Kíchakavadha); the sixth, "the peace-proposals" (Sámavarṇana); the seventh, "the defeat of the Kauravas;" and the eighth, "the victory of Yudhishṭhira over Duryodhana." The work is written in the Áryágíti metre, and each half verse is adorned with a Yamaka, or rhyme of four syllables. Its literary value is about the same as that of the Nalodaya. Its author is not named. One of my Śástrís told me that he had heard it mentioned by his teacher as an old and rare work.

No. 18, the *Rájavinoda,* "Amusement of the King," or Jarabakshapátaśáhíśrímahamúdasuratránacharita. "The life of Sultan Mahmúd" (Begadhá of Ahmedabad), by Udayarája, is quite a literary curiosity. The author, who declares himself to be the son of Prayágadása, and the pupil of Rámadása, celebrates Mahmúd, popularly reputed to have been the most violent persecutor of Hindus and Hinduism, as if he were an orthodox Hindu king. He calls him "the crest jewel of the royal race" (rájanyachúḍámaṇi) as if he were a Kshatriya, and he asserts that Śrí and Sarasvatí attend on his footsteps, that he surpasses Karṇa in liberality, and that his ancestor, *Muzaffar Khán, assisted Kṛishṇa against Kali.* The Charita is divided into seven Sargas. The first (ślokas 29), entitled "Surendra's and Sarasvatí's colloquy" (Surendrasarasvatísaṃváda), is introductory, and relates how Brahmá sent Indra to look after Sarasvatí, and found her in the halls of Mahmúd Sháh, and how she sang the praises of Mahmúd. The second (vaṇśánukírtana, ślokas 31) gives the genealogy of Mahmúd, beginning with Muzaffar Khán. The statements made appear to be historically correct. The third (sabhásamágama, ślokas 33) describes Mahmúd's entry into the durbar-hall. The fourth (sarvasára, ślokas 33) relates what princes and people were received in durbar. The fifth (saṅgítaraṅgaprasaṅgá, ślokas 35) describes a Nách given by the Sultan. The sixth (vijayayátrotsava, ślokas 36) and the seventh (vijayalakshmílábhá, slokas 37) are devoted to a rhapsodic description of Mahmúd's warlike exploits. The frequent allusions to the Pádisháh's liberality make it probable that the author either had received, or hoped to receive, dakshiṇá from him.

No. 26, the *Dharmapradípa,* is not identical with the Bhojasmṛiti, stated to be one of the works of Dhárá. It was written at the order of Bhoja, the son of Bharamalla, who ruled over Kachh some centuries ago. This king is the same to whom the Bhojavyákaraṇa of Vinayaságara, which occurs in my catalogue of manuscripts from Gujarat, is dedicated. The Dharmpradípa treats of Áchára, or the rule of conduct only. The manuscript comes from Kachh.

No. 27, the *Náradasmritibháshya* of *Kalyáṇabhaṭṭa*, is the most important acquisition of the year among the works on Dharma. It gives a full explanation of the first eight Adhyáyas of the Smṛiti, and helps greatly to settle the text of this interesting but difficult law-book, of which very few copies are procurable. Kalyáṇa says in the introductory verses that his work is based on an older but corrupt commentary.* The manuscript has been written in Benares, and has been procured from the library of the Rájá of Bundí, through the kind offices of the Political Assistant in charge of Haraoti.

Nos. 29 and 30.—These two copies of the old *Dharmasútra* of Vasishṭha are complete and very correct. The first was presented to me by Professor Bálaśástrin of Benares College, and the second by Dámodaraśástrin of Bhúj. Like all similar presents, I accepted them for Government.

No. 36 is a large fragment of the ancient *Gárgí saṃhitá* first discovered by Dr. Kern, and described in the preface to his edition of the Váráhísaṃhitá.

No. 37, the *Pañchasiddhántiká* of *Varáhamihira*, is one of those rare works which have been sought after for a long time. The copy which I have procured is a transcript made from a manuscript belonging to Sadaráma Joshí of Sojítrá, who was good enough to lend me his copy for some time. The original is unfortunately so incorrect that it is hardly possible even to make out the general drift. The work is a *karaṇa*, which gives the substance of five older works, the Siddhántas ascribed to Pauliśa, Romaka, Vasishṭha, Súrya, and Pitámaha.

It is written in the Áryá metre, and contains, I suppose, 18 Adhyáyas.

The first, called Karaṇávatára (slokas 25), contains the well-known verses giving the details about the older Siddhántas (verses 2 to 4), and the date Śáka 427, which forms the base of the subsequent calculations (verse 8). Next follow 83 verses, which are not divided into Adhyáyas, but at the end of which are placed the words Chandragrahaṇaṃ shashṭho 'dhyáyaḥ, Eclipses of the moon, Adhyáya VI.

The following Adhyáyas appear to be in good order: they are—Adhyáya VII, on eclipses of the sun, according to Pauliśa, iti pauliśasiddhánte ravigrahaṇaṃ saptamo 'dhyáyaḥ (ślokas 6): Adhyáya VIII, on

* Drishtvá saháyarachitaṃ náradabháshyaṃ kulekhakápabhrashṭaṃ kalyáṇena kriyate—práktanam eva tad viśodhya punaḥ.

eclipses of the sun, according to Romaka, iti romakasiddhánte 'rkagrahaṇam ashṭamo 'dhyáyaḥ (ślokas 18); Adhyáya IX, on eclipses of the sun, according to Súrya, siddhánte 'rkagranahámá (?) navamo 'dhyáyaḥ (ślokas 22); Adhyáya X, on eclipses of the moon, chandragrahaṇe daśamo 'dhyáyah (ślokas 7); Adhyáya XI, Avarṇanátyekádaśo 'dhyáyah (?) (ślokas 6); Adhyáya XII, on lunar and solar years according to Pitámaha, iti pitámaha-siddhánte dvádaso 'dhyáyaḥ (ślokas 5); Adhyáya XIII, on the order of the universe, trailokyasaṃsthánanáma trayodaso 'dhyáyaḥ (ślokas 40).

In this chapter occurs, verse 6, the refutation of the opinion of those who hold that the earth moves:

Bhramati bhramasthiteva kshitir ity apare vadanti noḍugaṇaḥ—
Yady evam śyenádyá na khát punaḥ svanilayam upeyuḥ.

"Others contend that the earth, standing as if in an eddy, turns round, not the crowd of the stars. If that were the case, falcons and other birds could not return from the sky to their nests."

Adhyáya XIV describes the chhedyakayantras (ślokas 58).

Adhyáya XV is called Jyotishopanishad (verse 13).

Adhyáya XVI contains the correction of the position of the stars and planets, tárágrahasphuṭíkaraṇaṃ shoḍasho 'dhyáyaḥ (ślokas 28).

After that follow seventy-eight ślokas without any division, and the conclusion of the whole is, ityácháryavaráhamihirakṛitáyám pañchasiddhántiká samáptá (*sic*).

Sadaráma Joshí states that he obtained his manuscript from Benares, and that better copies and a commentary are to be had there.

No. 38 is a manual for indigenous schoolmasters. Its author, Kshemendra, was the son of Bhúdhara, a Nágara Bráhman of Rájanagara, and wrote his treatise by order of Śaṅkaralála, Chief of Pitlad (Pedlád, manuscript).

No. 39 is a letter-writer, giving the proper formulas for addressing persons of all ranks.

5. Among the Jaina books, two deserve special notice. The first is the nearly complete copy of the *Trishashṭiśalákápurushacharita* (bought in Bhúj), which contains also the life of Mahávíra, the reputed founder of Jainism. It gives a great many hitherto unknown details regarding the saint's life. The second remarkable acquisition is the old copy of the *Páialachhínámamálá.* This manuscript is correct and accurate. I have already published a note regarding it in the *Indian Antiquary*, and have shewn that the author's name was *Dhanapála*. An edition of the book has

been prepared. I shall print it as well as Hemachandra's Deśíkosha, as soon as I find a little of that leisure and quiet which are absolutely necessary for serious work of the kind.

6. During 1874-75, as in former years, manuscripts have been furnished to various Indian and European scholars, partly such as belong to Government, and partly such as could be borrowed from owners of private libraries.

Professor Kielhorn has received copies of the Vákyapadíya, Máṇḍúkí, and Náradíyá Sikshás, as well as some less important works of the same description; Mr. Śaṅkar P. Pandit, copies of the Bharataśástra, the Setubandha (acquired last year), and of a commentary on the Vikramorvaśí; Mr. Káśináth T. Telang, several copies of the Mudrárákshasa; Professor Thibaut, at Benares, a copy of the Mánavaśulvasútra; Professor Bálaśástrin, in Benares, copies of the last two Adhyáyas of the Kásiká; Babu Rájendralála Mitra, in Calcutta, copies of Sáyaṇa's Aitareyáraṇyakabháshya and of Śaunaka's Vṛihaddevatá; Professor Aufrecht, copies of Trivikrama's Nalachampú; Professor Eggeling, of London, a copy of the Gaṇaratnamahodadhi; Professor Weber, of Berlin, a copy of Hála's Saptaśatí; Professor Goldschmidt, in Strassburg, a copy of the Setubandha. Various other demands of European scholars will be satisfied shortly.

I have also, in accordance with the permission granted to me by Government in 1872, bought about fifty manuscripts of works already represented in our collection for the Prussian Government.

No.	Title.	Author.	Page.	Lines.	Age of Manuscripts.	Remarks.
	I.—BRÁHMANICAL BOOKS.					
	(A) Vedic Works.					
1	Rishidevatáchhandáṇsi	......	70	8	1845	Complete.
2	Gáyatríbháshya	Śankaráchárya	2	11	......	„
3	Náradíyaśikshá	Nárada	...	...	......	„
4	Mantrasaṃhitá (used at the Gṛihya rites of the Ṛigvedins).	......	194	10	1865	„
	(B) Puráṇa and Itihása.					
5	Bhágavatapuráṇa, explanation of the first śloka.	Madhusúdanasarasvatí	13	12	......	„
6	Bháratamañjarí	Kshemendravyásapáda	211	15	1669	„
7	Rájávali, a list of kings taken from a Puráṇa	......	15	10	New copy	„
8	Váyupuráṇa	......	412	10	......	„
	(C) Kávya and Náṭaka and Alaṅkára.					
9	Anyokti	......	9	11	......	„
10	Anyoktiparichchheda	......	44	19	1844	„
11	Kaṇsavadhanáṭaka	Śeshakrishṇa	37	15	......	„
12	Kaṇsavadhaṭiká	......	26	10	1756	„
13	Kaṇsavadhaṭippaṇapadakaumudí	......	71	11	......	„
14	Durghaṭakávya	......	20	12	Śáka 1729	„
15	Dútáṅgadanáṭaka	Subhaṭa	18	12	1684	„
16	Naishadhíyadípiká	Chándúpaṇḍita	401	11	Śáka 1473	Incomplete: a portion of the Introduction, and Sargas X, XIII—XVII, lost.
17	Yudishṭhiravijayakávya	......	45	13	1707	Incomplete: 1st and 5th leaves wanting.

No.	Title.	Author.	Page.	Lines.	Age of Manuscripts.	Remarks.
	I.—Bráhmanical Books—*contd.*					
	(*C*) *Kávya and Náṭaka and Alankára*—contd.					
18	Rájavinoda	Udayarája	28	8	......	Complete.
19	Rasaratnadípiká	Mallarája	51	7	......	"
	(*D*) *Vyákaraṇa and Koshas.*					
20	Ekárthanámamálá	Saubhari	11	7	New copy	
21	Dvyaksharaṇámamálá	"	10	9	"	
	(*E*) *Dharma.*					
22	Achárárka	Divákara	73	9	......	
23	Kuṇḍakaumudí	Viśvanátha	37	10	......	
24	Kuṇḍamaṇḍapasiddhi	Viṭṭhala	5	10	......	
25	Kuṇḍamaṇḍapavivṛiti	"	20	15	......	
26	Dharmapradípa	Bhojadeva of Kachha	55	9	1726	
27	Narádityadharmaśástraṭíká	Kalyáṇabhaṭṭa	90	10	1926	
28	Pratishṭhápaddhati	Trivikramabhaṭṭa	91	11	1822	"
29	Vasishṭhasmṛiti	Vasishṭha	27	9	......	"
30	"	"	36	10	1599	"
31	Vasishṭhábháshya	Vedamiśra	24	13	New copy	"
	(*F*) *Púrva and Uttaramímaṇsá.*					
32	Nyáyaprakáśa	Apadeva	61	12	1873	"
33	Ramagítá saṭíká	... ...	11	15	......	"
34	Vedastutiṭíká	Raghunáthachakravartin	36	10	......	"
35	Vedastutiṭíká Anvayabodhiní	Kavichúḍámaṇichakravartin.	63	10	......	"

No.	Work	Author	Leaves	Lines	Date	Remarks
	(G) Jyotisha.					
36	Gárgisamhitá	Garga	79	8	New copy	„
37	Pañchasiddhántiká	Varáhamihira	49	15	„	„
	(H) Miscellaneous.					
38	Lipiviveka	Kshemendra	23	8	„	„
39	Lekhanaprakára	......	9	8	„	„
	II.—Jaina Works.					
	(A) Dharma.					
40	Jamálisútra (M.)	......	21	10	„	„
41	Tattvárthavṛittisukhabodhiká (S.)	Yogadeva	151	8	...	1st 3 leaves wanting.
42	Bṛihachchhántiṭíká (S.)	Harshakírtti	57	17	1676	Complete.
43	Yogaśástra with Bálávabodha (S. G.)	Hemachandra; Somasundara.	112	13	1531	„
44	Vichárapañchásíkávachúri (S.)	Vijayavimala	5	18	...	„
45	Siddhapañchásiká saṭíká (M. G.)	......	10	14	...	„
	(B) Poetry.					
46	Vairágyaśataka with Tabá (M. G.)	......	14	11	...	„
	(C) Biography, Legends.					
47	Trishashṭiśalákápurushacharita (S.)	Hemachandra	715	15	...	Incomplete: Parvas I, II, IV missing.
48	Rúpasenacharitra (S. M.)	Jinasúri	23	19	...	Complete.
	(D) Miscellaneous.					
49	Kárakavichára and Gujaráti-Sanskṛit Kosha (S. J.)	......	9	15	...	„
50	Taurushkinámamálá (S. U.)	......	4	13	...	„
51	Dhátutaranginí (S.)	......	4	18	...	Incomplete.
52	Páialachhínámamálá (P.)	Dhanapála	...	...	...	Complete.
53	Párasínámamálá (S. Pers.)	......	6	19	...	„
54	Bhádrabáhaví Saṃhitá (S.)	Bhadrabáhu	93	10	New copy	Incomplete.

From J. GEOGHEGAN, Esq., Under-Secretary to the Government of India, Home Department, to C. GONNE, Esq., Secretary to the Government of Bombay,—No. 2333, dated Simla, the 17th May 1869.

I am directed to request that, with the permission of His Excellency the Governor in Council, the accompanying printed list of books in the library of the late Rájá of Tanjore may be forwarded to Professor Bühler, and that he may be asked to favour the Governor-General in Council with his opinion, at an early date, as to the propriety of purchasing the Sanskṛit portion of the works enumerated therein, or any portion thereof.

From F. S. CHAPMAN, Esq., Chief Secretary to the Government of Bombay, to the Secretary to the Government of India, Home Department,—No. 1851, dated the 4th August 1869.

I am directed to acknowledge the receipt of Mr. Under-Secretary Geoghegan's letter No. 2333, dated the 17th May last, and in reply to forward herewith copy of one, dated the 26th ultimo, from Professor Bühler, and of its accompaniment, containing his opinion on the propriety of purchasing the Sanskṛit portion of the works enumerated in the printed list, which accompanied Mr. Geoghegan's letter, of the books in the library of the late Rájá of Tanjore.

2. In returning the printed list, I am directed to state that Mr. Geoghegan's letter was misdirected to England, and was not received here till the 16th ultimo; hence the delay which has taken place in replying to it.

From G. BÜHLER, Esq., Acting Educational Inspector, Northern Division, to the Chief Secretary to the Government of Bombay,—dated Surat, the 26th July 1869.

IN reply to Government Resolution No. 1692 of the 19th instant, I have the honour to submit the following remarks.

2. On examining the list of the Sanskṛit manuscripts which belonged to the late Rájá of Tanjore, I find that it contains a great many useful, and a number of *very rare*, or *nearly unique*, books (*vide* the annexed list). I am therefore of opinion that it would be in the interest of Sanskṛit philology if the Government of India decided to buy the whole collection, with exception of the portions headed in the catalogue—*Stotras*, pages 14 to 17 and page 44; *Extracts from Aksharakáṇḍa*, page 17. Should this be impossible, I beg strongly to recommend that at least the works

contained in the list may be bought, many of which are quite *unknown*, or procurable only with great trouble and expense (*vide* remarks in the list).

Dharmaśástra, or Hindu Law.

Work	Remarks
Subodhiní	A complete copy of Himádri's writings like this is very rare, and worth Rs. 4 to 6 per 1,000 ślokas, according to the age of the manuscripts.
Kaulahimádri	
Vratahimádri	
Dánahimádri	
Śántihimádri	
Śráddhahimádri	
Práyaśchittahimádri	
Mádhavavyavahárakáṇḍa.	
Smṛitichandrikásaṇskárakáṇḍa	Not obtainable in the Bombay Press.
Smṛitichandrikávyavahárakáṇḍa	
Smṛitichandrikáśráddhakáṇḍa	
Gotrapravaranirṇaya	
Madanaratna.	
Nirṇayámṛita.	
Sarvasmṛitisangraha.	
Vyavahárárthasmṛitisárasamuchchaya.	
Viśveśvarasmṛiti.	
Dattanirṇaya	Rare.
Ápastambasútra, Commentary by Ujjvala	Rare.
Smṛitisindhu.	
Gautamadharma.	
Pravaradípiká.	
Pravaramañjari.	
Manvarthachandriká	Rare.
Pulastyasmṛiti.	
Manusmṛitiṭiká.	
Vṛiddhayamasmṛiti	If really Vṛiddhayama, unique.
Vṛiddhaśankhasmṛiti.	If really Vṛiddhaśankha, unique.
Viśvámitrasmṛiti	Rare.
Kaushítakigṛihyasútra.	
Vasishṭhasmṛiti	If complete, very rare.
Dattamañjari.	
Vyavahárapraká́śakáṇḍa.	
Kámandakiníti.	
Gobhilagṛihyabháshya	Rare.
Áśvaláyanagṛihyabháshya	This must be Ápastamba's Gṛihyasútra, with Haradatta's Commentary, very rare.
Áśvaláyanagṛihyavṛitti	

Tarkaśástra, or Logic.

Title	Remarks
Vyáptikhaṇḍa, Gadádhari	A *complete* Gadádharí is rare, and worth Rs. 3 to 4 per 1,000 ślokas.
Upádhiváda	
Bhúyodarśanaváda	
Siddhántalakshaṇa	
Chaturdaśalakshaṇí	
Pakshatáváda	
Parámarśaváda	
Hetvábhása	
Sámányabhávasádhana	
Vyadhikaraṇadharmávachchhinnábháva	
Avayavaváda	
Sangatyanumiti	
Avachchedakatvaniruktilingakaraṇatáváda	
Púrvapakshavyápti	
Gadádharí Śabdakhaṇḍa	
Prámáṇyaváda	
Vyutpattiváda	
Vyáptigrahopáyaṭippaṇa.	

Vyákaraṇaśástra, or Grammar.

Title	Remarks
Paribháshávṛittivyákhyána.	
Vyákaraṇasútravyákhyámahábháshya	If complete, a good manuscript is worth Rs. 150.
Mahabháshyavyákhyá	Ditto.
Kaiyaṭaṭíká	Ditto.
Káśiká Vṛittiḥ.	
Commentary on the Kásiká Vṛittiḥ, Padamañjarí.	
Paribháshábháskara.	
Paribhásháv ṛitti.	

Mímáṇsáśástra, or Rules by which Vedic Texts are expounded.

Title	Remarks
Tantravárttika	Rare.
Tantraṭíká.	

Puráṇas, or Sacred History of the Hindu Gods, &c.

Title	Remarks
Bhavishyapuráṇa	Very rare.
Vámanapuráṇa.	
Ágneyapuráṇa	If a good copy, very useful; now required by the Asiatic Society of Bengal.
Śámbapuráṇa.	
Ádityapuráṇa	Rare.

Puráṇas, or Sacred History of the Hindu Gods—concld.

Bháratasubodhiní.	
Bháratadharmárthadípiká	Rare.
Bháratáṅkutachandriká	Rare.
Bhárataratnávali, by Ánandapúrṇamunîndra.	
Commentary on the Mahábhárata, by Paramánandabhaṭṭácharya.	
Commentary on the Mahábhárata, by Vimalabodha.	

Sangítaśástra, or Science of Music.

Bharataśástra, by Raghunáthaprasáda.
Bharataśástra, by Nandakeśvara.

Kávya, or Poetry and the Drama.

Commentary on Mágha, by Vardhamánácharya.	Not heard of before.
Commentary on Naishadhacharitra, by Mallinátha.	Very rare, and much wanted.
Commentary on Kumárasambhava, by Narahari.	
Vikramásanachampú.	
Patañjalitacharitra	Very rare.
Commentary on ditto.	
Śankarácháryacharita.	
Śivarájacharitra.	
Commentary on Meghasandeśa.	
Bṛihatkathámañjarí.	
Sasharya.	
Mayúraśataka.	
Commentary on the Mayúraśataka.	
Commentary on the Amaruśataka.	
Pannalavarṇana.	
Bhuṇsalavaṇśávali.	
Cháṇakyavarṇana.	
Sáhañjirájachúrṇiká.	
Kamandakanítisára.	
Pañchatantra.	
Sphuṭaśloka.	
Commentary on the Mudrárákshasanáṭaka .	Rare.
Commentary on the Málatímádhavaprakaraṇa	Rare.
Nágánandanáṭaka	Rare.

Kávya, or Poetry and the Drama—concld.	
Chaṇḍakauśikanáṭaka	Rare.
Commentary on the Málavikágnimitra . .	Unique.
Ratnávalináṭiká.	
Dhanañjayavilása.	
Sarasvatíkaṇṭhábharaṇa.	
Jyotisha, or Astrology.	
Somasiddhata	If real, unique.
Vedánta.	
Gauḍapádíyaṭíká.	
Várttikabháshya.	
Bhagavadgitávyákhyána, by Madhusúdana.	
Ditto, by Śankaráchárya.	
Ditto, by A'nandagiri.	
Bhagavadgítá, Brahmánandagiri.	
Śrauta, or Religious Observances.	
Śulvasútravyákhyána.	
Kapurthyabháshya	Rare.
Paribháshásútravyákhyána.	
Vedas.	
Niruktabháshya	Rare.
Nighaṇṭubháshya	Very rare.
A'tharvaṇavedasaṃhitá.	
A'tharvaṇabráhmaṇa	Rare.
Káṭhakabráhmaṇa	Rare.
Yajurvedabháshya	This commentary is new to me.
Saṃhitopanishad	
Táṇḍyabráhmaṇapañchapañchaka.	
Shaḍviṇśabráhmaṇa.	
Sámavidhánabráhmaṇa.	
Daivatádhyáya.	
Shaḍviṇśabráhmaṇa.	
Pushpasútra.	
Sámaśrautabaudháyanasútra.	
Nighaṇṭu, or Dictionaries.	
Amaravyákhána, or Commentary on the Amarakosha, by Sarvánanda.	New to me.
Vaijayanti	Very rare.
Pañchánananighaṇṭusára	Very rare.
Sañjívanínighaṇṭu	Very rare.
Padasaṅgrahanighaṇṭu	Very rare.
Durghaṭanighaṇṭu	Very rare.

Nighaṇṭu, or Dictionaries—concld.

Káláyudhanighaṇṭu	
Bhojanighaṇṭu	
Indranighaṇṭu	
Nánárthaśabdánuśásana	
Mayúranighaṇṭu	
Vákyanikáyanighaṇṭu	
Trirúpakosha	
Daśadipanighaṇṭu	
Daśanirṇaya	
Linganirṇayanighaṇṭu	Very rare.
Jaiminínighaṇṭu	
Shaṇmukhanighaṇṭu	
Agastyanighaṇṭu	
Vikramanighaṇṭu.	
Kávyasañjíviní	
Dharmarájanighaṇṭu	
Muráriníghaṇṭu	
Bhuvanapradípa	
Bhárgavanighaṇṭu.	
Śabdachandriká	
Gaṇamañjarí.	
Sanatkumáríya.	

Dharmaśástra, or Hindu Law.

Vyavahóramañjarí.	
Bodháyanagṛihyasútra	Rare.
Bodháyanadharmasútravyákhyána	If real, unique. I want it very much.
Gautamadharmavyákhyána.	
Mitákshará.	
Bharadvájasútravyákhyána, Śráddhakáṇḍa	Rare.
Rájadharmasárasangraha	Rare.
Bharadvájasmṛiti.	
Manusmṛitivyákhánanandiní.	
Bhárgavasmṛiti	Rare.
Vṛiddhatrayasmṛiti	If real, unique.
Sárvabhaumasmṛiti.	

Sabdaśástra, or Etymology.

Padamañjarí, Vyákhyánamañjarímakaranda.	
Bháṇḍírabháshábhúshaṇa	New to me.
Bháṇḍírabháshávyákaraṇa	
Prákṛitavyákaraṇavyákhána, Prákṛitamañjarí, by Kátyáyana, Uṇádidípiká.	

Mímáṇsáśástra.

Ráṇaka	Very rare.

Vaidyaśástra, or Medical Science.

Aśviśástra.

Śilpaśástra, or Architecture.

Vimánavidyá	Nearly all new to me.
Viśvkarmíya	
Sángítaśástra, or Musical Science, on Cadjans.	
Bháratíyanáṭyalakshaṇa	
Bháratíyanáṭyalakshaṇa, Abhinaya . . .	
Múlabhárata	

Vedas on Cadjans.

Saṃhitábháshya	New.
Parakshudrabháshya	New.
Káṭhakabháshya	If real, unique.
Áruṇabháshya	New.
Mantrapraśnabháshya.	
Chaturviṇśatisútra	New.
Prákṛitaṛigbháshya	Unique.
Prákṛitakuláchára	Very rare.
Pratihárasútra.	
Kalpasútra.	
Upagranthasútra.	
Kalpasútrabháshya.	
Pratiháradaśavidhanyáyavyákhyána.	

Kávya on Cadjans.

Gúḍhachintámaṇi.	
Sahasránkacharitra	New, and probably very important.
Achyutarámábhyudaya.	
Śriharshacharitra	Very rare; only four incomplete copies known.
Vasucharitrachampú.	
Víranáráyaṇacharitra.	
Śailendravilása.	
Prákṛitasetukávya.	
Prákṛitasaptáśiti.	
Prákṛitaśataka.	

G. BÜHLER,
Acting Educational Inspector,
Northern Division.

P.S.—To these may be added the whole division entitled—

Madhvaśástra, or Treatises of the Mádhavas, pages 33 to 35.

The Mádhavas are most unwilling to shew or sell their books, and I do not think it will be often that so fine a collection of their works is for sale.

From the Hon'ble W. HUDLESTON, Chief Secretary to the Government of Madras, to A. C. LYALL, Esq., Secretary to the Government of India, Home Department,—No. 263, dated Ootacamund, the 25th August 1873.

ADVERTING to your Officiating Under-Secretary's letter, dated the 7th July 1873, No. 2248, and the correspondence to which it refers, I am directed to transmit, for the information of the Government of India, copy of the Proceedings of this Government of this date, No. 262, which embodies a letter from Mr. Burnell, reporting on the progress made by him with the Catalogue of the Sanskṛit Manuscripts of the Library of the late Rájá of Tanjore.

Extract from the Proceedings of the Government of Madras in the Educational Department,—No. 262, dated the 24th August 1873.

Read the following—

From A. C. BURNELL, Esq., to the Hon'ble W. HUDLESTON, Chief Secretary to the Government of Madras,—dated Bangalore, the 6th August 1873.

WITH reference to the memorandum, dated 7th July 1873, from the Under-Secretary (Home Department) to the Government of India, I have the honour to state as follows, what I have done in regard to the Sanskṛit manuscripts of the Palace Library at Tanjore. As the Madras Government had not required me to report further than I had already done on occasions, I misunderstood the Proceedings of February 11th, 1873, as referring to the completion of my catalogue, and therefore did not reply.

2. I was appointed to this work in March 1871 by His Excellency Lord Napier. The little information I could procure at Madras about the Library, and my own impressions left by having seen (for a few minutes only) part at Tanjore in 1866, made me estimate the total number of manuscripts at not more than 1,200, and I thus concluded that a month or six weeks would suffice; but on my commencing the work (March 24th, 1871) at Tanjore, I found that I had been entirely misled,

Educational Department, 16th March 1871, No. 33.

and that the total number of manuscripts amounted to upwards of 18,000, and these in eleven distinct alphabets, being from all parts of India. It was thus obvious that a much longer time was required, and this was granted by the Government.

Educational Department, 24th August 1871, No. 61.

3. It was entirely left to me to do what I thought fit in respect of these manuscripts; and as I soon ascertained the collection to be perhaps the largest and most important in the world, I suggested (as one did not exist) the preparation of a regular catalogue, which was approved. I began by examining each manuscript, separately numbering it, and then entering its description and contents on a slip of paper. As the work progressed, these slips were sorted, and all referring to one class of literature put together, and then, after a fresh comparison of the several manuscripts of one work as far as appeared necessary, the general description was drawn up. In the case of new, or of little-known and important works as yet undescribed, I have given extracts to shew the nature of the book, or to give information as to the time of its composition and the sources used by its author, and, in addition to the information given by the divisions of the catalogue, I have added enough to enable any person of ordinary reading to identify the work and ascertain its contents. The immense extent of the collection, and the number of manuscripts of the same book (often twenty or thirty), rendered it imperatively necessary to substitute for the plan of the catalogues published for Government at Calcutta and Bombay, a different one, as a catalogue of this Library compiled on that plan would extend to such a size as to be useless; and, for the same reason, it was necessary to omit all that is already well known. A catalogue of Sanskṛit manuscripts is not now-a-days intended for beginners, and it is worse than useless to attempt to characterise important works in a few lines. I have, however, added references to published works. I believe that this plan was approved, and I trust that (as shewn by the specimen pages enclosed, A and B), it will now be considered sufficient.

As it was at first arranged that the catalogue should be printed at the Government Press at Madras, I chose the Roman character, because the amount of Devanágarí type there is very small. The selection of this character in preference to Devanágarí is of no importance as far as this Presidency is concerned, as it is fast coming into use in preference to the various and complicated alphabets used in different districts. The general scheme of the catalogue is annexed (C).

4. I continued eleven months at work in Tanjore. During this time I examined myself every manuscript—some but cursorily, others in greater detail—and wrote out fair for the Press the greatest part of the catalogue. At my removal to Mangalore in February 1872, the catalogue was nearly complete; the examination of the numerous manuscripts of the Bhárata and Rámáyaṇa (on palm-leaves), and of a few palm-leaf manuscripts referring to the Jyotiḥśástra, Sangítaśástra, and Tantras, only remaining to be done. Since then I have not been able to do as much as I expected, though on the whole the work has advanced. This is owing to two causes:—

(1) At first it was intended that the catalogue should be printed at Madras; but after about forty pages had been composed, the quantity of type available of the peculiar kinds required was found to be so limited as to preclude the work being finished in a proper way. The authorities in charge of the Government Press did all they could to help; but, as the difficulty could only be removed by the purchase of a quantity of type which would probably be in future useless, it was determined to get it printed in Europe, and Messrs. Austin of Hertford were selected, and an arrangement was made by me with them which obtained the approval of Government. As I stated at the time, it then became necessary to get a transcript made of my fair copy. While I was at Tanjore, it was possible to send (registered) to the Press at Madras portions of my original manuscript; but I was advised by experienced persons that I could not do so with safety if the manuscript had to be sent to Europe, and my experience here has fully proved the point, for I scarcely ever receive any book-post parcel that is not wet, or much injured, and many have been lost which I have sent. I have only lately been able to find a copyist, and he can work only in the morning. The first part (Vedic manuscripts) is, however, now complete, and requires only final comparison with the original slips before it can be put into the printer's hands. The copying of the second part (Modern Sanskṛit Literature) is progressing; but it will probably take a year to finish. My original estimate was that the whole book (catalogue, introduction, and indexes) would amount to 800 pages royal octavo. My manuscript at present contains enough to fill 600 pages. If I am able (as I propose) to enter upon the question of the different recensions of the epic poems which are found in the Tanjore Library, I fear that the estimate will be exceeded to the extent of 50 to 100 pages.

Educational Department, 6th December 1877, No. 15.

There is no reason why the printing should not now commence. I have only to remind the Government that it will be necessary to provide a corrector in England, for Messrs. Austin cannot afford to send proofs out to me here.

(2) The second cause of delay is the distance at which I am from Tanjore, and the difficulty and delay of getting additional information when necessary. During my stay there, I organised a system of copying extracts which I might consider necessary; but since my arrival here, and especially of late, these copyists have become so careless as to cause me a deal of trouble. I cannot get others, or I would discharge them, and, though they are paid by piece-work, most have got advances, and yet will not even work them out. One of the best has disappeared since a year with about Rs. 15 advance, and I can learn nothing about him.

The whole of my leisure time is devoted to the finishing of the catalogue; but, apart from hindrances already mentioned, I have not much leisure at my disposal. As the Administration Report will shew, the District Court of South Canara is one of the heaviest, if not the heaviest, in the Presidency; and as, since my arrival here, two out of the three subordinate Courts have been abolished, there is much more work for me to do than had to be done by my predecessors. At Tanjore I was able to devote twelve to fourteen uninterrupted hours a day to the work, as I had nothing else to do; here I can only give one or two hours, and that subject to interruption. From the beginning, the whole of the work has been done by me. I have myself examined the original manuscripts, and made all the *short* extracts I required; and both the rough and fair copy of my catalogue are in my own hands. If the time (several years) that has been taken by a scholar like Professor Aufrecht, to compile a catalogue of a library of not above 1,000 manuscripts, be considered, I think the Government will find that I have not wasted any time.

5. It may, perhaps, be asked if the Library is worth the labour spent on it. I can answer unhesitatingly that it is. It is now a recognised fact that nearly all Sanskṛit works of importance exist in different recensions. The Tanjore Library is unrivalled in this respect; it contains several good manuscripts of all the most important ones known as yet, including a few that are new. The number of new works it contains is less than might be expected; but I may be excused if I point out that my private labours for several years previous to 1869 are the chief cause of this. From my arrival in India in 1860 up to my departure in October 1868, I spared no trouble

to ascertain what new Sanskṛit works could be found in this Presidency, and formed a considerable library of such manuscripts. In 1870, on my return to India, I presented my collection to the India Office Library, and my discoveries thus became public property. The Tanjore Library, however, contains additional manuscripts of most of the works which I had discovered elsewhere, and this is a matter of great importance.

I believe that this library must, sooner or later, escheat to the Government; the preparation of this catalogue will therefore protect property of enormous value. Sanskṛit manuscripts have long been very dear, and the cost of making proper transcripts is now very heavy. As far as I can judge, it would not be possible to form a collection like that at Tanjore at a less cost than £50,000; but many manuscripts are unquestionably unique.

6. I may add that, as the Government has expressed a wish to promote Sanskṛit studies, I have already, to some extent, anticipated the publication of my catalogue by procuring transcripts of manuscripts for scholars. Several have been sent to Calcutta, Bombay, and Europe; and I often receive applications and requests for information which I have tried to satisfy.

C.

PLAN OF CATALOGUE.

PART I.

Vedic Literature.

I. Saṃhitá and Bráhmaṇa—
- *a.* Ṛigveda . . . . Finished.
- *b.* Yajurveda (black) . . . . ,,
- *c.* Yajurveda (white) . . . . ,,
- *d.* Sámaveda . . . . ,,
- *e.* Atharvaveda . . . . ,,

II. Sútra, &c.—
- *a.* Sútra—CC and general prayogas referring to special sútras
- *b.* Prayoga—special prayogas . . . . . ,,

III. Upanishad.

IV. General Works, Vedánga, &c.

PART II.

Sanskṛit Literature.

I. Epic Poetry—
- *a.* 1. Rámáyaṇa . . . . Partly finished.
- 2. Mahábhárata . . . . . ,,

	b. 1. Puráṇas	Finished.
	2. Upapuráṇas	„
II.	Metaphysics—Religious systems of Philosophy—	
	1. Púrvamímáṇsá	Finished.
	2. Vedánta	„
	a. Vedánta of Śaṅkara.	„
	b. Rámánuja	„
	c. Mádhava (Ánandatírtha). . . .	„
	d. Śaivavedánta (of Nílakaṇṭha and Apyaya)	„
	3. Yoga	„
	4. Sáṅkhya	„
	5. Nyáya	„
III.	Dharmaśástra—	
	a. 1. Original Smṛitis	„
	2. Nibandha, or digests and parts of them .	„
	b. Pṛithakpújá	Partly finished.
IV.	Vyákaraṇa—	
	1. *a.* School of Páṇini, and works relating to it	Finished.
	b. Sárasvatavyákaraṇa	„
	c. School of Vopadeva	„
	2. Prákṛit Grammar	„
	3. Sanskṛit Treatises on Telugu Grammar . .	„
V.	Kosha	„
VI.	Chhandas	„
VII.	Artificial Poetry—	
	a. Mahákávya	Finished.
	b. Kávya	„
VIII.	Náṭaka	„
IX.	*a.* Alaṅkáraśástra. *b.* Kámaśástra	„
X.	Vaidyaśástra	„
XI.	Jyotiḥśástra	Not finished.
XII.	Saṅgítaśástra	„
XIII.	Tantric literature	„

The foregoing letter, together with its enclosures, will be submitted for the information of the Government of India, with advertence to the communications noted in the margin.

From Officiating Under-Secretary to Government of India, Home Department, dated 18th June 1872, No. 2566.
Ditto, ditto, 11th Feb. 1873, No. 531.
Ditto, ditto, 7th July 1873, No. 2248.

2. The Governor in Council is of opinion that the scheme of the catalogue, and the system in which it is being prepared, are in every way suitable. The progress made is also highly satisfactory, considering the

very small amount of leisure which Mr. Burnell is now able to devote to the work.

3. As it appears that some portions are sufficiently advanced to be placed in the printers' hands, Mr. Burnell will be authorised to have a commencement made under the arrangement entered into with Messrs. Austin and Co. of Hertford, and also to take steps for the nomination of a corrector of the Press in England.

4. His Excellency in Council desires to place on record his high appreciation of Mr. Burnell's disinterested services.

A Classified Index to the Sanskrit Manuscripts in the Palace Library at Tanjore.

FIRST SECTION—VEDIC LITERATURE.

I.—SAṂHITÁS AND BRÁHMAṆAS, AND WORKS RELATING TO THEM.

I.—*Ṛigveda.* Text. Edited by Dr Aufrecht (in the Roman character), and with Sáyaṇa's Commentary by Dr. Max Müller.

A. *Saṃhitápáṭha.*

1. (2,341) D. *Ashṭaka* i., *Adhyáya* 1, 14 ff. b—*a* 2, 16 ff. c—*a* 3, 17 ff. d—*a* 4, 18 ff. e—*a* 5, 18 ff. f—*a* 6, 18 ff. g—*a* 7, 20 ff. h—*a* 8, 20 ff.

2. (2,342) D. *Ashṭaka* ii., *Adhyáya* 1, 22 ff. b—*a* 2, 19 ff. c—*a* 3, 17 ff. d—*a* 4, 16 ff. e—*a* 5, 17 ff. f—*a* 6, 17 ff. g—*a* 7, 17 ff. h—*a* 8, 17 ff.

3. (2,343) D. *Ashṭaka* iii., *Adhyáya* 1, 19 ff. b—*a* 2, 16 ff. c—*a* 3. 17 ff. d—*a* 4, 17 ff. e—*a* 5, 17 ff. f—*a* 6, 17 ff. g—*a* 7, 17 ff. h—*a* 8, 18 ff.

4. (2,344) D. *Ashṭaka* iv., *Adhyáya* 1, 18 ff. b—*a* 2, 18 ff. c—*a* 3, 19 ff. d—*a* 4, 20 ff. e—*a* 5, 17 ff. f—*a* 6, 17 ff. g—*a* 7, 19 ff. h—*a* 8, 17 ff.

5. (2,345) D. *Ashṭaka* vi., *Adhyáya* 1, 17 ff. b—*a* 2, 18 ff. c—*a* 3, 17 ff. d—*a* 4, 19 ff. e—*a* 5, 17 ff. f—*a* 6, 16 ff. g—*a* 7, 17 ff. h—*a* 8, 15 ff.

6. (2,346) D. *Ashṭaka* vi., *Adhyáya* 1, 7 ff. b—*a* 2, 17 ff. c—*a* 3, 21 ff. d—*a* 4, 26 ff. e—*a* 5, 15 ff. f—*a* 6, 17 ff. g—*a* 7 (Pav. *a* 1) 8 ff. h—*a* 8, (Pav. 2) 13 ff.

7. (2,347) D. *Ashṭaka* vii., *Adhyáya* 1 (Pav. 3) 13 ff. b—*a* 2, (Pav. 4) 9 ff. c—*a* 3, 18 ff. d—*a* 4, 17 ff. e—*a* 5, 18 ff. f—*a* 6, 8 ff. g—*a* 7, 16 ff. h—*a* 8, 16 ff.

8. (2,348) D. *Ashṭaka* viii., *Adhyáya* 1, 17 ff. b—*a* 2, 17 ff. c—*a* 3, 18 ff. d—*a* 4, 91 ff. e—*a* 5, 17 ff. f—*a* 6, 16 ff. g—*a* 7, 22 ff. h—*a* 8, 22 ff. This manuscript (written about 1830) is accented throughout in red. The

borders are illuminated with gold and flowers; on the first page of each chapter is a picture from the modern Hindu mythology. All these ornaments are beautifully executed.

9. (2,349) D. *Ashṭakas* i—iv. A similar manuscript; but the illuminations only extend to *a* 4 of A. iv.

10. (2,350) D. *Ashṭakas* iv.—viii. Not accented.

11. (2,351) D. *Ashṭakas* i.—iv. Accented.

12. (2,352) D. *Ashṭakas* v.—viii. Accented.

13. (2,353) D. A. vii. 3—8. Not accented.

14. (2,354) D. A. i., ii., iv.—viii. An old imperfect manuscript, much worn.

15. (2,362) Purushasúkta (A. viii. 4, 17, &c.) D. ff. 2. Accented.

16. (2,363) Purushasúkta D. ff. 4. White letters on a black ground.

17. (2,429) Extracts from the Ṛ. V.

18. (2,430) Ditto.

19—29. (2,432) to (2,441) do.

30—59. (2,442) to (2,471) do. These Extracts consist of the *Purushasúkta, Pavamána* hymns, *Śrísúkta,* &c.

60. (8,969) Te. 25 ll. Unaccented. U. ix. 1, 1. ll. 1. and 2 are injured, and the manuscript is a little worm-eaten.

B. *Padapáṭha.* Edited in Prof. Max Müller's great edition of the Ṛ. V. with Sáyaṇa's C.

61. (2,355) D. A. i.—viii. An old and worn manuscript. A. ii. and v. are from another copy.

62. (2,356) D. A. i.—iii., v.—viii. Accented. A. ii.—vi and viii. are imperfect. This copy includes a second manuscript of A. viii. (unaccented), which wants the beginning and end.

63. (2,357) D. complete, except A. vii., which is imperfect, partly accented. Much worn.

64. (2,358) D. i.—v. and 3 copies of vii. Only a few pages are accented. A. ii. is imperfect. In very bad condition.

65. (2,359) D. A. iii. (3 copies); iv. (3 copies); v. (2 copies); viii. (2 copies). Partly accented. More or less imperfect.

66. (8,966) Te. 241 ll. A. i—iv. imperfect and unaccented. This manuscript is so much worm-eaten and broken as to be quite useless.

67. (8,967) Gr. 349 ll. A. i.—viii. Unaccented. Last line broken. Worm-eaten in parts. Written about 1800.

68. (8,968) Gr. 119 ll. Válakhilya hymns and M. vi. 63—end. The last few ll. are broken. Written about 1700.

II.—WORKS RELATING TO THE TEXT OF THE ṚIGVEDA.

A. *Śaunaka's Prátiśákhya.*—This has been edited with a German translation by Dr. Max Müller, and with a French translation by M. Regnier.

69. (2,423) D. ff. 5. A fragment.

Párshadavyákhyá. A commentary on the *Ṛ. V. Prátiśákhya* by Uaṭa (Uvaṭa)-*Bhaṭṭa,* son of *Vajraṭa,* and an inhabitant of Ánandapura (Benares?). In 18 paṭalas. The introduction has been given by Prof. Roth in his *Zur Literatur und Geschichte des Weda,* 1846. It attributes the work to *Vishṇumitra,* son of *Vedamitra,* but the colophon assigns it to *Uaṭa,* who is also known as a commentator on the White Yajurveda.* This C. is not the oldest. Dr. Eggeling (v. Preface to Prof. Max Müller's Ṛigvedaprátiśákhya) has discovered one which is certainly more ancient than Uaṭa's Work.

70. (2,417) D. ff. 239. Recent.

Śatapathabráhmaṇa. Edited (in the Mádhyandina Text) by Professor Weber, in vol. ii. of his edition of the *White Yajurveda.*

265. (9,082) Gr. ll. 226. The first 14 ll. (*adhyáyas* 1 and 2) and some ll. at the end are much injured. Written in the 17th century. Not accented.

a. Rájasúyakáṇḍa (viii) adhyáya—1 (?); 2—1. 12; 3—15, b; 4—21; 5—23.

b. Ukhasambharaṇakáṇḍa. (vii.) *a,* It begins: Asad vá idam agra ásíd áhuḥ kiṃ tad—1. 26; 2—29, b; 3—34; 4—38, b; 5—?; 6—45, b; 7—49, 6; 8—54.

c. Hastighaṭakáṇḍa (ix) *a,* 1—athá 'to nairritir haranty etad vai devá gárhapatyam—1. 59, b; 2—63, b; 3—67, b; 4—70, b; 5—74, b; a few lacunæ in the last two chapters.

d. Chitikáṇḍa (x.) *a,* 1—práṇabhṛita upádadhati práṇá vai práṇabhritaḥ —1. 78; 2—81; 3—86, b; 4—88, b; 5—93; 6—96, b; 7—101.

e. Agnirahasyakáṇḍa (xii) *a,* 1—agnir esha purassaras tach chíyate samvatsara uparishtán mahadukthyaṃ śasyate—1. 104, b; 2—107, 6; 3—112; 4—114, b; 5—119; 6—124, b.

---

* Weber's White Y. V., vol. i., p. viii.

f. Sautrámaṇikáṇḍa (xiii. ?) a. 3 (?)—Yad bálaka idaṃ trivṛid—126; 4—128, b; 5—131. This section appears to want two chapters.

g. Chayanabráhmaṇa (?) *a*, 1—etasmád yajñát purusho jayate—1. 136, b. *(Three Bráhmaṇas)*. Ends 1. 143.

h. Havyaváhakáṇḍa (ii.) *a*, 1—sa vai vratam—1. 144; 2—149; 3—155; 4—160, b; 5—164, b; 6—168, b; 7—174; 8—180.

i. Sambhárakáṇḍa (i.) a, 1—sa vai sambharan sambharati yad vá enam iccha—187; 2—192; 3—198; 4—203, b; 5—208, b; 6—212, b. Ends 1. 217, b. The last chapter is not inked, and is much injured.

j. This section begins: Sa yatra hava eshah prathamam. The ll. containing the continuation of this k. are not inked, and are much injured.

This manuscript contains part of the *Káṇva* text of the *Śatapatha-bráhmaṇa,* which differs much from that published.* Except at the beginning and end, the text is in very fair order. But few Bráhmans in Southern India follow the White Y. V., and these are all originally from Northern India, though some families have been settled near Madras and Madura for several centuries. The old enmity† between the followers of the two texts of the Yajurveda has given rise to a curious fiction, namely, that followers of the White Y. V. cease to be Bráhmans for a certain period at noon every day. This has no doubt arisen from the name *Mádhyandina,* which is that of the most common *Sákhá* of this *Veda.* This fiction has reduced the followers of the White Y. V. so low that other Bráhmans will not associate with them.

Charaṇavyúha. Printed in the Śabdakalpadruma, ("V. Veda,") and edited by Professor Weber in I. S. iii.

266 (2,410) D. ff.
267 (2,411) D. ff.
268 (2,412) D. ff.
269 (2,413) D. ff.
270 (2,414) D. ff.
271 (2,415) D. ff.
272 (2,416) D. ff.

These manuscripts are all recent and unfortunately far from correct. Nos. 2,410, 1, 2, 3, 5, 6, represent one text. No. 2,414 is much shorter and differs considerably from the other. I much regret that I am not able to give the collation with the text published by Dr. Weber, as the only

* White Yajur Veda, by Dr. Weber, II., p. ix. MSS. of this text are rare.

† A. S. L., p. 350.

copy accessible to me of the I. S. wants parts 2 and 3 of vol. iii. The Śabdakalpadruma is also inaccessible to me. Both texts begin Atha charaṇavyúhaṃ vyákhyásyámaḥ. Tatra yad uktaṃ cháturvaidyam. Chatváro vedá vijñátá bhavanti ṛigvedo yajurvedaḥ sámavedo,'tharvavedaś cheti. Tatra ṛigvedasya 'shṭau bhedá bhavanti—charchá śrávakaḥ charchakaḥ śravaṇíyapáṭhaḥ kramapáthaḥ kramajátaḥ kramarathaḥ kramadaṇḍaś cheti. The lists of Śákhás, &c., are as follows: A=2,410; B=2,414.

I. Ṛ. V. A. A'śvaláyanas, Sáṅkhyáyanas, Śákalas, Báshkalas, Máṇḍúkeyas. B. Śákalas, Váshkalas, A'śvaláyanas, Śáṅkháyanas, Máṇḍúkáyanas. B. omits nearly all the details of the numbers of Vargas, &c.

II. Y. V. Black. A. Charakas, A'hárakas, Káṭhas, Kápishṭhalakáṭhas, Cháráyaṇíyas, Váratantavíyas, Śvetáśvataras, Upamanyus, Maitrávaruṇíyas. As the number is stated to be twelve, some are omitted by the transcriber.

B. 12: Charakas, A'hvárakas, Práyaskáṭhas, Kápishṭhalakáṭhas, Cháráyaṇíyas, Váratantavíyas, Śvetáśvataras, Apamanyus, Pátas, Aindineyas, Maitráyaṇíyas.

The last are divided by A. into seven sub-divisions: Mánavas, Dundubhas, Śaikeyas, Váráhas, Háridraveyas, Śyámas, Śyámáyaníyas.

And by B into six: Mánavas, Várábas, Dundubhas, Chhágaleyas, Háridravíyas, Śámáyaníyas.

White Yajurveda. A. Jábálas, Bandhayas, Káṇvas, Mádhyandinas * * * víyas, Sthápaníyas, Kápálas, Páṇḍaravatsas, A'vatikas, Paramávatis, Parachareyas, Vaidyeyas, Vaineyas, A'ndyeyas, Gálavas, Vaijakas, Kátyáyaníyas.

B. 15. Jábálas, Bándháyanas, Káṇvas, Mádhyandinas, Śápheyas, Tápaníyas, Kápotas, Pauṇḍaravaśyas, A'vatikas, Paramávatikas, Páráśaras, Vaineyas, Vaidheyas, Addhábodheyas.

B. divides the Káṭhas into Práchyas, Udíchyas and Nirṛityas. In A this is omitted.

The Pariśishṭas are, according to A., Upajyotisha, Saṅgalakshaṇa, Pratijñánuvákya, Parisaṅkhyáta, Charaṇavyúha, Śráddhakalpa, Pravarádhyáya.

According to B. 18: Yúpalakshaṇa, Chhágalakshaṇa, Pratijñánuvákya, Sáṅkhya, Charaṇavyúha, Śráddhakalpa, Śulvikáni, Párshada, Ṛigyajúṃshi Ishṭakápúraṇa, Pravarádhyáya, Ukthaśástra, Kratusaṅkhyá, Nigama, Yajñapárśva, Paurvika, Prasavotthána, Kúrmalakshaṇa.

III. Sámaveda. A. A'suráyaṇíyas, Vartantareyas, Práñjalis, Ṛigvarṇas, Práchínayogyas, Jñánayogyas, Ráṇáyaníyas. The last divided into Ráṇáyaníyas, Sáṅkhyáyaníyas, Saptamudgalas, Khalyalas, Maháklialyalas, Lángalas, Kauthumas, Gautamas, Jaiminíyas.

B. Ráṇáyaníyás divided into seven: Ráṇáyaníyas, Śátyamugryas, Kálopas, Mahákálopas, Láṅgaláyanas, Śárdúlas, Kauthumas; and the Kauthumas into seven: A'suráyaṇas, Vátáyanas, Práñjalidvaitabhṛits, Práchínayogyas, Nekeyas, Kauthumas (one name is thus omitted).

IV. Atharvaveda. A. 9: Paippalas, Dántas, Pradántas, Autas, Brahmádas, Báládas, Śaunakis, Devadarśins, Charaṇavidhas.

B. 9: Pippalas, Śaunakis, Dámodas, Tottáyanas, Jábálas, Bráhmapaláśas, Kunakhinas, Devadarśinas, Charaṇavidyas.

A. 5 Kalpas: Nakshatrakalpa, Vidhánakalpa, Vidhividhánakalpa, Saṃhitákalpa, Śántikalpa, and Pravarádhyáya.

B. do. Nakshatrakalpa, Vidhánakalpa, Saṃhitávidhi, Abhichárakalpa, Śántikalpa.

I have let several obvious errors remain to shew how incorrect the manuscripts are. There are thus two texts of the Charaṇavyúha, which differ not only in the lists of Śákhás, but also of the divisions and number of verses in the Vedas. The text represented by B. seems to be that followed in the Śabdakalpadruma, so far as can be judged from the quotations in A. S. L. This tract is so evidently written in the interest of the followers of the White Y. V., that it, perhaps, little deserves the importance which has been attributed to it.

From T. J. Chichele Plowden, Esq., Officiating Under-Secretary to the Government of India, Home Dept., to the Chief Secretary to the Government of Madras,—No. 3434, dated the 31st October 1873.

I am directed to acknowledge the receipt of your letters No. 263, dated the 25th August last, and No. 283, dated 12th September 1873, with enclosures, shewing the progress made by Mr. Burnell in preparing a catalogue of the Sanskṛit manuscripts in the library of the late Rájá of Tanjore.

2. In reply, I am desired to express the full concurrence of the Government of India in the praise bestowed on Mr. Burnell for his disinterested services, and to say that His Excellency the Governor-General in Council hopes to see this important work soon completed.

From the Hon'ble D. F. CARMICHAEL, Officiating Chief Secretary to the Government of Madras, to the Secretary to the Government of India,—No. 373, dated Ootacamund, the 5th November 1874.

WITH reference to your letter, dated the 7th September, No. 2304, I am directed to forward, for the information of the Government, copy of a letter* from Mr. Burnell, stating that he has not yet been able to complete the catalogue of the Sanskṛit manuscripts in the Library of the late Rájá of Tanjore.

* Dated 29th October 1874.

From A. C. BURNELL, Esq., PH.D., to the Officiating Chief Secretary to the Government of Madras,—dated Tanjore, the 29th October 1874.

WITH reference to G. O. dated 16th September 1874, No. 318 (Educational), I have the honour to state that I have not been able, as yet, to complete the revision of my manuscript (fair copy) of the catalogue of the Tanjore Palace Library; but I hope, now that I am near the Library, to be able to get on much faster, provided my health continues to permit me to do extra work, as I have done as yet. The rough copy is finished, and the greater part of the fair copy.

From the Hon'ble D. F. CARMICHAEL, Officiating Chief-Secretary to the Government of Madras, to the Secretary to the Government of India,—No. 200, dated Ootacamund, the 24th June 1875.

WITH reference to your No. 921 of 1st June, instant, I have the honour to enclose copy of a letter† from Dr. Burnell, shewing the state of progress in which the cataloguing of the Sanskṛit manuscripts of the late Tanjore Ráj now stands.

† Dated 21st June 1875.

From A. C. BURNELL, Esq., PH.D., to the Officiating Chief Secretary to the Government of Madras,—dated Tanjore, the 21st June 1875.

WITH reference to your memorandum No. 177, dated 9th June 1875, (Educational Department), I have the honour to state (as I have done already several times), that I am getting on with the completion of the fair copy of my catalogue of the Tanjore manuscripts as fast as I possibly can.

2. You will be aware that I have had the duties of a District and Sessions Judge to perform since three years, and that I have had very little leisure, being in charge of very heavy Courts the whole of that period. To do such work as this properly, much time is obviously necessary. I need scarcely say that I shall be glad to complete it as quickly as is consistent with the standard of completeness now required.

3. I may add that part of the introduction has been already printed by me ("Elements of South Indian Palæography," octavo, Mangalore and London, 1874), a copy of which has been laid before the Madras Government.

From L. NEILL, Esq., Under-Secretary to the Government of India, to the Secretary to the Government of Madras,—No. 1850, dated Simla, the 9th October 1877.

WITH reference to the correspondence ending with your letter No. 200, dated the 24th June 1875, I am directed to enquire into the present state of progress of Dr. Burnell's catalogue of the Sanskṛit manuscripts of the late Tanjore Ráj.

From C. G. MASTER, Esq., Secretary to the Government of Madras, to the Secretary to the Government of India,—No. 411, dated the 9th November 1877.

REFERRING to your letter, dated the 9th October 1877, No. 1850, I am directed to forward, for the information of the Government of India, copy of a letter* from Dr. Burnell, stating the progress that has been made with his catalogue of the Sanskṛit manuscripts of the late Tanjore Ráj.

* Dated 22nd October 1877.

2. Dr. Burnell's proposal to issue "what is done as a first part" has been approved by this Government.

From A. C. BURNELL, Esq., PH.D., to the Chief Secretary to the Government of Madras, dated Tanjore, the 22nd October 1877.

WITH reference to G. O. No. 389, dated 17th October 1877, I have the honour to inform you that my catalogue has been printed as far as the article "Kosha," but that I am not now in a position to go on with the necessary revision, as I cannot find leisure to visit the Palace Library and refer to the original manuscripts.

2. You will be aware that, in July 1876, the Courts of North and South Tanjore were united, and the whole work thrown upon me. I had very little leisure before, and now I have none.

3. I hope to be able to finish the revision of my manuscripts to the end of the section "Technical Literature," during the leave in December and January. With your approval, I would then ask Messrs. Trübner to issue what is done as a first part. Delay in publication will (I need hardly say) seriously affect the value of my work, and, though I have already published some of the most important results at which I have arrived ("Elements of South Indian Palæography," 1874; "On the Aindra School of Sanskṛit Grammarians," 1875), there is much in my catalogue which will be no longer new, if the publication is further delayed. It will also be as well to pay Messrs. Austin for what they have printed.

4. Under the circumstances already referred to, and considering my unsatisfactory state of health, which my medical advisers attribute to overwork, I am quite unable to make any promises for the future.

From L. Bowring, Esq., C.S.I., Chief Commissioner of Mysore, to the Secretary to the Government of India, Foreign Department,—No. 298, dated Bangalore, the 8th October 1869.

Referring to the extract from the Proceedings of the Government of India in the Home Department (Public), No. 4345, dated the 3rd November 1868, I have the honour to forward herewith, for submission to His Excellency the Viceroy and Governor-General in Council, copy of a classified catalogue of Sanskṛit works in the Library of His Highness the Mahárája of Mysore.

Classified Catalogue of Sanskṛit Works in the "Sarasvatibháṇḍáram" Library of His Highness the Mahárája of Mysore.

Number.	Number in the old Catalogue.	Names of Works.	Name of the Author.	Character in which written.	Remarks.
		CLASS I.			
		VEDAS.			
		Ṛigveda.			
1	1207	Ṛigvedasaṃhitá, V, VI Ashṭakas	......	Nágarí.	
2	344	Ṛigvedapada, Eight Ashṭakas	......	Telugu	Complete.
3	814	Ṛigvedamahábráhmaṇa	......	Grantha	,,
		Yajurveda.			
4	330	Yajurvedasaṃhitá, Káṇḍas I, II, III, IV	......	,,	,,
5	812	,, Káṇḍas V, VI, VII	......	,,	,,
6	1048	Yajurveda, Ashṭaka I	......	,,	,,
7	334	,, Ashṭaka II	......	Nágarí	,,
8	329	,, Ashṭaka III	......	Grantha	,,
9	337	Yajurveda, Áruṇa and Káṭhaka	......	,,	,,
		Sámaveda.			
10	340	Sámaveda, Prakṛiti and Úha, Four Parvans	......	,,	
11	342	Sámaveda, Prakṛiti (another copy)	......	Nágarí.	
		Atharvaveda.			
12	974	Átharvaṇaveda, Three Káṇḍas	......	Grantha.	

		Upanishad.			
13	1292	Ashṭottaraśatopanishadaḥ	......	Telugu	„
14	927	Dvátriṇśad Upanishadaḥ	......	Nágarí.	
15	926	(Another Copy)	......	Kanarese.	
16	325	(Another Copy)	......	Telugu.	
17	326	Íśávásyádyupanishadaḥ	......	„	
18	343	Chhándogya Upanishad	......	„	
19	341	A'yurveda	......	Grantha.	
		VEDABHÁSHYA.			
		Connected with Class I.			
20	327	Yajurvedabháshya	Bhaṭṭabháskaramiśra	„	„
21	328	Yajurvedakáṭhakabháshya and A'ruṇabháshya	„	„	„
22	817	Yajurvedabháshya to first Ashṭaka	„	„	This volume comprises also a totally distinct work called Védántasiddhánta-siddhajṅána.
23	820	Yajurvedabháshya from third to eighth Praśna	„	„	
24	332	Yajurvedakáṭhakabháshya	„	„	
25	333	Yajurvedabháshya to second Káṇḍa	„	„	
26	331	Yajurvedaparáyatabháshya	„	Telugu.	
27	813	Yajurvedamantrápannabháshya	Haradattamiśra	Grantha	Complete.
28	338	Sámavedabháshya	......	Nágarí	„
		CLASS II.			
		KALPASÚTRA.			
29	301	A'śvaláyanasútra	A'svaláyana	Grantha.	
30	1113	A'pastambasútra, eighteen Praśnas	A'pastamba	„	„
31	319	„ fifteen Praśnas	„	„	
32	312	A'pastambachayanántaprayoga	„	„	
33	306	Bodháyanasútram Aptoryámaparyantam	Bodháyana	„	
34	316	Satyásháḍhakalpasútra, sixteen Praśnas	Satyásháḍha	„	
35	315	Bháradvájasútram, Somántam	Bharadvája	„	
36	311	Kátyáyanasútra, thirty-two Adhyáyas	Kátyáyana	„	Complete.

Number.	Number in the old Catalogue.	Names of Works.	Name of the Author.	Character in which written.	Remarks.
		CLASS II—*concld.*			
		KALPASÚTRA—*concld.*			
37	317	Dhúrtasvámibháshya to Ápastambasútra, Three Paṭalas in the Ninth Praśna.	Dhúrtasvámin . .	Grantha.	
38	824	Dhúrtasvámibháshya to Śrautasútra . .	„ . .	„	
39	310	„ to Ápastambasútra (Another Copy)	„ . .	„	
40	318	„ „ (Another Copy)	„ . .	„	
41	323	Ápastambadharmápanna, with Ujjvalavyákhyáṇa up to eleventh Paṭala in the second Praśna.	Haradattamiśra . .	„	
42	1118	Ápastambadharmápanna, with Ujjvalavyákhyána	„ . .	Telugu.	
43	901	Yállajiyavyákhyána to Ásvaláyanasútra . .	Yallaja . . .	„	This volume comprises also a totally distinct work called Kámandakanítiśástra with Vyákhyána and Vyákaraṇanakshatravedávali.
44	304	Bodháyanasútravyákhyána	Vishṇubhaṭṭa . .	„	
45	305	(Another Copy)	„ . .	Grantha.	
46	902	(Another Copy)	„ . .		
47	302	Bháshya to Bodháyanasútra	Bhavasvámin . .	„	
48	307	Trikáṇḍachayanántaprayóga	Keśavasvámin . .	„	
49	321	Sautrámaṇipaśubandhaprayogaratna . .	Vasudeva . . .	„	
50	1016	Śuklayajuḥsútrakáriká	......	„	
		CLASS III.			
		ŚIKSHÁ.			
51	825	Bháradvájaśikshá, Siddhántaśikshá, Áraṇyakaśikshá and Sarvapráyaśchitta.	Bharadvája . . Bálasúri.	„	
52	819	Vyásaśikshá to Yajurveda, with Commentary .	Vyása.		
		Rávaṇabheda, with Commentary . . .	Rávaṇaśúra . .	Telugu.	
		Vaidyanáthabheda	Vaidyanátha.		
		Saptalakshaṇa, Uchchodárkya, and Bháradvájaśikshá, with Commentary	Bharadvája . .	Grantha.	

53	823	Yajurvedaprátisákhya	Páṇini	Telugu	This volume comprises also a totally distinct work, the Virátaparvan of the Mahábhárata.
54	821	Yajurvedadarpaṇa and Aningyapádavyákhyána			
55	822	Prátisákhyavyákhyána, Vaidikábharaṇa, ten Adhyáyas.	Gárgyagopalabhaṭṭa	Grantha	This volume comprises also a totally distinct work called Vedántapárásaryavijaya.
56	816	Prátiśákhyavyákhyána. Tribháshyaratna	......	,,	This volume comprises also a totally distinct work called Madhuránandíya.
57	818	Varṇakramadarpaṇa and Yogibháshya	......	,,	
58	339	Sámavedachaṇḍésvaravishaya	......	Nágarí.	
		CLASS IV. NIRUKTA. (No Works in this Class).			
		CLASS V. CHHANDAS. (No Works in this Class).			
		CLASS VI. SMṚITI.			
59	978	Vásishṭha, Páráśaríya, Bárhaspatya, Angirasa, Daksha, Yama, Saṃvartha, Śátátapa, Atreya, and Vyása Smṛitis.	Authors as named in the works.	Telugu	This volume comprises also a totally distinct work called Śivatattvaviveka.
60	541	Parásara, Daksha, Gautama, and Śáṇḍilya Smṛitis.	Authors as named in the works.	Grantha	Complete.

Number.	Number in the old Catalogue.	Names of Works.	Name of the Author.	Character in which written.	Remarks.
		CLASS VI—*contd.*			
		SMṚITI—*contd.*			
61	542	Vásishṭha, Prajñáhárita, Yama, Bárhaspatya, Smṛitis.	Authors as named in the works.	Grantha and Telugu	Complete.
62	540	Śankha, Likhita, Devala, Pulastya, Átreya, Yama, Bṛihaspati, Brahma, Daksha, Śátátapa, Ápastamba, Nárada, Buddha, Smṛitis.	Authors as named in the works.	Grantha	This volume comprises also a totally distinct work called Sandhyábháshya of Náráyaṇa.
63	0	Manusmṛiti, with English translation	Sváyambhuvamanu	Nágarí.	
64	517	Hemádridánakáṇḍa	Hemádri	Telugu.	
65	958	,, (Another Copy)	,,	,,	
66	1017	,, ,,	,,	Grantha.	
67	963	,, ,,	,,	Telugu.	
68	518	,, ,,	,,	,,	
69	1220	Hemádrivratakáṇḍa	,,	,,	
70	1219	,, (Another Copy)	,,	,,	
71	1038	Hemádripráyaśchittakáṇḍa	,,	,,	
72	1218	,, (Another Copy)	,,	Grantha.	
73	1217	,, ,,	,,	,,	
74	1205	,, ,,	,,	,,	
75	895	Smṛitichandrikávyavahárakáṇḍa	Yájñikadevabhaṭṭa	Telugu.	
76	524	,, (Another Copy)	,,	Grantha.	
77	1200	,, ,,	,,	,,	
78	507	Nirṇayasindhu, and a portion of Hemádripráyaśchittakáṇḍa.	Kamalákarabhaṭṭa	Kanarese.	
79	1106	,, Three Parichchhedas	,,	Grantha.	
80	510	,, (Another Copy)	,,	,,	
81	508	,, Ácharakáṇḍa and Smṛitichandrikácharakáṇḍa	,,	Kanarese.	
82	1008	,, Two Parichchhedas	,,	Grantha.	
83	509	,, ,, (Another Copy)	,,	Nágarí.	

84	535	Śúdradharmakamalákara	,,	Telugu.
85	523	Vaidyanáthiyáchárakáṇḍa	Vaidyanátha	Grantha.
86	893	,, (Another Copy)	,,	,,
87	511	,, Aśauchakáṇḍa	,,	,,
88	894	,, ,, and Śráddhakáṇḍa	,,	Nágarí.
89	950	,, ,, (Another Copy)	,,	Grantha.
90	955	,, Śráddhakáṇḍa	,,	,,
91	512	,, ,, and Smṛitiratnákaráchárakáṇḍa	Yájñikadevabhaṭṭa	Telugu.
92	543	Páráśaramádhavíya, Achárakáṇḍa	Vidyáraṇya	Nágarí.
93	522	,, and Vaidyánáthíya	,,	Kanarese.
94	521	,, Achárakáṇḍa and Hémadri Práyaśchittakáṇḍa	,,	,,
95	904	,, Práyaśchittakáṇḍa	,,	Grantha.
96	1126	Śuddhivilochana	Vaidikasárvabhauma	,,
97	948	,, Aparaprayoga	,,	,,
98	1116	(Another Copy)	,,	,,
99	531	Pitṛimedhasára	,,	,,
100	527	Smṛitiratnákara	,,	Telugu.
101	520	Vivádabhangárṇavadáyabhága	Jagannáthapañchánanabhaṭṭa	Grantha.
102	519	,, Mádhavíyavyavahárakáṇḍa and Vaidyanáthíyáśauchapráyaśchittakáṇḍa	,,	,,
103	0	Vivádabhangárṇava Indranílákhyanavamanidhi	,,	Nágarí.
104	0	,, ,, A portion	,,	,,
105	0	Nítimayúkha		
106	529	Dánamayúkha, Práyaśchittamayúkha, Samayamayúkha, Pratishṭhámayúkha, Śántimayúkha, and Varadarájíyavyavahárakáṇḍa	Nílakaṇṭhabhaṭṭa and Varadarája	Grantha.
107	977	Dánamayúkha	Nílakaṇṭhabhaṭṭa	,,
108	1102	(Another Copy)	,,	,,
109	530	Aśauchaśataka, with Commentary	Veṅkaṭeśa	Telugu.
110	525	Sarasvatívilása	Pratáparudra	,,
111	500 {	,, Dáyabhága	,,	,,
		,, Dattamímáṃsá and Dattachandriká	Haradatta	,,

Number.	Number in the old Catalogue.	Names of Works.	Name of the Author.	Character in which written.	Remarks.
		CLASS VI—*concld.*			
		SMṚITI—*concld.*			
112	1026	Prayogapárijáta up to Ankurárpaṇa, and Śráddhapaddhati	Lakshmínarasiṇha	Nágarí.	
113	533	Gautamadharmápannavyákhyánamitákshará	Haradatta	Telugu.	
114	505	Karmavipákamahárṇava	Visveśvarabhaṭṭa	,,	
115	506	(Another Copy)	,,	,,	
116	504	(Another Copy)	,,	Nágarí	This volume comprises also a totally distinct work called Jyotishayogárṇava.
117	1107	Karmavipáka	,,	Grantha.	
118	503	,, Yogárṇava, Three Adhyáyas	,,	Telugu.	
119	502	,, Bṛihannáradíya	First part by the above	,,	
120	995	,, and Vratakalpádiprayógadarpaṇa	,,	Grantha.	
121	516	Vijńánéśvara Vyavahárakáṇḍa	......	,,	
122	972	(Another Copy)	......	,,	
123	514	(Another Copy)	......	Kanarese.	
124	898	Smṛitisangraha	......	Nágarí.	
125	1197	Smṛitipradípiká	......	,,	
126	987	Prapannadharmasárasamuchchayasmṛiti	Vaikuṇṭhanátha and Yájńavalkya.	Grantha.	
		Chandriká and Yájńavalkyasmṛiti	......	......	
127	1204	Tithichandriká	......	Nágarí	This volume comprises also totally distinct works called Agnéyatuláḱávérímáhátmya, Bhavishottara Pushkaramáhátmya and Skánda Haimávatívaiśákhamáhátmya.
128	962	Aśauchavidhánasangraha	......	Grantha.	
129	532	Dharmapravṛitti, Áchárakáṇḍa	Náráyaṇabhaṭṭa	Nágarí.	
130	528	Madanaratnadípiká, Dánakáṇḍa and Śántikáṇḍa	Rájanarasiṇhadeva	Grantha.	
131	534	Sucharitrasudhánidhi	Vedantácharya	Telugu.	
132	900	Pravaranirṇaya and Parásaramádhavíya	......	,,	

133	899	Yatidharmasamuchchaya, Yatyanushṭhánaprayoga, and Sautrámaṇiprayoga	Yádavaprakáśa	Grantha	This volume comprises also a totally distinct work called Vaidyaśárirakasútra by Bilhaṇa, and Mímáṇsá Śomanáthíyá.
134	536	Rájochitavyavahāramáliká and Yájñavalkyasmṛiti	Visveśvarabhaṭṭa	,,	
135	1312	Dánadarpaṇapaddhati, Vratas and Karmavipáka	......	Telugu.	
136	501	Tulábhárapaddhati and Ubhayamukhígodánapaddhati	Śivaśarman	,,	
137	787	Tírthayátrákrama and Yantroddhárakrama	Varadarájayati	Kanarese.	
138	1050	Vratavalli	......	Grantha.	
139	537	Śaunakádyuktaśánti	......	Nágarí.	
140	538	Śántisára	......	Grantha.	
141	539	Śanti and Vastukalpa	......	Telugu & Nágarí.	
142	1083	Śánti, Vratas and Aśauchavidhána	......	Kanarese & Telugu.	
143	489	Aśvinyádinakshatraśánti	......	Telugu.	
		CLASS VII.			
		ÁGAMA, ITIHÁSA, PURÁṆAS.			
		Ágamas.			
144	1006	Páñcharátra, Nátvatasaṃhitá	......	Kanarese.	
145	943	,, Sátvatasaṃhitá, twenty-five Parichchhedas	......	Grantha.	
146	1031	,, Aniruddhasaṃhitá, thirty Adhyáyas, and Vásudevasaṃhitá	......	,,	
147	1019	,, Parameśvarasaṃhitá, sixty-two Adhyáyas, and Chittraśikhaṇḍisaṃhitá, two Adhyáyas	......	,,	
148	903	,, Bháradvájasaṃhitá	......	Nágarí.	
149	1040	,, Jayasaṃhitá, Second Part	......	Kanarese.	
150	967	,, Paramasaṃhitá and Náráyaṇasaṃhitá	......	Grantha.	

Number.	Number in the old Catalogue.	Names of Works.	Name of the Author.	Character in which written.	Remarks.
		CLASS VII—*contd.*			
		ÁGAMA, ITIHÁSA, PURÁṆAS—*contd.*			
		Ágamas—contd.			
151	1037	Pancharátra, Jnánapáda and Lakshmítantrádi	......	Grantha.	
152	988	Prayogamaṇidípiká	......	,,	
153	956	Pádmasaṃhitá, Four Pádas	......	,,	
154	624	Lakshmínáráyaṇasaṃhitá, thirty- Adhyáyas	......	Telugu.	
155	440	Śeshasaṃhitá	......	Grantha.	
156	964	Paráśarasaṃhitá	......	,,	
157	990	Ahirbúdhnasaṃhitá	......	,,	
158	1003	Paushkarasaṃhitá, from 30th to 45th Ádhyáyas	......	,,	
159	944	Uchchavasaṃhitá	......	,,	
160	945	Márkaṇḍeyasaṃhitá	......	,,	
161	0	Pádmasaṃhitá and Agastyasaṃhitá	......	,,	
162	1043	Náradíyasaṃhitá	......	,,	
163	314	Vaikhánasasútra, Eleven Praśnás	Vaikhánasa	,,	
164	1138	Bhṛigusaṃhitá, Second Part	,,	,,	
165	292	Śaivágama Paushkarasaṃhitá	......	,,	
166	294	Vátulágama	......	Telugu.	
167	299	,, (Another Copy)	......	,,	
168	296	,, Sudhákhyatantra	......	Nágarí.	
169	297	Pratishṭhákalpa, Ásurikalpa, Śvetáśvatarakalpa and Cháturmásyavidhána	......	,,	
170	469	Kaumárasaṃhitá and Vaináyakasaṃhitá	......	Telugu.	
171	442	Dakshiṇamúrttisaṃhitá, Thirty-three Paṭalas Tulárṇavasaṃhitá, Seventeen Paṭalas and Surendrasaṃhitá	......	Grantha.	
172	642	Káraṇágama	......	,,	

173	295	Pushkaratantra, Jñánapádavyákhyána	......	Telugu.	
174	298	,, ,,	......	,,	
		Itihása,—Rámáyana.			
175	0	Rámáyaṇa, seven Káṇḍas	Válmiki	Kanarese	Complete.
176	877	,, (Another Copy)	,,	,,	,,
177	1103	,, ,,	,,	Nágarí	,,
178	591	,, ,,	,,	,,	,,
179	1215	,, ,,	,,	Telugu	,,
180	1143	,, six Káṇḍas	,,	Grantha.	
181	12	,, (Another Copy).	,,	Nágarí.	
182	703	,, Ayodhyákáṇḍa	,,	Telugu.	
183	704	,, Bála, Ayodhyá, Araṇya Káṇḍas	,,	,,	
184	705	,, Sundarakáṇḍa	,,	Grantha.	
185	657	Rámáyaṇavyákhyána	Maheśvaratírtha	Kanarese.	
186	692	,, Íśvaradíkshitíya	Íśvaradíkshita	Grantha.	
187	716	,, Haripaṇḍitíya, six Káṇḍas	Haripaṇḍita	Telugu.	
188	1092	,, Govindarájíya, Bála, Ayódhyá Káṇḍas	Govindarája	,,	
189	1094	,, Govindarájíya, Araṇya, Kishkindhá, Sundara Káṇḍas.	,,	,,	
190	1201	,, Govindarájíya, Yuddhakáṇḍa	,,	,,	
191	1288	,, ,, Uttarakáṇḍa	,,	,,	
192	9	Tattvasangraharámáyaṇa, seven Káṇḍas	Rámabrahmánandasarasvatí.	Kanarese	,,
193	11	Adhyátmaramáyaṇa, seven Káṇḍas	Vyása	,,	,,
194	10	(Another Copy)	,,	,,	,,
195	13	,,	,,	Nágarí	,,
196	1118	Jaiminirámáyaṇa, sixty-seven Adhyáyas	Jaimini	Grantha.	
197	0	Mahábhárata, eighteen Parvans	Vyása	Kanarese.	
198	39	,, Ádipañchaka	,,	Grantha.	
199	40	,, Bhíshma, Droṇa, Karṇa, Śalya Sauptika, Strí, Áśvamedhika Parvans	,,	,,	
200	41	,, Śánti, Anuśásana, Aśvamédha, Áśramavása, Mausala, Maháprasthána, Svargárohaṇa, Parvans.	,,		

Number.	Number in the old Catalogue.	Names of Works.	Name of the Author.	Character in which written.	Remarks.
		CLASS VII—*contd.*			
		A'GAMA, ITIHÁSA, PURÁNAS—*contd.*			
		Itihása—contd.—*Mahábhárata.*			
201	42	Mahábhárata A'di, Sabhá, Aranya Parvans	Vyása	Kanarese.	
202	43	" Viráta, Udyóga, Bhishma Parvans	"	"	
203	45	" Śántiparvan, Rájadharma	"	"	
204	46	" Śántiparvan, Mokshadharma	"	"	
205	47	" Anuśásana, Aśvamédha, A'śramavása, Mausala, Maháprasthána, Svargárohaṇa Parvans.	"	"	
206	60	Harivanśa	"	Telugu.	
207	61	Śeshadharma	"	"	
208	1335	Mahábháratavyákhyána, A'di and Sabhá Parvans.	Nílakaṇṭhabhaṭṭa	"	
209	1336	" Araṇya, Viráta Parvans	"	"	
210	1337	" Udyoga, Bhishma Parvans	"	"	
211	1341	" Droṇaparvan	"	"	
212	1342	" Karṇa, Śalya, Sauptika, Strí Parvans.	"	"	
213	1343	" Sántiparvan, Rájadharma, and A'paddharma.	"	"	
214	1345	" Anuśásanaparvan	"	"	
215	1346	" Asvamedha, A'sramavása, Mausala, Maháprasthána, Svargárohaṇa Parvans.	"	"	
216	...	" with Nílakaṇṭhiyavyákhyana, eighteen Parvans, Bengal edition, 6 volumes	Vyása and Nílakaṇṭhabhaṭṭa	Nágarí	Complete.
217	1330	Harivanśavyákhyána	Arjunamiśra	Kanarese	"

218	...	,,	Nílakaṇṭhabhaṭṭa	Nágarí.	
219	90	Bhagavadgítá, with Commentary	Krishṇasúri	Telugu	,,
220	97	,, with Subodhaníyavyákhyána	......	Nágarí.	
221	94	,, with Rámachandrasarasvatíyavyákhyána	Rámachandrasarasvatí	Telugu	,,
222	96	,, (Another Copy)	,, ,,	,,	,,
223	97	,, with Rághavánandatírthíyavyákhyána	Rághavánandatírtha	Grantha.	
		Puráṇas.			
224	1289	Matsyapuráṇa, one hundred and fifty-two Adhyáyas	Vyása	Telugu.	
225	1282	(Another Copy)	,,	Grantha.	
226	153	(Another Copy)	,,	Kanarese.	
227	155	Kúrmapuráṇa	,,	Grantha.	
228	729	,, First Part	,,	,,	
229	156	,, and Vámanapuráṇa	,,	Kanarese.	
230	154	,, and Vámanapuráṇa (Another Copy)	,,	,,	
231	159	Varáhapuráṇa	,,	Grantha.	
232	130	Skandasutasaṃhitá	,,	Nágarí.	
233	129	,, (Another Copy)	,,	Kanarese.	
234	127	,, (Another Copy)	,,	,,	
235	115	Śaṅkarasaṃhitá	,,	Telugu.	
236	1012	,, (Another Copy)	,,	Kanarese.	
237	1188	,, (Another Copy)	,,	,,	
238	785	Umásaṃhitá	,,	Nágarí.	
239	164	Bráhma, Saura, Sanatkumára Saṃhitás	,,	Grantha.	
240	909	Káśikáṇḍa, twenty Adhyáyas	,,	Telugu.	
241	165	Káñchímáhátmya	,,	,,	
242	167	Śríśailamáhátmya	,,	,,	
243	788	Hálasya máhátmya	,,	,,	
244	632	Skandapuráṇa, Śivarahasyasambhavakáṇḍa and Asurakáṇḍa	,,	Telugu.	
245	637	,, Kalahastimáhátmya	,,	,,	
246	1159	,, Six Aṇśas of the First Part	,,	Grantha.	

Number.	Number in the old Catalogue.	Names of Works.	Name of the Author.	Character in which written.	Remarks.
		CLASS VII—*concld.*			
		ÁGAMA ITIHÁSA PURÁNAS—*concld.*			
		Purános—concld.			
247	1160	Skandapuráṇa, Śivarahasyasambhavakáṇḍa VIII, X, XI Aṇśas	Vyása	Grantha.	
248	1162	„ IX Aṇśas	„	„	
249	1291	„ Three Aṇśas in the First Part	„	Telugu.	
250	1290	„ IV, V, VI Aṇśas	„		
251	1293	„ VII, VIII Aṇśas	„	„	
252	1294	„ IV, X Aṇśas	„	„	
253	1296	„ XI, XII Aṇśas	„	„	
254	1279	„ Pañchánandamáhátmya	„	Grantha.	
255	466	„ Śivakavacha, Śivapújávidhimahiman, Annamaya, Malhaṇa and Haláyudhastava	„	Nágarí.	
256	635	„ Śivadharmottara, First Part, fifty-five Adhyáyas	„	Telugu.	
257	636	„ Second Part, seventy-five Adhyáyas, and Vishṇudharmottara, twenty-seven Adhyáyas	„	„	
258	231	„ Sútasaṃhitávyákhyána	Vidyáraṇya	„	
259	172	Brahmáṇḍapuráṇa, Jñánamaṇḍapamáhátmya	Vyása	Nágarí.	
260	174	„ Venkaṭagirimáhátmya	„	Kanarese.	
261	623	„ Venkateśamáhátmya, one hundred Adhyáyas	„	Telugu.	
262	1313	„ Śivakáñchímáhátmya and Lalitayantroddhára	„	Grantha.	
263	180	„ Champakáraṇyamáhátmya, Adhyáyas 61 to 68, and Harivaṇśaśésha, Dakshiṇadvárakámáhátmya, Adhyáyas 61 to 63	„	„	

264	168	Padmapuráṇa, Mághamáhátmya . . .	„ . . .	„	
265	169	„ Puṇḍaríkapuramáhátmya . .	„ . . .	„	
266	1167	„ A'dibhúmibrahmakhaṇḍa . .	„ . . .	Telugu.	
267	1168	„ Pátálasrishṭikhaṇḍa . . .	„ . . .	„	
268	1169	„ Uttarakhaṇḍa	„ . . .	„	
269	160	Márkaṇḍeyapuráṇa, seventy Adhyáyas . .	„ . . .	„	
270	965	Vámanapuráṇa, sixty-five Adhyáyas . . .	„ . . .	Grantha.	
271	107	„ Hanumatśarabhasubrahmaṇya-mantra.	„ . . .	„	
272	162	A'gneyapuráṇa	„ . . .	„	
273	1030	„ Tulakáverímáhátmya, thirty Adhyáyas.	„ . . .	„	
274	1121	„ Tulakáverímáhátmya (Another Copy).	„ . . .	Telugu.	
275	108	Váyupuráṇa, Mághamáhátmya, ...	„	„	
276	185	Vásishṭha, Lainga, Bhárgava, Śámbha, Váruṇa, Mánava, Puráṇas.	Authors as named in the works.	Grantha.	
277	640	Bhágavatapuráṇa, twelve Skandhas . . .	Vyása.	Telugu	Complete.
278	77	„ (Another Copy)	„	„	
279	76	„ (Another Copy)	„	Grantha.	
280	80	Devíbhágavatapuráṇa, twelve Skandhas . .	„	Telugu.	
281	152	Vishṇupuráṇa, six Aṇśas	„	„	
282	940	„ „ (Another Copy) . .	„	Grantha.	
283	1121	„ Vishṇupuráṇavyákhyána . .	Vishṇuchitta.		
284	1137	„ Vishṇupuráṇasárasangraha . .	......	„	
285	1275	Devíbhágavatapuráṇa with Commentary, first five Skandhas.	Nílakaṇṭhabhaṭṭa.	Telugu.	
286	1277	„ Skandhas VI to IX . . .	„	„	
287	1275	„ Skandhas X to XII . . .	„	„	
288	81	Bhágavatapuráṇa, with Commentary, twelve Skandhas, except XI.	Śrídharácharya . .	Grantha.	
289	679	„ XI Skandhas . . .	„ . .	„	
290	1317	„ Skandhas from I to IV .	„ . .	Kanarese.	
291	1318	„ Skandhas from V to IX .	„ . .	„	
292	1310	„ Skandhas from X to XII .	„ . .	Telugu.	
293	1324	„ Toshiṇívyákhyáṇa, Daśamaskandha.	Káśináda . . .	„	

Number.	Number in the old Catalogue.	Names of Works.	Name of the Author.	Character in which written.	Remarks.
		CLASS VIII.			
		VYÁKARAṆA.			
294	979	Ashṭádhyáyí Savárttiká	Páṇini and Vararuchi	Grantha.	
295	861	Mahábháshya, eight Adhyáyas	Patañjali	Telugu	Complete.
296	369	Mahábháshyavyákhyána, First and Second Adhyáyas.	Kaiyaṭopádhyáya	Grantha.	
297	371	,, Third Adhyáya	,,	,,	
298	370	,, Fourth, Fifth, and Sixth Adhyáyas.	,,	,,	
299	867	,, Śabdabṛihati, VI, VII Adhyayas.	......		
300	862	Padamañjarí, First Adhyáya	Haradatta	,,	
301	863	,, Fifth and Sixth Adhyáyas	,,	,,	
302	865	,, ,, ,,	,,	,,	,,
303	364	Káśikávṛitti, first four Adhyáyas	Vámanácharya	,,	,,
304	365	,, Adhyáyas V to VIII	,,	,,	
305	363	Siddhántakaumudí	Bhaṭṭojidíkshita	Nágarí.	
306	367	Siddhántakaumudívyákhyána, Tattvabodhiní, First Part.	Jñánendrasarasvatíyati.	Grantha	,,
307	368	Siddhántakaumudivyákhyána, Tattvabodhiní, Second Part.	Jñánendrasarasvatíyati.	,,	,,
308	361	Siddhántakaumudívyákhyána, Tattvabodhiní, Second Part.	Manorama (*sic*) Bhaṭtojidíkshita.	,,	
309	859	Siddhántakaumudí	Manorama (*sic*) Bhaṭtójidíkshita.	Telugu.	
310	375	Śabdenduśekhara, First Part	Nágojibhaṭṭa	,,	
311	860	Padasmṛiti	Yajñadíkshita	Grantha.	
312	857	Tiṅantaśirómaṇi	......	Nágarí.	
313	1240	Dhátumálá	Mádhavácharya	Kanarese.	
314	378	Sumanoramá, First Part	Daśáhadvárin	Grantha.	
315	377	Laghukaumudí	......	Nágarí.	

CLASS IX.

Nyáyaśástra.

316	696	Chintámaṇi, Pratyakshakhaṇḍa, Anumánakhaṇḍa, with Commentary	Gaṅgeśamiśra and Dharmarájadíkshita.	Telugu.	
317	1007	Chintámaṇi Śabdakhaṇḍa	Gaṅgeśamiśra . .	Grantha.	
318	1148	,, Vyákhyána Pratyakshakhaṇḍa .	Ruchidatta . .	,,	
319	393	,, ,, (Another Copy) . .	,, ...	,,	
320	846	,, ,, (Another Copy) . .	,, ...	,,	
321	397	,, ,, Anumánakhaṇḍa . .	,, ...	Telugu.	
322	844	,, ,, Śithikaṇṭhíya, Pratyakshakhaṇḍa	Jánakínátha . .	,,	
323	1112	,, ,, (Another Copy) . .	,, . . .	Nágarí.	
324	...	Śiromaṇivyákhyána	Jagadíśabhaṭṭa .	,,	
325	...	Vyutpattivádártha	Gadádharabhaṭṭáchárya.	,,	
326	849	Mathuránáthíya, Anumánaparichchheda . .	Mathuránátha . .	Grantha.	
327	850	,, Śabdaparichchheda . . .	,, . .	,,	
328	399	,, Śirómaṇi Anumánakhaṇḍa .	,, . .	,,	
329	943	Varadarájíya, four Parichchhedas . . .	Varadarája . .	,,	
330	957	Tarkabháshávyákhyána	Chennabhaṭṭa . .	,,	
331	395	,, (Another Copy) . .	,, . .	,,	
332	1110	Gaurikántíya	Gaurikánta . .	Nágarí.	
333	401	Akhaṇḍánandíya	......	,,	
334	392	Maṇisára	......	Kanarese.	
335	1032	,, (Another Copy)	......	Grantha.	
336	1149	,, Pratyakshakhaṇḍa	......	,,	
337	400	Maṇisára, Śabdakhaṇḍa	......	,,	
338	948	Maṇisáradarpaṇa	......	,,	
339	398	Tarkachúḍámaṇi	Dharmarája . .	,,	
340	1028	(Another Copy)	,, . .	,,	
341	856	Muktávali	Viśvanátha . .	,,	
342	1111	Muktávalivyákhyána	Dinakara . . .	Nágarí.	
343	396	Śaśadhara, with Prabhávyákhyána . . .	Tárkikasiṃha . .	Grantha.	
344	853	Bhavánandíyavyákhyána	Vajraṭaṅkaśástrin .	Nágarí.	

Number.	Number in the old Catalogue.	Names of Works.	Name of the Author.	Character in which written.	Remarks.
		CLASS IX—*concld.*			
		NYÁYAŚÁSTRA—*concld.*			
345	848	Śiromaṇi, Anumánakhaṇḍa, Evakáravádártha and Visishṭavaisishtyavádártha	Harirámabhaṭṭa	Nágarí.	
346	852	Yallabhaṭṭíyanyáyapárijáta, Jagannáthadíkshitíya, Dharmarájadíkshitíya, and Nyáyasiddhántamañjari.	Yallabhaṭṭa, Jagannáthadíkshita, Dharmarájadíkshita.	Telugu.	
347	1035	Tarkabhásháyyákhyána, IV Parichchhedas	Gopínadamiśra	Nágarí.	
348	854	„ Anumánakhaṇḍa	Akhaṇḍánandabhaṭṭa	„	
349	1190	Annambhaṭṭíya	Annambhaṭṭa	Grantha.	
		CLASS X.			
		MÍMÁNSÁŚÁSTRA.			
350	386	Mímáṇsásankarshaṇakáṇḍa, Adhyáyas XIII—XVI, and Mímáṇsákaustubha up to the second Páda of the third Adhyáya.	Khaṇḍadeva	„	
351	387	Bháṭṭarahasya	„	„	
352	868	Mímáṇsásútravárttika	Kumárilasvámin	Telugu.	
353	999	Mímáṇsátantraratna, Adhyáyas VI—IX	Párthasárathimiśra	„	
354	388	Śástradípiká, Tarkapáda	„	Grantha.	
355	389	Śástradípiká	„	„	
356	872	„ Eight Adhyáyas	„	„	
357	390	„ Somanátha's Commentary, Twelve Adhyáyas and Mímáṇsávárttika with Ráṇaka, First Adhyáya.	Somanadadíkshita, Kumárilasvámin, Someśvaramiśra.	„	

358	1137	Sástradípikávyákhyána, Mayúkhamáliká, two Adhyáyas.	Somanáthadíkshita	Grantha.	
359	869	Mímáṇsáśabarabháshya, three Adhyáyas	Śabarasvámin	„	
360	871	Upakrama, Parákrama and Vidhirasáyana	Apyayadíkshita	„	
361	384	Vidhirasáyaṇa and Bháṭṭadípavyákhyána, Bhaṭṭachandrodaya, six Pádas.	„	„	
362	385	Mímáṇsákutúhala, four Adhyáyas	Vasudeva	„	
363	1099	Śástradípikávyákhyána, fourth, fifth and sixth Adhyáyas and Advaitaratnakosha.	Viśvanáthabhaṭṭa, Vasudévayatíndra.	Telugu.	
364	391	Tantraśikhámaṇi, from sixth Páda of sixth Adhyáya to twelfth Adhyáya.	Chúḍámaṇidíkshita	Grantha.	
365	873	Mímáṇsánayavivéka, four Adhyáyas	Bhavanáthamiśra	Grantha and Telugu.	
366		Jaimininyáyamálávistara, six Adhyáyas	Vidyáraṇya	Nágarí.	

CLASS XI.

Vedánta, Advaitavedánta.

367	402	Śankarabháshya and Átmánátmavivekachúḍámaṇi.	Śankarácharya	Grantha	This volume comprises also the Kápilasánkhyasútravṛitti and Sánkhyasaptati.
368	457	Vishṇusahasranámabháshya	„	Nágarí.	Complete.
369	1140	Gítábháshya	„	Grantha.	„
370	415	Daśopanishadbháshya	„	„	„
371	1124	Triṇśatibháshya	„	„	„
372	443	Nṛisiṇhatápaníyopanishadbháshya	„	„	„
373	649	Śankarabháshyaṭíká	Váchaspatimiśra	„	
374	413	„ fourth Adhyáya	„	Telugu.	
376	444	Sámánvayasútra	„	Grantha.	
377	422	Adhikaraṇaratnamálá, four Adhyáyas	Vidyáraṇya.	Telugu.	
378	1261	Pañchadaśí, with Commentary	„	Kanarese.	
379	426	„ „	„	„	
380	1229	Dhyánadípiká with Commentary	„	„	
381	1331	Śivakathámṛitasára, Śankaravijaya	„	Telugu.	„

Number.	Number in the old Catalogue.	Names of Works.	Name of the Author.	Character in which written.	Remarks.
		CLASS XI.—*contd.*			
		VEDÁNTA, ADVAITAVEDÁNTA.—*concld.*			
382	828	Advaitasiddhi	Madhusúdanasarasvatí.	Grantha.	
383	833	Advaitaratnakosha	......	,,	
384	412	Vákyasudhátíká, Vásudevamánana, Hastámalakatátparya, Drigdriśyaviveka	Brahmánanda	Telugu.	
385	420	Hastámalakatátparya, Vedántavárttikasárasangraha, Atmánátmaviveka, Tattvasudhá, Uttaragítá, Átmabodha, Aparokshánubhúti, Vivekasáravyákhyána, Vásudevamánana	Náráyaṇabhaṭṭa	Kanarese.	
386	928	Ajñánatamobháskarasudhá	Śankaráchárya	,,	
387	830	Vedántavivaraṇasára	Yajñeśvaradíkshita	Nágari.	
388	416	Vedántavivaraṇa	,,	,,	
389	432	Átmánátmaviveka, Nirvikalpavádártha.	......	,,	This volume also comprises the Sánkhyabháshya and the Yogabháshya. Complete.
390	421	Vyákhyána to Śankarabháshya, Adhyáyas I, II.	Náráyaṇendrayati.	Grantha.	
391	464	Lalitasahasranámabháshya	Ánandanátha	,,	
392	425	Advaitadípiká	Nrisiṇhayati	Telugu.	
393	459	Śivasahasranámavyákhyána.	Alankárikadíkshita	Nágarí.	
394	411	Siddhántasiddhajñána	Krishṇánandayati	Grantha.	
395	1321	Tattvamuktávalivyákhyána	Ánandapaṇḍita	Telugu.	
396	1191	Bhedádhikára	......	,,	
397	1194	Śivasútravárttika with Commentary, Víraśaivasiddhántachúḍámaṇi.	Maheśvaráchárya náthánanda.	Kanarese.	
398	300	Trayodaśabhuvanavichárapaṭala, Mrigendravritti, thirteen Paṭalas.	Vidyánáráyaṇakánta	Telugu.	
399	1176	Jñánavásishṭha with Commentary, Utpattiprakaraṇa.	Válmíki and Ánandabodhasarasvati.	,,	
400	1222	Jñánavásishṭha with Commentary, Sthitiprakaraṇa and Upaśamanaprakaraṇa.	,,	,,	

401	1216	Jñánavásishṭha with Commentary, Nirváṇaprakaraṇa.	,,	,,	
402	772	(Another copy)	,,	Kanarese.	
403	1322	Sútratátparyanirṇaya	......	,,	
404	423	Vedántapadárthanirṇayavyákhyána	Ánandajñánayati	,,	
405	831	Nyáyarakshámaṇi, Adhyáya I, Páda II.	Apyayadíkshita	Telugu.	
406	406	Vedántaparibháshávyákhyána	Rámakṛishṇadíkshita	,,	
407	1002	Mádhavíya, first Adhyáya and portion of the second.	Vidyámádhava	,,	
408	1231	Śivadarpaṇa, First Part	......	,,	
409	427	Brahmasútrabháshya	Nílakaṇṭha	Nágarí.	
410	721	Uttaragítávyákhyána, three Adhyáyas	Gauḍapádáchárya	Grantha.	
411	922	Vishṇusahasranáma, Ślokarúpavyákhyána.	Gambhírabhárati	Nágarí.	
412	1331	Vishṇusahasranáma, Vyákhyánapraśnáñjali	,,	Grantha.	
413	136	Átmapuráṇa, Upanishadratna	Śaṅkaránanda	Kanarese.	
414	1338	Kálajñána	Vidyáraṇya.		
		VIŚISHTÁDVAITAVEDÁNTA.			
415	403	Śríbháshya	Rámánujáchárya	Grantha	Complete.
416	996	(Another Copy)	,,	,,	,,
417	937	Gítábháshya	,,	,,	,,
418	938	(Another Copy)	,,	,,	,,
419	409	Śrutaprakáśiká	Sudarśanáchárya	,,	
420	1104	Śrutaprakáśiká, Another Copy	,,	,,	
421	1044	,, first Adhyáya	,,	,,	
422	834	Śrutaprakáśikávyákhyána, Bhávaprakáśiká	Varadavishṇu	,,	
423	951	(Another Copy)	,,	,,	
424	1203	(Another Copy)	,,	,,	
425	839	Rahasyatrayasára	Vedántácharya	Telugu.	
426	101	Gítátátparyachandriká	,,	Grantha.	
427	407	Śatadúshiṇí, Ágamaprámáṇyavyákhyána, Vedántadípa, Chaṇḍamáruta, Pañcharátrarakshá, Satcharitrarakshá.	,,	,,	
428	408	Tattvamuktákalápa, Sarvárthasiddhi, Nyáyasiddhajñána, Nyáyapariśuddhi, Saptagranthanibarhaṇa.	,,	,,	

Number.	Number in the old Catalogue.	Names of Works.	Name of the Author.	Character in which written.	Remarks.
		CLASS XI.—*concld.*			
		VIŚISHTÁDVAITAVEDÁNTA.—*concld.*			
429	829	Vedántakaustubha	Surapura Venkatácháárya.	Grantha	Complete.
430	436	Nyáyaratnávali, Siddhántachintámaṇi	„	Kanarese.	
431	410	Chandrikákhaṇḍana, Rámánujasiddhántavijaya.	„	Grantha.	
432	414	Tattvamártaṇḍa	Surapura Śrínivásácháárya.	„	„
433	1022	Vedántavijaya	......	„	„
434	836	Páráśaryavijaya	„	„	„
435	1039	Śríbháshyavyákhyána, Nyáyaprakáśiká	......	„	
436	110	Adhikaraṇachintámaṇi, Adhikharaṇasáráralí	Varadáchárya, Vedántáchárya.	„	
437	1018	Upanishadvákyavivaraṇa, Rámánujapadaviraksh á	......	„	
438	171	Pramáṇasangraha	......	Telugu.	
439	840	Taptamudrávilása, nine Parichchhedas	Nṛisiṇhácharya	„	Complete.
		DVAITAVEDÁNTA.			
440	596	Sarvamúla	Madhváchárya	Nágarí	„
441	404	Brahmasútrabháshya	„	„	„
442	435	Daśopanishadbháshya	„	„	„
443	433	Nyáyasudhá, second Adhyáya	Jayatírtha	„	„
444	434	Pramáṇapaddhatí, Nyáyakalpalatá	„	„	„
445	1146	Chandrikávyákhyána, second Pada	Rághavánandatírtha	„	
446	405	Tantrasáravyákhyána	Śesháchárya		
447	461	Dvádaśastotra, Nṛisiṇhastuti, Śivastuti with Commentary.	Madhváchárya, Náráyaṇapaṇḍita, Śesháchárya	„	
448	1147	Nyáyámṛitavyákhyánataranginí	Rámácharya	Grantha.	

449	465	Ashṭamahámantra, &c.	......	Telugu.	
450	428	Bṛihattáratamya, Gajendramoksha, Vishṇusahasranáma, Váyustuti, Náráyaṇavarman, Mádhavastavarája, Dvádaśastotra, Sadácharasmṛiti, Mangaláshṭaka, Dadhivámanastotra, Urdhvapuṇḍravidhi, Prabhátapañchaka, Anuváyustuti.	......	,,	
		CLASS XII.			
		SÁNKHYA.			
375	316	Sánkhyatattvakaumudí	Váchaspatimiśra .	Grantha.	
		CLASS XIII.			
		YOGAŚÁSTRA.			
451	799	Yogapátañjalasútravyákhyána	Rámayogin . .	Telugu.	
		CLASS XIV.			
		JYOTISHAŚÁSTRA.			
452	473	Bárhaspatyasaṃhitá, Muhúrtavidhána, Náradíyasaṃhitá Gandharvanagaralakshaṇaparyantá, Kaśyapasaṃhitá, Jaiminisútravyákhyána.	Nṛisiṇhadeva . .	Nágarí . .	
453	490	Kálaprakáśiká	Nṛisiṇhasúri . .	Grantha . .	
454	475	,, seventy-three Adhyáyas . .	......	Telugu . .	
455	494	Narapativijaya	......	Grantha and Nágarí.	This volume also comprises a totally distinct work called Svarasástra.
456	483	Kálavidhánavyákhyána, Bhárgavasútravyákhyána.	Paráśara, Śrídhara .	Grantha.	
457	492	Shoḍaśatantravyákhyánamanoramá, Sarvárthachintámaṇi.	Vaidyanátha, Śástraviveka.	,,	
458	482	Jyotishárṇavataraṅgiṇí, thirty-two Adhyáyas .	......	Nágarí.	
459	484	Kákasvara, Gauliphala, Varshaphaṇin . .	......	Kanarese.	
460	486	Nakshatrachúḍámaṇi	......	,,	
461	481	Vṛiddhapáráśarya, Kálavidhána, Upadeśasútra .	Paráśara	Grantha.	
462	474	Sarvárthachintámaṇi, Ashṭakavargadaśaphala .	......	Kanarese.	

Number.	Number in the old Catalogue.	Names of Works.	Name of the Author.	Character in which written.	Remarks.
		CLASS XIV—*concld.*			
		JYOTISHAŚÁSTRA—*concld.*			
463		Bhúgolavistara, Navagrahavivaraṇa	......		
464	487	Lambaka, five Adhyáyas	......	Kanarese.	
465	479	Phalaratnamálá, thirty-two Adhyáyas	Kṛishṇamiśra	Grantha.	
466	1267	Jyotishasárasaṅgraha, Náradíyasaṃhitá	Śríharshadeva	Nágarí.	
467	97	Bṛihajjátakavyákhyána, Jagachchandriká	Bhaṭṭotpala	,,	
468	472	Bṛihajjátaka, Laghuprakáśiká	Varáhamihira, Vidyámádhava.	,,	
469	496	Bṛihajjátakavyákhyána, Jagachchandriká	Bhaṭṭotpala	Grantha.	
470	493	Saṃhitárṇava, eight Tarangas	......	,,	
471	762	Súryasiddhántavyákhyána, Subodhaníya, eleven Adhyáyas.	Rámakṛishṇárádhya	Telugu.	
472	471	,, ,,	,,	,,	
473	1120	,, ,, Yallajíya	Yallaja	Kanarese.	
474	763	Gárgyasaṃhitá, Jyotishapravarakhaṇḍana	......	Nágarí.	
475	761	Kálámṛita and Nakshatrádiśánti	......	Grantha.	
476	1122	Śrípatíyavyákhyána	Bháskarácharya	Nágarí.	
477	495	Bhárgavanadi	......	Grantha.	
478	497	Pañchapakshíya, Ashṭakavarga, Praśnabhága	......	Nágarí.	
479	1092	Daivajñavilása, sixty-three Adhyáyas, Kálanirúpaṇa.	Yallácharya	......	
480	477	Sámudrikalakshaṇa	......	Kanarese.	
		CLASS XV.			
		MANTRAŚÁSTRA.			
481	440	Śrívidyábhuvanálankárasañjívanibháshya	Śankarácharya	......	Complete.
482	441	(Another Copy)	,,		
483	448	Tantrarája, thirteen Adhyáyas	Parameśvara	......	,,

484	437	Saubhágyaratnákara, thirty-six Tarangas . .	Śrívidyánandanátha.		
485	439	Mahálakshmíratnakosha	......	Grantha.	
486	444	Lakshmínáráyaṇahṛidaya	......	Kanarese.	
487	1192	Mantramahodadhi	Nṛisiṇhakavi . . .	Telugu.	
488	438	,, (Another Copy) . . .	,, . . .	Grantha.	
489	450	,, With Setubandhavyákhyána .	Bháskaráchárya . .	,,	
490	451	,, ,, (Another Copy)	,, . . .	,, . . .	Complete.
491	452	Yoginísútra, three Stavakas, Ratnasútrí, eight Paṭalas.	......	Kanarese.	
492	453	Rudrayámila	......	Telugu.	
493	446	Navagrahakalpa	......	Kanarese.	
494	449	,, Vírabhadrajapavidhána .	......	Grantha.	
495	485	Grahachcshṭávidhána	Deveśvara . . .	Telugu . . .	This volume comprises also a distinct work called Kavikalpalatá.
496	455	Pratyangiramantra, Mahálakshmíratnakosha, Devívishaya, Guptavatímantra.	......	Grantha.	
497	1123	Mantradevatáprakáśiká, fifteen Paṭalas, Mantradíkshávidhána, Vasishṭatryambakakalpa, seven Paṭalas.	......	Nágarí.	
498	803	Sudarśana, Shaḍaksharímálámantra, Yantra .	......	Telugu.	
499	463	Párthiveśvarapújá, Śivakavachamantra, &c. .	......	Nágarí.	
500	1256	Pañcháksharíkalpa	......	,,	
501	754	Devapújáratnakrama, Samprokshaṇa with Prayoga.	......	Telugu and Grantha.	
502	789	Śáligrámalakshaṇa, Múrtidhyána	......	Telugu.	
503	753	Bṛihannyása, Aupaśamaprayoga	......	Nágarí.	
504	744	Gáṇapatyastotra, with Vrata and Sahasranáma, Anantavratodyápana, with Dosharáyaschitta, Sankaṭaharagaṇapatívrata.	......	Kanarese.	
505	781	Mṛitasañjívinikalpa	......	Nágarí . . .	This volume also comprises a distinct work called Karmavipáka.
506	...	Kámaratna, Vásyádishaṭprayoga, Nidhipradípiká, Nidhyañjanádiprayoga.			
507	742	Jayalakshmívrata, with Udyápana . . .	......	Kanarese.	
508	798	Kártavíryagaṇapati, Bhairavakalpa, Shaṭprayoga Añjanasiddhi.	......	Nágarí.	
509	1323	Ardhanáríśvarádivrata, Siṇhásanagajáśváyudhapújárájyapátrábhisheka, Sahasrakalaśábhisheka, Vṛiddhyabhisheka, Ugraratha, Bhímarathaśánti.			

Number.	Number in the old Catalogue.	Names of Works.	Name of the Author.	Character in which written.	Remarks.
		CLASS XVI.			
		VAIDYAŚÁSTRA.			
510	358	Sútrasthána, Padárthaśuddhi and a portion of Rájamrigánka.	......	Grantha.	
511	1020	Báhaṭavyákhyána	Hemádri	Telugu.	
512	1235	Vaidyasárasamudra, with Kanarese Translation	Śeshádrisúnu	Kanarese	Complete.
513	349	Vaidyasárasangraha	......	Grantha and Nágari	
514	779	Jívarakshámṛita	Śríkánta	Kanarese.	
515	359	Nṛisiṇhasaṃhitá, Vaidyasárasangraha with Kanarese Translation.	Rámasvámin	Telugu	,,
516	352	Vaidyasárachintámaṇi	......	,,	,,
517	346	Ánandakhaṇḍa, with Kanarese Translation	......	Kanarese	,,
518	845	(Another Copy)	......	,,	,,
519	600	(Another Copy)	......	,,	,,
520	351	Rasadípikásárasangrahasútra, with Tamil Translation.	......	Grantha	,,
521	354	Netravaidya, Shaḍrasanighaṇṭu, with Tamil Translation.	......	,,	,,
522	353	Śataśloka, Vaidyámṛitachikitsá, with Kanarese Translation.	......	Kanarese	,,
523	356	Abhidánamañjarí	......	Nágarí.	
524	347	Vaidyasárasangraha, Gáṇapatya, with Commentary	......	Kanarese.	
525	350	Dhanvantarinighaṇṭu, Chintámaṇi	......	Telugu.	
526	348	Vaidyanighaṇṭu, Ákárádinighaṇṭu	......	Kanarese.	
527	644	Rájanighaṇṭu	......	Telugu.	
528	357	Śvetabháskara, Śvásanidhána	......	Grantha.	
		CLASS XVII.			
		DHANURVEDA.			
		(No Works in this Class.)			

		CLASS XVIII.				
		GANDHARVA.				
529	752	Saptasvaralakshaṇa, Rágalakshaṇa, Svarachúḍámaṇi.	......	Kanarese.		
530	277	Sangítaratnákara, Sangítasarvasva, with Kanarese Translation.	......	,,		
531	1095	Bharataśástra	Śárngadhara . .	Telugu.		
532	239	Ashṭapadívyákhyána, Śrutiranjiní.				
		CLASS XIX.				
		ŚILPAŚÁSTRA.				
533	289	Śilpanighaṇṭu, Ágamoddhára, two Adhyáyas, Kriyákramadípiká.	Aghoraśástrin . .	Grantha.		
534	219	Śilpaśástrabhúśalya	......	,,		
535	791	Devatáśilpa, with Telugu Translation . . .	......	Kanarese.		
536	790	Máyávastulakshaṇa, Bráhmaṇakshatriyavaiśyaśúdragrihanirmáṇalakshaṇa, Vápíkúpataḍágádilakshaṇa.	......	,,		
537	288	Śilpaśástrasútra with Bháshya, sixty-nine Adhyáyas.	Viśvakarman and Śeshaśarman.			
538	1051	Vimánasára	......	Grantha.		
		CLASS XX.				
		NÍTIŚÁSTRA.				
		(No Works in this Class.)				
		CLASS XXI.				
		SÁHITYA.				
539	559	Raghuvaṇśa with Commentary, Sargas XI—XIX	Kálidása, Peḍḍabhaṭṭa	Grantha.		
540	947	Raghuvaṇśa, Meghasandeśa, Kumárasambhava .	Kálidása . . .	Nágarí.		
541	1228	Kumárasambhava, second Sarga, Mághakávya .	,, Mágha .	,,		

Number.	Number in the old Catalogue.	Names of Works.	Name of the Author.	Character in which written.	Remarks.
		CLASS XXI—*contd.*			
		SÁHITYA—*contd.*			
542	1052	Naishadha	Sríharsha	Malayalam.	
543	1891	„ with Commentary on second and third Sargas.	„ and Peḍḍabhaṭṭa	Grantha.	
544	1117	Naishadhavyákhyána, Sargas X—XVII	„	Nágari.	
545	1046	Mágha, Sargas II, V, VI	Mágha	Telugu.	
546	998	Haṃsasandeśa	Vedántácharya	Grantha	Complete.
547	1135	Pádukásahasra	„	Nágari.	„
548	578	Kirátárjuníya with Commentary	Bháravi and Peḍḍabhaṭṭa.		
549	260	Bhairaveśvarakávya	Bhairaveśvara	Kanarese.	
550	339	Kṛishṇarájaprabhavodayakávya	Śrínivása	Grantha	„
551	244	Śankaravijaya	Vidyáraṇya	Kanarese	„
552	544	Amaruśatakavyákhyána	......	„	„
553	765	Bhartṛihari	Bhartṛihari	„	
554	1082	Bhojacharitra, Daśakumárakathá	Daṇḍin	Telugu	„
555	272	Sudarśanaśataka, with Commentary	Náráyaṇayati	Grantha	„
556	1286	Parakálasvámin Ashṭottara, Kṛishṇarája Ashṭottaratriśatí and Sahasranáma.	Kṛishṇarája, Kṛishṇajoshya.	Kanarese	„
557	1179	Sánkhyaratnakosha, with Prabhávalivyákhyána, Chámuṇḍikalaghunighaṇṭu with Commentary Grahaṇadarpaṇa.	Kṛishṇarája	„	„
558	1	Śrítattvanidhi, Chámuṇḍikalaghunighaṇṭu	„	„	This volume comprises also distinct works called Svarachuḍámaṇi and Rágalakshaṇa.

559	1296	Chámuṇḍikanakshatramáliká, Śivanakshatramáliká, Gaṇapatinavaratnamáliká, Rámakṛishṇastotra.	,,	Nágarí	Complete.
560	1315	Devatánámakusumamañjaristotra, Mangala	,,	Grantha	,,
561	190	Saugandhikapariṇaya, thirty-six Adhyáyas	,,	Kanarese	,,
562	1141	Śivasthapativyákhyána	,,	,,	This volume comprises also a distinct work called Sangítagangádharíya, with the Commentary called Śravaṇanandiní.
563	634	Sánkhyaratnakosha with Commentary, Laghunighaṇṭu with Commentary, Navagrahadaśavibhágapádaka, Samudramathanakathá.	Kṛishṇarája	Kanarese.	
564	1326	Sánkhyaratnakosha with Commentary, Grahaṇadarpaṇa, Pratibhágidaśavibhágapádaka	,,	,,	Complete.
565	1266	Śiváshṭaka, Śankaráshṭaka, Devípañcharatna, Śaivadíkshávidhi.	,,	,,	,,
566	467	Áryadvisatí, Śivastotra, Múkapañchaśati	......	Telugu	,,
567	1128	Bṛihatkathámañjarí	Bhaṭṭasomadeva	Grantha	,,
568	247	Śivakathámṛitasárasangraha, Śankaravijayavilása, sixty-four Adhyáyas.	Vidyáraṇya	,,	,,
569	279	Ratirahasya, nine Parichchhedas	Káñchinátha	Telugu	,,
570	218	Battísputalíkathá	Chikka Upádhyáya	Kanarese	,,
571	724	Śivabhaktivilása, with Ekámṛitanáthastavavyákhyána.	Śrínivása, Nṛisiṇhadíkshita.	Nágarí	,,
572	206	Śríkṛishṇarájavaṇśaratnaprabhá	Tammaiya Śástrin	Telugu	,,
573	1174	Śríkṛishṇarájavaṇśaratnákara with Kanarese Translation.	......	Kanarese	,,
574	543	Śivatattvaratnákara	Keralívásava	,,	,,
575	888	Champúrámáyaṇa, Yuddhakáṇḍa	Lakshmaṇakaví	Telugu	
576	776	Uttarachampú, Harischandravijayachampú	Venkatácháryasvámiśástrin.	,,	

Number.	Number in the old Catalogue.	Names of Works.	Name of the Author.	Character in which written.	Remarks.
		CLASS XXI—*concld.*			
		SÁHITYA—*concld.*			
577	777	Viśvaguṇádarśa	Venkatácharya	Telugu.	
578	770	Bháratachampúvyákhyá, Stavakas VI—X	Nṛisiṇhakavi	Nágarí.	
579	555	Bháratachampúvyákhyá	,,	Grantha.	
580	553	Bháratachampúvyákhyá	Anantabhaṭṭa	Nágarí.	
581	556	Púrvakádambarí	Báṇakavi	Grantha.	
582	557	Uttarakádambarí	Báṇaputra	,,	Complete.
583	810	Bhágavatachampú with Commentary	Abhinava, Kálidása	Nágarí	,,
584	919	Keralábharaṇa	Rámachandradíkshita	Kanarese	,,
585	548	Mállikamárta	Uddaṇḍakavi	,,	
586	564	Anargarághava with Commentary	Murári and Tripurári	Telugu	,,
587	551	Málatímádhava with Commentary	Bhavabhúti and Tripurári.	Grantha and Telugu.	
588	547	Chaṇḍakauśiká	Śriharsha.		
		Ratnávalí			
		Anargharághava	Murári.		
		Veṇisaṃvaraṇa	Bhaṭṭanáráyaṇa.		
		Mudrárákshasa with Commentary	Vaiśákhadatta	Grantha.	
589	571	Śákuntala	Kálidása	Telugu.	,,
590	546	Kamalanikalahaṇsa	Rájachúḍámaṇi.		
		Uttararámacharitra	Bhavabhúti.		
		Málavikágnimitra	Kálidása.		
		Prabodhachandrodaya	Krishṇamiśra.		
		Jánakípariṇaya	Rámabhadradíkshita.		
		Mudrárákshasa	Viśakhadatta.	Grantha.	
591	772	Sankalpasúryodaya	Vedántácharya	Telugu	,,
592	664	Mahánáṭaka			
593	771	Śṛingárararatnákarabháṇa	Sundaratathyácharya	Grantha.	
		Prasannarághava	Jayadeva.	Nágarí.	

594	780	Śáradatilaka	......	Kanarese.	
595	1316	Pañchayuddhaprapañchabháṇa	Trivikramaśástrin .	Telugu.	
596	570	Kávyaprakáśiká	Mammaṭa.		
597	565	Alankárasangraha	Amṛitánanda . .	,,	
598	973	Kuvalayánanda	Apyayadikshita . .	Grantha.	
599	569	Kuvalayánandachandriká	Vaidyanáthasúri .	,,	
600	573	Rasagangádhara	Paṇḍitaráya . .	Kanarese.	
601	563	Alankáramaṇidarpaṇa	Venkaiya, Sampatkumára.	,,	
602	562	Pratáparudríya	Vidyánátha . .	Telugu.	
603	567	,, with Commentary	,, Kumárasvámin	,,	
604	1125	Daśarúpaka	Dhanikakavi . .	Kanarese.	
605	1240	Námalingánuśásana	Amarasiṇha . .	,, ...	Complete.
606	549	Amarasudhá	Párivrájakáchárya .	,, ...	,,
607	1283	Amarapadapárijátavyákhyá	Ahobala . . .	Telugu.	
608	576	Śabdaratnákaranighaṇṭu	Vámaṇabhaṭṭa . .		
		Dhanañjayanighaṇṭu	Dhanañjaya . .		
		Haláyudhanighaṇṭu	Haláyudha . . .		
		Viśvaprakáśanighaṇṭu	Maheśvarakavi . .	Grantha.	

G. B. MALLESON,
Guardian to His Highness the Mahárája of Mysore.

GUARDIAN'S OFFICE,
Mysore, 1st October 1869.

No. 2342, dated the 30th November 1869.
Endorsed by the Foreign Department.

FORWARDED to the Home Department, with reference to the resolution from that Department, No. 4348, dated 3rd November 1868.

From L. BOWRING, Esq., C.S.I., Chief Commissioner of Mysore, to E. C. BAYLEY, Esq., Secretary to the Government of India, Home Department,—No. 451, dated Bangalore, the 27th January 1870.

REFERRING to Mr. Under-Secretary Geoghegan's docket No. 2920, dated the 25th June 1869, I have the honour to forward, for submission to His Excellency the Viceroy and Governor-General in Council, the accompanying two printed copies of a classified catalogue of Sanskṛit works in the Library of His Highness the Mahárája of Mysore.

Vide Proceedings No. 92, dated 19th March 1870.—Index No. 211.

From L. BOWRING, Esq., C.S.I., Chief Commissioner of Mysore, to the Secretary to the Government of India, Foreign Department, No. 449, dated Bangalore, the 27th January 1870.

ADVERTING to my letter No. 298 of the 8th October 1869, I have the honour to forward, for submission to His Excellency the Viceroy and Governor-General in Council, the accompanying five printed copies of a classified catalogue of Sanskṛit works in the Library of His Highness the Mahárája of Mysore.

No. 283 G., dated the 14th February 1870.
Endorsed by the Foreign Department.

FORWARDED to the Home Department, in continuation of the docket from this office, No. 2342, dated 30th November 1869, together with five copies of the classified catalogue.

From J. GEOGHEGAN, Esq., Under-Secretary to the Government of India, Home Department, to the Chief Secretary to the Government of Bombay,—No. 1201, dated the 3rd March 1870.

WITH reference to your letter No. 1976, dated the 18th August last, and previous correspondence, on the subject of the preservation of the records of ancient Sanskṛit literature, I am directed to request that, with the permission of His Excellency the Governor in Council, Dr. Kielhorn may be asked to submit a report on the enclosed copy of a classified catalogue of Sanskṛit works in the Library of His Highness the Maháràja of Mysore.

From J. Geoghegan, Esq., Under-Secretary to the Government of India, Home Department, to the Secretary to the Asiatic Society, Calcutta,—No. 1202, dated the 3rd March 1870.

With reference to the resolution of this Department, dated the 3rd November 1868, relative to the discovery and preservation of the records of ancient Sanskṛit literature in India, I am directed to forward, for the information of the Asiatic Society, copy of a classified catalogue of Sanskṛit works in the Library of His Highness the Maháràja of Mysore.

From E. C. Bayley, Esq., C.S.I., Secretary to the Government of India, Home Department, to the Secretary to the Government of India, Legislative Department,—No. 1203, dated the 3rd March 1870.

I am directed to forward herewith, for your information, a copy of a classified catalogue of Sanskṛit works in the Library of His Highness the Maháràja of Mysore.

From the Government of India, to the Secretary of State for India,—No. 34, dated the 15th March 1870.

We transmit herewith three copies of a " Classified Catalogue of Sanskṛit works in the Sarasvatíbháṇḍáram Library of His Highness the Maháràja of Mysore." We beg that a copy may be forwarded to the Royal Asiatic Society.

Extract from the Proceedings of the Government of Bombay, General Department,—No. 791, dated the 2nd April 1870.

Read—

Letter from the Director of Public Instruction, No. 4887, dated 25th March 1870, forwarding a letter from Dr. Kielhorn, in which he reports on the catalogue of Sanskṛit works in the Library of His Highness the Maháràja of Mysore, forwarded with Government Resolution No. 627, dated the 10th idem; and requesting instructions as to the amendments which that gentleman suggests in the method of compiling and printing catalogues of Sanskṛit manuscripts now in force.

Resolution.—Dr. Kielhorn's report to be forwarded to the Government of India, with reference to Mr. Under-Secretary Geoghegan's letter No. 1201 of the 3rd ultimo.

No. 792.

FORWARDED for the information of the Government of India, with a copy of Mr. Peile's letter and accompaniment.

From J. B. PEILE, Esq., Director of Public Instruction, to the Officiating Chief Secretary to the Government of Bombay, General Department,—No. 4887, dated Poona, the 25th March 1870.

I have the honour to forward a report by Dr. Kielhorn on the copy of a catalogue received with Resolution No. 627 of 10th March, General Department, and to solicit instructions as to the amendments which he suggests in the method of compiling and printing catalogues of Sanskṛit manuscripts now in force.

From DR. F. KIELHORN, Superintendent of Sanskṛit Studies, Deccan College, to the Director of Public Instruction, Bombay,—No. 122, dated Poona, the 22nd March 1870.

IN compliance with your letter No. 4798 of 1869-70, I have the honour to submit to you, for the information of Government, the following report on a "Classified Catalogue of Sanskṛit works in the Sarasvatíbháṇḍáram Library of His Highness the Mahárája of Mysore."

2. In order to execute the orders of Government, I will (1) endeavour to state which of the works contained in the catalogue under report are already printed or to be found amongst the manuscripts of the various public libraries in Europe; (2) comment on the manner in which this catalogue has been prepared, and suggest how, in my opinion, similar catalogues should be prepared and arranged to be of real use; and (3) submit such observations on the practice of printing the catalogues of Sanskṛit manuscripts which are now being prepared in various parts of India, as have occurred to me since I have been engaged myself in carrying out in the Southern Division of this Presidency the Resolution of the Government of India, No. 4339, dated 3rd November 1868.

3. With a view to discover which of the works contained in this catalogue are unknown, or at least inaccessible, to European scholars, I have compared it with the catalogues of the Sanskṛit manuscripts of the India Office Library, of the Bodleian Library at Oxford, of the Royal Library at Berlin, and with some smaller catalogues, such as that of the Sanskṛit manuscripts of Trinity College, Cambridge, &c. The result of this comparison

is, that of the 608 works of the catalogue under report, 468 are already in Europe. Among these :—

Nos. 1, 2, 4, 5, 10, 11, 17, 18, 28, 42, 44, 50, 59, 143, 175, 293, 295, 298, 300, 310, 315, 321, 324, 328, 330, 332, 341, 342, 344, 347, 359, 363, 365, 396, 399, 414, 440, 538, 567, 542, 545, 549, 551, 553, 554, 540, 569, 575, 583, 586, 605, and 608.

4. But, in making this statement, I would guard against the belief that all the remaining 140 works of the catalogue under report have, up to the present, been inaccessible to European scholars. On the contrary, I have the strongest suspicion that many of the remaining works are likewise already to be found in Europe, and that only the circumstance of their not having been described in the present catalogue with sufficient care and accuracy prevents me from recognising them again in the catalogues of European libraries; *e. g.*, I suspect that No. 3, which is put down as Mahábráhmaṇa, *i. e.*, the great Bráhmaṇa, is nothing else than the Aitareyabráhmaṇa of the Ṛigveda, which is well known and printed. No. 13, Ashṭottara Satopanishats (which should have been written Ashṭottaraśatopanishad), means merely 108 Upanishads, and it is impossible to say whether any of the 108 Upanishads contained in this work are as yet unknown in Europe. Or, to bring an instance of a somewhat different nature, it is easy to conjecture that the commentator who, under Nos. 539, 543, and 548, is called Peḍḍabhaṭṭa, is the same scholar who commonly goes by the name of Mallinátha; but the truth or falsehood of this conjecture cannot be ascertained except by a reference to the manuscripts. Again, it is impossible to discover from the statements made under Nos. 20 to 27, to which portions or branches of the Yajurveda the commentaries mentioned in the catalogue refer, &c.

5. I would therefore suggest that an intelligent Pandit should be employed to re-catalogue the following manuscripts :—Nos. 3, 6, 9, 12, 16, 19, 27, 43, 51, 58, 144, 174, 294, 299, 311, 314, 322, 323, 329, 333, 340, 343, 345, 346, 360, 362, 364, 397, 398, 415, 439, 539, 543, 544, 546, 548, 550, 552, 555, 566, 568, 570, 574, 584, 585, 606, and 607; and I need not say that I shall be glad again to report on a new catalogue of these manuscripts should the Government of India desire me to do so.

6. The catalogue under report gives more information regarding the manuscripts described in it than is usually found in Native lists, but it is deficient in some important particulars. It contains no information regarding the age of the works catalogued, nor any statements concerning

their bulk; moreover, in many cases, the titles of the works seem to me to have been transcribed from the outside of the first or last leaf of the manuscripts, while they should have been given as found in the introductory or the last lines of the works themselves. Under No. 316, a work is catalogued as Chintámaṇi, whereas its real title is Tattvachintámaṇi. Under No. 314, we find a work called in the catalogue Śiromaṇivyákhyána, while its true name appears to be Anumánamaṇidídhitiṭippaṇí. Finally, the catalogue seems to have been transcribed in Roman character by a person ignorant of Sanskṛit. For only thus can I account for such errors as, *e.g.*, that committed under Nos. 308 and 309, where Manorama is given as the name of the author of a commentary on the Siddhántakaumudí, whereas it is really the title of that commentary.

7. As it is of great importance that the catalogues of Native libraries which are now being prepared in this country should be as accurate as possible, and should give the greatest possible and the most trustworthy information regarding the books catalogued, within the smallest compass, I venture to suggest that whenever any Native owners of books will permit their books to be catalogued, the following rules should be strictly observed:—

(*a*). All catalogues should be prepared by Sanskṛit scholars, Native or European; when prepared by Native scholars, they should be written (if possible) in the Devanágarí character, and not be transcribed in Roman character.

(*b*). The catalogues should give the following information:—

(1). The title of the work.

(2). The name of the author.

(Both should be taken from the introductory or the closing lines of the work catalogued; *e.g.*, a work may on its outside bear the title Paribháshá, but in the interior it may be called Paribháshenduśekharaprakáśiká; if, in this case, the work is catalogued as Paribháshá, the information to be derived therefrom is extremely small, whereas the title Paribháshenduśekharaprakáśiká would inform us at once that the work is a commentary on the Paribháshenduśekhara of Nágojibhaṭṭa. Wherever it may be difficult or impossible to make out the title or the author's name, the introductory and final lines of the work to be catalogued should be carefully given in the catalogue in the Devanágarí character.)

(3). The number of the leaves, the average number of lines on each page, and the number of ślokas, to be calculated in the Native fashion.

(4). The age of the manuscripts. Under this head it should be distinctly stated whether the year in which the manuscript was written is given in the manuscript, and if so, according to what era, or whether the person cataloguing it infers the age from the appearance of the work, the paper, the handwriting, &c.

(5). Substance on which written, and character.

(6). Where deposited, and in whose possession.

(7). Remarks.

(*c*). All works catalogued should be classified according to their contents in one uniform manner. As a model for such a classification, I propose for Vedic works the classification adopted by Professor Weber in his catalogue of the manuscripts of the Royal Library at Berlin, and, for other Sanskṛit works, that followed by Professsor Aufrecht in his catalogue of the Sanskṛit manuscripts of the Bodleian Library at Oxford. The more uniform the arrangement of the works catalogued in India is with that of the catalogues of the great European Libraries, the easier it will be to decide which of the manuscripts catalogued are already within reach of European scholars, and which are not yet accessible to them, and should therefore be either purchased or copied.

I am aware that my plan for cataloguing manuscripts will, at the outset, entail more labour and expense than that hitherto adopted; but experience has convinced me that its adoption will save much useless labour and expense in the end.

8. Finally, I venture to submit a few observations on the practice of printing the catalogues of manuscripts of Native libraries. According to paragraph 2 of the letter No. 4350 from the Officiating Secretary to the Government of India, to the Secretary to the Government of Bombay, dated Simla, the 3rd November 1868, all procurable unprinted lists of Sanskṛit manuscripts in the Native libraries should be printed. I take the liberty to suggest that much unnecessary expense will be incurred, and much labour uselessly expended, if this order be carried out to its full extent. Experience has taught me that, of the works catalogued in Native lists, generally at least half the number are duplicates, and of the remaining half at least two-thirds are either printed or otherwise within reach of

all Sanskṛit scholars. I am, therefore, humbly of opinion that it would be both in the interest of Government, and also in that of those Sanskṛit scholars who are likely to use the catalogues of manuscripts printed in India, to direct those who superintend the printing of catalogues in the various parts of this country to strike out of the lists all duplicate copies (except in the case of very important manuscripts), and to leave out likewise all those works which are already to be found in the great Sanskṛit Libraries of Europe, *i. e.*, the Library of the India Office, the Bodleian Library at Oxford, and the Royal Library at Berlin.

From E. C. BAYLEY, Esq., C.S.I., Secretary to the Government of India, Home Department, to the Secretary to the Government of Bombay,—No. 3705, dated Simla, the 9th August 1870.

I am directed to acknowledge the receipt of your communication, No. 792, dated 2nd April last, submitting a report by Dr. Kielhorn on the catalogue of Sanskṛit works in the Library of His Highness the Mahárája of Mysore; and, in reply, to state that his suggestions for re-cataloguing more carefully the 140 volumes indicated by him has been adopted, and the Chief Commissioner of Mysore has been asked to take the necessary steps for carrying it out.

2. Professor Kielhorn's general remarks as to the preparation of the catalogues of Sanskṛit manuscipts have the concurrence of the Governor-General in Council, who agrees in the conclusion that it is most desirable to have the lists prepared in the manner suggested, wherever practicable. But His Excellency in Council apprehends that it would be impossible, generally, to get sufficiently qualified scholars for the performance of the work.

3. The main difficulty would seem to be to obtain any lists of the Sanskṛit libraries at all; and it is but few persons—and these, of course, very often far from the best qualified—who at present can get access to them at all. It is, however, a great step to have even a rough catalogue prepared; for it enables a scholar like Dr. Kielhorn to say at once what works are, or are not, worth attention.

4. On the whole, His Excellency in Council thinks that the present method of preparing catalogues of the ancient Sanskṛit works is the best to insist upon, although, wherever a competent scholar can be found, Dr. Kielhorn's suggestion might be followed; and at any rate, if the writer

could, in each case, enter in his catalogue the first and last few lines of a manuscript, it would add great value to the lists; and this is so merely mechanical that His Excellency in Council believes that almost any one qualified to make a list can do it.

From E. C. Bayley, Esq., C.S.I., Secretary to the Government of India, Home Department, to the Chief Commissioner of Mysore,—No. 3706, dated Simla, the 9th August 1870.

With reference to your letter No. 451, dated the 27th January last, forwarding a classified catalogue of Sanskṛit works in the Library of His Highness the Mahárája of Mysore, I am directed to transmit herewith copy of a correspondence* with the Government of Bombay, with a report by Dr. Kielhorn on the catalogue in question, and to request that you will be good enough to cause the necessary steps to be taken for giving effect to Dr. Kielhorn's proposal to re-catalogue the 140 volumes indicated by him.

* To Bombay, No. 1201, dated 3rd March 1870.
From " " 792, " 2nd April " and enclosures.
To " " 3705, " 9th August "

From A. P. Howell, Esq., Officiating Under-Secretary to the Government of India, Home Department, to the Governments of Madras, Bombay, North-Western Provinces and the Punjab, and the Chief Commissioners of Oudh and the Central Provinces,—Nos. 6—398-403, dated the 6th March 1876.

I am directed to request that an annual catalogue of Sanskṛit manuscripts discovered in† may be submitted to the Government of India in the Home Department, in place of the quarterly catalogue called for in Home Department Nos. 4349-55,† dated 3rd November 1868. The form prescribed in the orders cited should, however, be retained.

† 4349, Madras.
4350, Bombay.
4351, N.-W. Provinces.
4352, Punjab.
4354, Oudh.
4355, Central Provinces.

No. 404.

Copy forwarded to Foreign Department, with a request that the necessary instructions may be given to the Agent, Governor-General, Rajputana.

From A. P. Howell, Esq., Officiating Under-Secretary to the Government of India, Home Department, to the Secretary to the Government of Bengal,—No. 6405, dated the 16th March 1876.

I am directed to request that an annual catalogue of Sanskṛit manuscripts discovered in Bengal may be submitted to the Government of India in the Home Department, instead of the quarterly catalogue asked for in Home Department No. 4353, dated 3rd November 1868. The present form in which the notices of Sanskṛit manuscripts are published by Babu Rájendralála Mitra, under the orders of the Government of Bengal, may be adhered to.

From J. A. Bourdillon, Esq., Officiating Under-Secretary to the Government of India, Home Department, to the Secretaries to the Governments of Madras and the Punjab, and the Chief Commissioners of Oudh and the Central Provinces,—Nos. 12—616-619, dated the 5th April 1876.

With reference to paragraph 3 of this office circular, dated 3rd November 1868, regarding the discovery and preservation of the records of ancient Sanskṛit literature, I am directed to request that a report may be submitted, as early as practicable, of the work actually done in* up to the end of 1875, towards carrying out the scheme set forth in the circular above cited.

* The Madras Presidency and Mysore, the Punjab, Oudh, the Central Provinces.

2. The report should shew the names of the Sanskṛit manuscripts acquired for Government, where they are deposited, and whether any manuscripts, and, if so, how many, and what, manuscripts have been supplied to Oriental scholars or institutions in Europe and elsewhere.

No. 620.

Copy forwarded to the Foreign Department, with reference to this office No. 4356, dated 3rd November 1868, and with a request that orders to the above effect may be communicated to the Governor-General's Agent in Rajputana.

From the Hon'ble W. Hudleston, Chief Secretary to the Government of Madras, to the Officiating Secretary to the Government of India, Home Department,—No. 391, dated Ootacamund, the 6th October 1876.

With reference to your Under-Secretary Mr. J. A. Bourdillon's letter, dated the 5th April 1876, No. 12—616, I am directed to forward, for the information of the

No. 1560, dated 7th June 1876.

Government of India, copy of a letter from the Director of Public Instruction marginally noted.

From the Director of Public Instruction, Madras, to the Chief Secretary to the Government of Madras,—No. 1560, dated Madras, the 7th June 1876.

I have the honour, with reference to G. O. No. 164 of the 5th May 1876, to submit the accompanying letter from the Professor of Sanskṛit, from which it will be seen that Dr. Oppert was not aware of the existence of G. O. No. 423 of the 16th December 1868, which he supposes was taken away by Mr. Pickford.

2. As I entered on my duties only last year, I can supply no information from personal knowledge, and find but little on record.

3. The duty of carrying out the instructions of the Government of India was committed to Mr. Pickford in December 1868; but Mr. Pickford was compelled by severe illness to return to Europe in March 1870, and never returned. Mr. Venkaṭa Subba Śástrí, who was appointed to act as Sanskṛit Professor, also fell ill and died in the following year, and a young graduate, Mr. Śeshagiri Aiyer, afterwards acted in this post until Dr. Oppert arrived in 1872.

4. Three of Mr. Pickford's reports are recorded in G. O. No. 84 of the 15th March 1869, No. 105 of the 1st April 1869, and No. 46 of the 10th February 1870. On referring to G. O. No. 32 of the 30th January 1873, which does not seem to have been communicated to Dr. Oppert, although he was then in India, it will be seen that the Government of India made enquiries regarding the distribution of the catalogues printed from time to time in this Presidency, and that Mr. Powell reported that no such catalogues had been printed, the only one which had been prepared having been taken to England by Mr. Pickford. Mr. Powell was directed to communicate with Mr. Pickford on the subject; and, on the 11th June 1873, he submitted to Government a copy of a letter which he had received from Mr. Pickford. Mr. Pickford stated that, when he left, he had two catalogues in hand; that one of these was fairly advanced and already in process of printing at the Foster Press; and that copies of both these catalogues were deposited in the library. Mr. Powell reported, however, that he had had a search made for these papers by the Hindu who was appointed to act for Mr. Pickford, and that they could not be found.

5. When Mr. Pickford left India, the post of Acting Sanskṛit Professor was offered to Mr. Lingam Lakshmaji Puntalu, of Ganjam, and declined by him. It will be seen, however, from G. O. No. 156 of the 12th May 1870, and No. 229 of the 14th July 1870, that he was authorised to institute a search for rare Sanskṛit manuscripts in the Northern Sircars, and that funds were provided for the transcription or purchase of such manuscripts as might be determined on, after comparing his list with the books in the Oriental Library. A few Sanskṛit manuscripts in the Uriya character were accordingly sent by Lingam Lakshmaji Puntalu to Madras, and these are believed to be now deposited in the Oriental Manuscript Library.

6. Dr. Burnell was appointed, in G. O. No. 71 of the 16th March 1871, to catalogue the Sanskṛit Library at Tanjore, and sanction for printing the catalogue in England was given in G. O. No. 371 of the 6th December 1871.

7. In G. O. No. 367 of the 23rd November 1870, Dr. Burnell's services were placed at the disposal of the Chief Commissioner of Mysore for the examination of the Sanskṛit manuscripts in Mysore, but I am nat aware with what result.

From the Professor of Sanskṛit, Presidency College, Madras, to the Chief Secretary to the Government of Madras,—dated Madras, the 22nd May 1876.

I much regret to report that the Government order containing the circular of the Home Department of the Government of India, dated 3rd November 1868, is not in the records of the Government Oriental Manuscript Library, and that its contents were unknown to me up to the 18th instant, when the Director of Public Instruction communicated them to me. Had I been acquainted with that order, I should have gladly acted according to it, the more so as I learnt there was a yearly allowance of Rs. 850 assigned to the library to fulfil the demands of that order.

2. How it came that my predecessor, Mr. Pickford, did not deposit it, I do not know; perhaps he regarded it as a matter concerning him personally as Professor of Sanskṛit. As the acting successors of Mr. Pickford also did not comply with that order, I presume they were also ignorant of it.

3. Mr. Pickford commenced to catalogue manuscripts at Tanjore, which work was, after the departure of Mr. Pickford, entrusted to Dr. Burnell (see G. O. dated 16th March 1871, No. 71). The only increase added to the

library was the purchase of Sanskṛit manuscripts for which were paid R90 (see G. O. dated 29th October 1872, No. 304).

4. When I assumed charge of the library on the 4th November 1872, I found it in a bad condition, and I reported on it on the 14th February 1873 (see G. O. dated 11th August 1873, No.250). Since then, the manuscripts have been nearly all catalogued and placed in good teakwood glass-cases, which I received in January this year.

5. Now that the manuscripts are safely housed and well taken care of, the grant for the extension of the library will be very welcome, and I shall use it to the benefit of that institution. I can even now devote more time to this purpose, as the duties of teaching and lecturing, which formerly devolved on me alone, are, since the end of last year, shared with a Native Assistant Professor of Sanskṛit.

6. I request you will kindly forward to me the Government order containing the circular above mentioned.

From J. W. Neill, Esq., Officiating Secretary to the Chief Commissioner of the Central Provinces, to the Officiating Secretary to the Government of India, Home Department,—No. 3131-139, dated Nagpur, the 15th August 1876.

I am directed to send, with advertence to your letter No. 1216, dated 22nd July, the accompanying copy of a letter from the Inspector-General of Education, regarding the preparation of the catalogue of Sanskṛit manuscripts in these Provinces. Mr. Browning's report gives all the information required, and I am to explain that, through inadvertence, the orders contained in your letter Nos. 12—616-620, of the 5th April, were not communicated to the Inspector-General, and the report required was therefore not furnished.

2. The Chief Commissioner agrees very generally in what the Inspector-General has said. He fears that few Sanskṛit manuscripts of any value are likely to be found in these Provinces, which are almost wholly wanting in a literary class.

3. With reference to the number of copies of the catalogue in store, I am to enquire whether copies for distribution among other Governments and Administrations should be sent to you, or whether the distribution should be made direct.

From C. A. R. Browning, Esq., M.A., Inspector-General of Education Central Provinces, to the Secretary to the Chief Commissioner of the Central Provinces,— No. 6071, dated the 2nd August 1876.

I have the honour to acknowledge the receipt of your enfacement No. 2987-135 of the 1st August, forwarding a copy of a letter No. 1216, dated 22nd July, from the Officiating Secretary to the Government of India, to which I have the honour to reply.

2. Letter No. 6-403 of 16th March 1876, from the Secretary to the Government of India, Home Department, to the Chief Commissioner, was received by me, and to that letter, and your enfacement No. 1120-49 of 24th March last, I duly replied; but no letter or circular Nos. 12—616-620 of the 5th April last, from the Home Department, has ever been received in my office.

3. It is now understood, for the *first time*, that a report is called for on the work actually done up to the end of 1875, shewing the names of manuscripts acquired for Government, where they were deposited, and whether any manuscripts, and, if so, how many, had been supplied to Oriental scholars and institutions in Europe and elsewhere. This report I now have the honour to submit.

4. On receipt of circulars Nos. 4349 and 4354, dated 3rd November 1868, forwarding Resolution of the Government of India on the preparation of catalogues of Sanskṛit manuscripts, and the purchase or transcription of such Sanskṛit manuscripts, the possession of which competent scholars deemed to be desirable as being "unique," "extremely old," or for other reasons, the Chief Commissioner issued General Circular No. 9 of the 13th January 1869, requiring Deputy Commissioners to ascertain the existence of Native libraries in any of the districts of the Central Provinces. On receipt of their replies with preliminary lists of existing manuscripts, a competent Native scholar, Mr. Vishṇuśástrí, was appointed to visit such libraries, and to prepare a list, to be edited by Professor Kielhorn. Full instructions were conveyed in your No. 3183-333 of the 27th December 1870. The list was completed, edited by Professor Kielhorn, and published in 1874. In the meantime, after the issue of the first instructions of the Government of India, and before the publication of the catalogue, three lists of learned Societies and Orientalists were sent by the Government of India, to whom copies of the catalogue were to be sent, namely the lists with No. 479C. of 23rd October 1872, with No. 1770 of 21st May 1873, and, finally with No. 665C. of 24th October 1873, from the Officiating Secretary to

the Government of India, Military Department, in charge of the Home Department. Accordingly, copies of the catalogue were sent to all the learned Societies and Orientalists named in the last-quoted list, and to the officers noted in the margin. I also remember to have addressed the Home Secretary demi-officially regarding the number of copies that would be required by the Home Department, and was, if I remember correctly, told that, as I had sent, or was about to send, all the copies to the Societies and Orientalists named in the list I have quoted, only five copies need be despatched to the Home Office. I accordingly directed the publishers to send five copies to the Home Office; and as, out of an edition of 250 copies, I received only 245, I suppose this was done. I still have, after sending five copies to the Home Office, 29 to the above-mentioned officers, and 131 to learned Societies and Orientalists, some 85 copies in store, and I have directed that four copies be now sent for the use of the Government of India, Home Department. In the absence of advice to the contrary, these four copies have been sent to Calcutta addressed to the Secretary to the Government of India, Home Department.

	Copies.
President, High School .	2
Pandit Vishṇuśástrí . .	1
Deputy Commissioners, Central Provinces . .	19
Curator, Nagpur Museum.	1
Circle Inspectors . .	3
Head Master, Zila School, Ságar	1
Assistant Inspector of Schools, Central Provinces	1
Inspector-General of Education, Central Provinces	1
	29
To Oriental scholars and Societies. . . .	131
To Home Department . .	5
	136
Total .	165
Printed .	250
Number in hand .	85

5. I have acquired in original no manuscripts for Government, but have obtained copies of the following manuscripts, which are placed in the Museum Library, Nagpur:—

1. Ratnamañjarí, by Rájaśekhara (drama).
2. Púrvamímáṃsásútra, by Jaimini.
3. Nyáyaprakáśaṭíká, by Anantadeva.

I have also sent copies of the above manuscripts to Professor Kielhorn, together with two copies of Harikárikávyákhyána by Heláràja (grammar), and I have sent two copies of manuscripts to Dr. Bühler, namely, Chandralokaṭíká (rhetoric) and Śekharanábha (drama). No other Oriental scholars have asked for any manuscripts excepting Captain Jacob, Inspector of Army Schools, Bombay, and he will receive a copy of the manuscript he requires.

6. I have not received any "desiderata," though it was supposed such would from time to time be forwarded: *vide* paragraph 4 of Nos. 4349

and 4354 of 3rd November 1868. I would add that, so far as I have had copies taken of manuscripts—generally themselves copies—I have found such manuscripts to be very incorrect. I do not for a moment believe that many manuscripts in addition to those already catalogued exist in the Central Provinces. There is not a single seat of ancient Sanskṛit learning in these Provinces. The few manuscripts that exist were probably brought from Northern or Western India by immigrant pandits—not, I should say, themselves very learned men, but rather adventurers, who accompanied invading Mahrattas. Even now there are only thirteen towns in the Central Provinces of more than 10,000 inhabitants. In other parts of India Sanskṛit learning is dying or dead; here it never existed, and is not likely now to commence. Dr. Haug, mentioned by the Officiating Home Secretary, is not, I believe, now in India. I have no doubt that Professors Kielhorn and Bühler do continually find fresh manuscripts of value in the Deccan, Gujarat, and Kaśmír, where Sanskṛit learning once flourished. Possibly they would be equally successful in Bengal and the North-Western Provinces; but even their learning and activity would, I am afraid, fail to detect manuscripts of value in these rudely rustic Provinces, where, in some places, a bamboo guitar is esteemed a treasure, bows and arrows weapons not to be despised, and the people are not Hindus, still less Bráhmans. It might be supposed that as, of late years, the Mahánadí and Narmadá have grown in reputed sanctity, the influx of Bráhmans with pilgrims would have introduced perhaps stray Sanskṛit manuscripts. But these directors of religious ceremonies are the most illiterate of their caste, and, even if they know a little Sanskṛit, only value their knowledge as it enables them "to eat a piece of bread." I believe it will be quite sufficient to direct Zila Inspectors to send in, once a year, reports of any Sanskṛit libraries they may have discovered and been able to examine; or when Pandit Vishṇuśástrí has finished his archæological work, he may once again be appointed to see what fresh Sanskṛit manuscripts he can bring to light. In this case, a grant of not less than R1,080 annually will be necessary, and I am much afraid that there will be no results commensurate with the outlay.

From Major A. Murray, Officiating Personal Assistant to the Chief Commissioner of Oudh, to the Officiating Secretary to the Government of India, Home Department,—No. 3015, dated Lucknow, the 5th July 1876.

I am directed to acknowledge the receipt of your letter No. 12—619, dated 5th April last, calling for a report of the work actually done up to the end of 1875 towards carrying out the scheme for the preservation of ancient Sanskrit literature set forth in Resolution of the Government of India in the Home Department, No. 4343, dated 3rd November 1868.

2. In reply, I am directed to submit the accompanying copy of letters Nos. 962, dated 17th June, and 1015, dated 23rd June, from the Director of Public Instruction, giving the particulars asked for.

3. On receipt of the above-quoted Resolution with your office letter No. 4354, dated 3rd November 1868, it was circulated to Deputy Commissioners, who were requested, with the co-operation of learned Natives, to prepare lists of Sanskrit literature in Oudh. These lists were received in 1871; they were very incomplete, and Mr. Browning, the Director of Public Instruction, was then requested to take the necessary measures for carrying into effect the wishes of the Government of India.

4. In answer to a reference on the subject to the Accountant-General, North-Western Provinces, the Chief Commissioner was informed by that officer, in a letter dated 21st June 1871, that the allowance of R1,600 per annum, which had been sanctioned for the purpose, had lapsed in the years previous to 1871-72, and that in that year the Government of India had sanctioned R900 only for the purchase of books, and purchase and transcription of manuscripts, out of R1,600 estimated; and of this Mr. Browning was informed. The measures taken by Mr. Browning to carry out the scheme are given in detail in Mr. Nesfield's letters, and it will be seen that lists have been prepared, but that very few manuscripts have been copied, and no original manuscripts have been purchased.

5. The amount now entered in the Educational budget in order to carry out the scheme is R1,012, and the Director of Public Instruction considers that the buying and transcribing of rare manuscripts cannot be effected within reasonable time, unless some pecuniary assistance can be rendered to his department, equal, at least, to half the allotment entered in his budget.

From the Director of Public Instruction in Oudh, to the Officiating Junior Secretary to the Chief Commissioner of Oudh,—No. 962, dated the 17th June 1876.

In compliance with your endorsement No. 1734, dated Lucknow, 15th April 1876, I have the honour to submit the report called for by the Government of India, shewing what has been done in Oudh up to the end of 1875 towards carrying out the scheme set forth in their Resolution dated 3rd November 1868. My delay in submitting this report has arisen from the fact that much of the information which I required before writing this report has been only very recently received in my office.

2. In order to shew what has been done in Oudh, and also to account for what has not been done, it will be necessary to make a few preliminary remarks as to the circumstances under which this Department was first commissioned to carry out the scheme, and the funds with which it was provided for that purpose.

3. The objects of the scheme set forth in the Government Resolution were—

(1) to purchase such manuscripts as the possessors were willing to sell at a reasonable rate;

(2) to employ copyists to transcribe copies which were unique, extremely old, or otherwise desirable, but which the possessors refused to part with; and

(3) to prepare and submit quarterly lists of the manuscripts ascertained to exist during the previous quarter.

To carry out these three objects, the Government of India provided from the Imperial Treasury R500 per annum for the travelling expenses of the scholar to be sent out on tour, R500 per annum for the purchase of manuscripts, and R600 for transcribing those manuscripts which could not be purchased. While ample allowance was thus made for the discovery, purchase, and transcription of manuscripts, no provision was made for the salary of the scholar to be employed.

4. From the date of the Government of India's Resolution up till 5th June 1871,—that is, for two years and seven months,—no orders relating to the scheme were received in this office; nor was any notice sent that such a scheme had been prepared. The first notice of any kind received by the late Director, Mr. Browning, was through Secretary to Chief Commissioner's docket No. 2710, dated 5th June 1871, in which a file of correspondence in original was forwarded for perusal, and the Director was requested first to make himself thoroughly acquainted with the wishes of Government, and then to take the necessary measures for carrying them into effect. As the file of correspondence was returned after perusal, all that I am myself able to say respecting it is, that it consisted of a series of letters on the subject of the scheme, which had passed between the Secretary to the Chief Commissioner and the divisional and district officers in the interim from November 1868 to June 1871, and that it contained lists of Sanskṛit manuscripts prepared in the same interval by the Deputy Commissioner of each district. These lists were retained by the Director of Public Instruction, but the correspondence was returned.

5. In his reply, this office No. 1060, dated 27th June 1871, to the above docket, Mr. Browning proposed that the scholar to be appointed "to search for additional manuscripts" and prepare the quarterly lists, should be Pandit Devíprasáda, Head Master of the Model School, Lucknow. Regarding the sum sanctioned by the Government of India, for Oudh, namely, R1,600, he suggested that it should be drawn annually for five years and formed into a fund, and that any savings which might accrue after a lapse of five years could be returned to the Treasury after the plan adopted in the North-Western Provinces. In the Secretary to Chief Commissioner's reply to this (No. 3246, dated 10th July 1871), the appointment of Pandit Devíprasáda for the search after additional manuscripts, and the preparation of quarterly lists, was approved of; but, in regard to the financial proposals respecting the annual allotment of R1,600 made by the Government of India, the Director was informed that the sums sanctioned for the years 1868-69, 1869-70, and 1870-71 had all lapsed, and that, in the current year's budget, R900 only had been provided.

6. In the letter of appointment sent by the Director, Mr. Browning, to Pandit Devíprasáda, the duties of the Pandit were thus defined:—

This office No. 1267, dated 14th July 1871.

"You are appointed under orders from the Government of India, No. 4354, dated 3rd November 1868, to procure lists of Sanskṛit manuscripts to be found in the several Native libraries that may exist in Oudh. It will be your duty to prepare, four times a year, a catalogue of all the manuscripts found by you in the previous quarter."

7. From what has been reported thus far, respecting the measures adopted in this province for working out the scheme under notice, four facts have been elicited—

(1) that no provision was made from the first by the Government of India for the salary of the scholar to be employed to work the scheme, and that, hence, the scholar selected by Mr. Browning was to receive his salary in the nominal capacity of Head Master of a school;

(2) that the provision of R1,600 made in 1868, partly for the travelling expenses of the scholar, partly for the purchase of manuscripts, and partly for the transcription of those manuscripts which could not be purchased, had, by July 1871, decreased to R900;

(3) that this allotment of R900 was not included in the Educational Provincial Services budget, but came from some source other than departmental funds, the Chief Commissioner himself undertaking to pay the travelling bills; and

(4) that, out of the three objects of the original scheme as described above, one only was taken in hand, namely, the discovering and codifying of Sanskṛit manuscripts; while the other two objects, namely the purchasing and the transcription of manuscripts, for which R500 and R600 had been provided, respectively, in the original grant, were either dropped or lost sight of.

8. I do not understand why, in his letter No. 1060, dated 27th June 1871, in which the late Director first submitted for approval his plans for working the scheme, he made no proposal for either copying or purchasing manuscripts, but confined himself simply to the project of discovering what manuscripts existed, and preparing quarterly lists. But the announcement made in your reply (No. 3246, dated 10th July 1871), that only R900 were available for working the scheme, would, in any case, have prevented him from doing much more than this. Nor is it understood in this office why, if the Educational Department was to work the scheme at all, it did not receive its commission to do so before June 1871. Doubtless, there were reasons for the delay; but the reduction of the allotment from R1,600 to R900 per annum, which occurred during the interim, was unfortunate.

9. After this preliminary explanation, I am now in a position to shew what this Department has done towards carrying out the scheme from June 1871 up to the end of the calendar year 1875, and also to account for what it has not done. The points to be reported on are the following:—

(1) what has been done towards discovering and compiling lists of Sanskṛit manuscripts;
(2) what has been done towards making copies of Sanskṛit manuscripts;
(3) what has been done towards purchasing original manuscripts;
(4) the names of the manuscripts acquired for Government;
(5) where the above are deposited; and
(6) whether any manuscripts, and, if so, how many, and what manuscripts, have been supplied to Oriental scholars or institutions in Europe and elsewhere.

10. First, as to the discovery of Sanskṛit manuscripts and the submission of lists. From June 1871 up to the end of the calendar year 1875—an interval of four years and a half—thirteen fasciculi, or lists of manuscripts, were compiled, or three, on an average, each year. The rule prescribed by the Government of India in their original scheme, that a new fasciculus should be sent up every quarter, was not carried out. One reason was, that the late Director could not spare Pandit Devíprasáda from his duties as Head Master of the Model School; consequently, only three fasciculi out of the thirteen were compiled from June 1871 up till Mr. Brown-

ing's departure from Oudh in October 1873—a space of two years and five months; and only R830 were paid by the Chief Commissioner on account of the Pandit's travelling bills. But it would have been difficult in any case to send up four valuable lists every year; for in Oudh there are no Sanskṛit ṭols (or universities, if the term may be used) such as exist, or did exist, in Lower Bengal. The libraries are not usually found in cities or in the larger towns, but have to be hunted for in villages and the more secluded towns, in the schools or houses of Pandits. The first of the thirteen lists or fasciculi alluded to, was merely a compilation of the lists furnished by Deputy Commissioners and forwarded to Mr. Browning under cover of your docket No. 2710, dated 5th June 1871. The rest are lists of manuscripts which have been discovered by the Educational Department through the agency of Pandit Devíprasáda. In the opinion of the late Director, Mr. Browning, the first is of less value than the two other lists which were prepared during his incumbency.

11. The following is a summation of all the manuscripts mentioned in the thirteen fasciculi, classified according to the method prescribed by Babu Rájendralála Mitra, of Calcutta, and followed, I believe, in other Provinces:—

	No. of Manuscripts.
I. Vedaśástra—	
a. *Saṃhitá* (Hymns)	11
b. *Bráhmaṇa* (Ceremonials)	33
c. *Áraṇyaka* (Ceremonials appropriate for forest-life)	5
d. *Upanishad* (Theology)	102
e. *Vaidika* (Sútras, Rituals, Phonetics, &c.)	65
II. Aitihásikaśástra—	
a. *Itihása* (History)	22
b. *Puráṇa* (Ancient legends)	87
III. Kávyaśástra—	
a. *Kávya* (Poems)	71
b. *Náṭaka* (Drama)	17
c. *Champú* (Poetical prose)	6
d. *Kosha* (Miscellaneous poetical collections)	2
e. *Upákhyána* (Tales and Romances)	6
IV. Abidhánaśástra (Lexicography)	14
V. Vyákaraṇaśástra (Grammar)	122
VI. Chhandaḥśástra (Prosody)	27
VII. Alankáraśástra (Rhetoric)	38

VIII.	Jyotiḥśástra (Astronomy and Astrology)	271
IX.	Smṛitiśástra (Law, Civil and Canonical)	130
X.	Sangitaśástra (Music)	9
XI.	Śilpaśástra (Art)	9
XII.	Kámaśástra (Erotics)	5
XIII.	Darśanaśástra (Philosophy)—	
	a. *Sáṅkhya* (Hylotheistic)	14
	b. *Nyáya* (Dialectics)	67
	c. *Vaiśeshika* (Physical)	59
	d. *Mímáṇsá* (Ritualistic)	24
	e. *Vedánta* (Monotheistic)	132
	f. *Yoga* (Theocratic)	17
	g. *Aparadárśanika* (Minor System of Philosophy)	3
XIV.	Bhaktiśástra (Faith)	123
XV.	Tantraśástra (Mysticism)	203
XVI.	Vaidyakaśástra (Medical Science)	87
XVII.	Jainaśástra (Jaina religion)	1
XVIII.	Bauddhaśástra (Buddhist religion)	8
XIX.	Anirdishṭa (Miscellaneous)	166

12. Eleven out of the twelve districts of Oudh were visited and partially traversed in order to discover the above manuscripts, and the libraries of the following gentlemen were examined :—

1.	Pandit Kálíprasáda of Itounja	Lucknow.
2.	Mahant Nandagopála of Malihabad	
3.	Pandit Káśinátha Kaśmírí, Lucknow City	
4.	" Krishṇanáráyaṇa, "	
5.	" Gangádhara, "	
6.	" Rámanáráyaṇa, "	
7.	" Bálagovinda, Maurawan	Unao.
8.	" Vṛindávana, "	
9.	" Śivagopála, Brondu	
10.	Mahant Gopáladása, Tilokpur	Bara Banki.
11.	Pandit Rámacharaṇa, Gaṇeśapur.	
12.	" Harasenaka, Bakhara	
13.	Mahant Chaingerigosvámí, Misrikh	Sitápur.
14.	Pandit Ayodhyáprasáda, Mahmúdabád	
15.	" Sabtáwan Lála, Hargam	
16.	" Vaṇśídhara, Behta	Kheri.
17.	" Vaṇśagopála, Íśanagar	
18.	" Jánakíprasáda, Kheri	
19.	Lokeśvara, Mallawan	Harduí.
20.	Pandit Bhairavaprasáda Piháni	

21. Mahárája Mánasiṇha, Sháhganj . . . .
22. Rája Rámanátha Siṇha, „ . . . .
23. „ Káśinátha Siṇha, „ . . . .
24. „ Haradatta Siṇha, „ . . . .
25. Śríyugulánanyaśaraṇa, Ayodhyá . . . . Faizábád.
26. Mahant Priyadása „ . . . .
27. Pandit Umádatta Trivedin, „ . . . .
28. Rája Rámasvarúpa Siṇha, „ . . . .
29. Pandit Haradatta Ráma, Atah . . . .
30. „ Lakshmínáráyaṇa, Balrámpur . . . . . . Gonda.
31. Mahant Maheśagiri, Dalmau . . . . Ráí Barelí.
32. Pandit Súryanáráyaṇa Ácharya, Lakshmaṇapur. . . . Sultánpur.
33. Pandit Devidína Ta'alluqdár, Gughor . . . . . . Partábgarh.

13. A few remarks as to the owners of manuscripts, the authenticity of the same, and the state of preservation in which they are found, may not be out of place before proceeding further. The only possessors of manuscripts are Pandits,—that is, Bráhmans. These may be divided into (*a*) Pandits of independent means, and (*b*) Pandits who live by their profession: of the former class, some are men of literary tastes, who preserve or collect manuscripts for the sake of studying them; others are illiterate men, who preserve the manuscripts bequeathed to them merely as sacred family furniture. In Oudh the only Native libraries that had been examined up to December 1875 are those possessed by literary Pandits belonging to class (*a*). It was best to begin with these, because the owners are more accessible to reason, and their example in opening their libraries would be setting a precedent for the rest to follow. Indeed, it has already been followed to some extent since December 1875.

14. As to the authenticity or correctness of the manuscripts discovered, it has been found that some are substantially correct, and, saving a few minor errors, bear the true impress of their original author. Others abound in errors, each generation of ignorant scribes having perpetuated the errors of its predecessors, and created new errors of its own in addition. The former will be the manuscripts most suitable for purchasing, if the owners will part with them. The latter are scarcely worth purchasing; and correct copies can only be made of them by a careful collation of several existing copies. Although there are glaring errors in many of the manuscripts existing in Oudh, there is no reason to think that intentional forgeries have been committed.

15. Manuscripts are almost always found written on paper, and not on the palm-leaf. Only one manuscript has yet been found written on the

palm-leaf. They are generally kept in the kind of box known as *pitára*. Considerable care is taken to preserve them from harm; but the constantly increasing use of the frail European paper, in the place of the more durable country paper which was formerly used, universally exposes them to much more rapid destruction by insects. There is reason to fear that, as fast as existing manuscripts are destroyed or lost, their places will not always be supplied by fresh copies. The Sanskṛit páṭhaśálás, or schools kept by professional Pandits, which are the only existing means for perpetuating Sanskṛit learning, are rapidly dying out. Sanskṛit learning does not pay in these days, and lithographed manuscripts do not find a ready sale. Pandits are becoming more and more ignorant, and the art of caligraphy, once so common, is now almost extinct. The natural result of all these changes is, that either fresh copies will not be taken at all, or, if they are taken, they will contain more errors than those which preceded them.

16. I come now to the second point on which I have to report, namely, what has been done towards taking copies of valuable manuscripts. In this we have done very little for the reasons already explained, namely, that no instructions to that effect were given to Pandit Devíprasáda by the late Director, and that, if they had been given, the loss of nearly half of the original allotment would have rendered it impossible to do much. The following is a list of the manuscripts of which copies have been taken up to December 1875:—

(1) Gítábhāṇḍa, a treatise on music, by Ahobalaśástrin. This was copied at the request of Babu Rájendralála Mitra, and the copy sent to the Tanjore Library.

(2) Dhátupáṭha, by Bhímasena, a glossary of Vedic verbal roots purporting to be as old as the tenth century. This was also sent to the Tanjore Library through Babu Rájendralála Mitra.

(3) Prákṛitachandriká, a Grammar of the Prákṛit language, written in verse. Author's name unknown. A copy of this was made for Babu Rájendralála Mitra's own private use.

(4) Śálihotra (author's name Nakula), a treatise on the different breeds of horses indigenous to India. One copy was made for Babu Rájendralála Mitra and one for Government.

(5) Prákṛitaprakáśa, a grammar of the Prákṛit language, in prose, and by a different author from Prákṛitachandriká. A copy of this was made for Babu Rájendralála Mitra's own private use.

(6) Aśvachikitsá, by Sámanta Jayadatta, a treatise on the medical treatment of horses. A copy of this was made for Babu Rájendralála Mitra's own private use.

Of the above six books, the two first were copied by Mr. Browning's orders; the four last by orders from me within the year 1875. No copy of any of the six books was made for Government, except that of the fourth. A copy of the fourth was taken for Government within the year 1875 by my orders. Copies of the other five are now being taken for Government: one is already finished, and the rest are in progress.

17. Regarding the remaining points mentioned above in paragraph 8, namely those numbered 3, 4, 5, 6, respectively, I have the honour to report that nothing has been done. No original manuscript has ever yet been purchased or otherwise acquired. I have already explained that Pandit Devíprasáda received no instructions from the late Director in his letter of appointment to make such purchases, and that, in any case, it would not have been possible to make purchases so long as the whole allotment was spent in paying the travelling expenses of the Pandit. In March 1875, it struck me that the mere preparation of lists, or fasciculi, without either copying or purchasing manuscripts, could not be all that the Government required. This led me to read over, for the first time, the original scheme prepared by the Government of India; and, finding that two-thirds of the scheme were not being carried out, I opened correspondence with Babu Rájendralála Mitra, and asked his advice as to how I should proceed with the limited funds at my disposal. He said that the funds were too small for carrying out simultaneously the three objects of travelling in search of manuscripts, copying manuscripts, and buying manuscripts; but he could give me no distinct advice as to what should be done. As he informed me that what had been done so far towards discovering and codifying existing manuscripts had been done well, and that it was very important to carry out this part of the scheme, I left the existing arrangements alone.

18. This completes all that I have to report respecting what has been, and what has not been, done in furtherance of the scheme up to the end of the calendar year 1875. The time within which the scheme can be completed will depend entirely upon the amount of funds assigned for its completion. The Government of India, as I have shewn already, initiated the scheme with a grant from their own revenues of R1,600 per annum. By the time that this Department received the commission which it now holds to work the scheme, the assignment had fallen from R1,600 per annum to R900. From June 1871 till December 1873, all the travelling expenses of the Pandit were paid by the Chief Commissioner (*vide* your letter

No. 5748, dated 6th December 1873). From December 1873 up till the present time, the Educational Department has had to bear the whole of this cost, and, since 1st April 1876, it has incurred the additional burden of making special provision for the salary of the Pandit (*vide* your office No. 318, dated 21st January 1876). The total sum now entered in the Educational Budget on account of the Sanskṛit scheme is R1,012, which exceeds the sum allotted by the Chief Commissioner in 1871 from other than departmental funds by R112. On looking back at the travelling bills countersigned in the Oudh Secretariat in the years 1871, 1872, and 1873, I find that the aggregate amount was only R830-8-0; whereas the amount spent on the same object by this Department from that time up to 31st March 1876 was R1,907-12-6, or more than double the former amount within nearly the same space of time. I have therefore spared no expense in pushing the scheme forward. The Pandit has been relieved of all other work. He no longer draws his salary in the capacity of a Head Master. Although the progress made within the last two or three years has been much greater than in the years preceding, yet up to this time very little has been done; nor do I see how the buying or transcribing of rare manuscripts can be effected within reasonable time, unless some pecuniary assistance can be rendered to this Department, equal, at least, to half the allotment of R1,000 which is now entered in the Educational Budget. If this imperial scheme is to be carried out thoroughly and promptly, some additional assignment should be made for the purpose.

From the Director of Public Instruction, Oudh, to the Officiating Junior Secretary to the Chief Commissioner of Oudh,—No. 1015, dated the 23rd June 1876.

SINCE sending up my report on the working of the Sanskṛit scheme by this office No. 962, dated 17th instant, I have the honour to inform you that I have discovered that the number of fasciculi prepared up to the end of the calendar year 1875 is twelve, and not thirteen, as I stated in paragraph 10 of the letter referred to.

From A. P. HOWELL, Esq., Officiating Secretary to the Government of India, to the Secretary to the Government of Bengal,—No. 1057, dated Simla, the 22nd June 1876.

I am directed to forward the accompanying copy of a letter,* with enclosure, from the Agent to the Governor-General, Rajputana, relative to an analytical catalogue of the Sanskṛit books belonging to the Mahárája of Bikanír, prepared by Hariśchandra Śástrí.

* No. 1027-742 G., dated 9th May 1876, to the Foreign Department of the Government of India.

2. Dr. Bühler, Educational Inspector in the Bombay Presidency, recommended that Hariśchandra Śástrí should be employed to prepare a short abstract of the catalogue; but the latter has since died, and the Agent to the Governor-General suggests that the arrangement of the work be placed in the hands of Mr. C. Tawney of the Bengal Educational Establishment. It is understood that Mr. Tawney is in Europe, and I am therefore to enquire whether the Bengal Government can recommend any one else who would undertake to bring out the work within a reasonable time, and on what terms.

No. 1058.

COPY forwarded to the Foreign Department with reference to their endorsement No. 1079G, dated 22nd ultimo.

From A. L. LYALL, Esq., Officiating Agent to the Governor-General in Rajputana, to the Officiating Secretary to the Government of India, Foreign Department,—No. 1027-742 G, dated Mount Ábú, the 9th May 1876.

I have the honour to acknowledge receipt of your office docket No. 797 G, dated 10th ultimo, transmitting copy of Home Department circular, dated 5th idem, calling for a report of the work actually done up to the end of 1875 toward carrying out the scheme set forth in the circular of that Department marginally quoted.

No. 4349-55, dated 3rd November 1868.

2. With reference to paragraph 2 of the Home Office circular, dated 5th April 1876, enclosed with the docket under acknowledgment, I transmit copy of a memorandum by Dr. G. Bühler, Educational Inspector in the Bombay Presidency, on the papers compiled by Hariśchandra Śástrí which have been bought for R1,000. The Śástrí has unfortunately died.

3. The materials which are now at Ábú might, with the approval of Government, be sent to Calcutta, where a competent person could be found to abstract and arrange them under proper supervision. Perhaps Mr. C. Tawney, of the Calcutta University, might be willing to receive charge of the documents, and to direct their arrangement.

Memorandum by DR. G. BÜHLER, Educational Inspector, Northern Division, on special duty in Rajputana,—dated Bikanír, the 1st March 1874.

HARIŚCHANDRA ŚÁSTRÍ has been engaged for a number of years in making a catalogue *raisonné* of the Sanskṛit books of the Maháràja of

Bikanír. I have examined both the library and his work, and believe that the latter might be used as a basis for a really useful catalogue fit for publication.

2. The library of the Mahárája contains in all about 1,400 manuscripts, and besides a good deal of trash, a few nearly unique, and a dozen or two of rare works. Its strongest points are the Vedas, Dharmaśástra or sacred law, Sangíta or the art of singing and dancing, and Mantra.

3. Hariśchandra has prepared a large voluminous compilation, in which he gives a catalogue, with abstract of contents, of about 1,200 works. The abstracts of contents are as full, for well-known and unimportant works, as for rare ones. The books, though professedly arranged according to Śástras or sciences, stand not always in their proper order. To print this compilation would be very expensive and nearly useless. It would, however, be of great interest to have a short abstract of it, in which the books should be arranged under each Śástra in alphabetical order, and the name, author, beginning and concluding ślokas, number of leaves and of lines on each page, and the date of the manuscripts, should be given. If the Śástrí would prepare such a compilation (and he is well qualified for the task), I would suggest that it might be bought from him, and that he might be given a lump sum, say R1,000, for all his materials. This latter suggestion I make, however, under the impression that his story of having worked for some years without pay is correct.

Hariśchandra ought to be able to finish the registration of the remaining 200 books of the library in four weeks.

No. 1079 G., dated Simla, the 22nd May 1876.

Endorsed by the Foreign Department.

FORWARDED to the Home Department for consideration, with reference to the endorsement thence No. 620, dated 5th April 1876.

From H. H. RISLEY, Esq., Acting Assistant Secretary to the Government of Bengal, Financial Department, to the Officiating Secretary to the Government of India, Home Department,—No. 2623, dated Calcutta, the 17th August 1876.

I am directed to acknowledge the receipt of your letter No. 1057, dated the 22nd June 1876, regarding the preparation of an abstract of the analytical catalogue of Sanskṛit books belonging to the Mahárája of Bikanír.

2. In reply, I am desired to submit herewith copies of the letters* received from the Asiatic Society of Bengal and the Director of Public Instruction on the subject, and to say that the Lieutenant-Governor believes that either Dr. Rájendralála Mitra, or the Rev. Dr. K. M. Banerjea, may be relied upon to perform the work in a thoroughly efficient manner.

* From Honorary Secretary to the Asiatic Society of Bengal, No. 487, dated 8th August 1876, and enclosure.
From the Director of Public Instruction, No. 4161, dated 9th August 1876.

From CAPTAIN J. WATERHOUSE, Honorary Secretary, Asiatic Society of Bengal, to the Assistant Secretary to the Government of Bengal,—No. 487, dated Calcutta, the 8th August 1876.

I am directed to acknowledge the receipt of your letter, Financial Department, No. 2012, dated 1st July, forwarding a copy of a letter from the Government of India, Home Department, No. 1057, dated 22nd June 1876, with its enclosures, enquiring in what time, and on what terms, the Society would undertake to bring out an analytical catalogue of Sanskṛit works belonging to the Mahárája of Bikanír.

In reply, I am directed by the Council of the Asiatic Society of Bengal to inform you that the papers were referred to Dr. Rájendralála Mitra for consideration and opinion, and to enclose a copy of his reply.

From BABU RÁJENDRALÁLA MITRA, to CAPTAIN J. WATERHOUSE, Honorary Secretary, Asiatic Society of Bengal,—dated Calcutta, the 15th July 1876.

IN the absence of all information about the bulk of the Śástrí's catalogue, it is impossible to say in what time it can be printed, and what would be the cost. It is said to be "very voluminous," but this is not definite enough for an estimate.

Believing, out of the 1,200 works it describes, at least two-thirds to be what have been already catalogued and analysed by Weber in the Berlin Catalogue, by Aufrecht in the Bodleian Catalogue, by Taylor in his Analyses of the Mackenzie Manuscripts, or by me in my "Notices," and that, of the remainder, at least one-half is made up of mere tracts, I assume 200 to be about the number of copies that will require detailed notices; and, allowing at an average three pages to each, I arrive at 600 pages as the probable size of the catalogue.

The printing at, say, R3 per page of royal octavo, uniform with my "Notices," will thus be R1,800, or, with the cost of binding, R2,000. The time for writing up the English portion, and printing, will be about a year.

The cost of editing will in a great measure depend upon the quantity of new matter to be supplied in English. I believe that, except in the case of the rarest and most valuable, of which there are not likely to be 30 or 40 at the outside, the amount of English given in the Society's Catalogue, or the amount of Latin given in Aufrecht's Catalogue, will suffice. The Oxford University has just offered me £4 a sheet, or R5 a page, for translations from the Sanskṛit; and, as the Catalogue work will be of the same character, I fancy we may calculate the price at the same rate. The total cost thus, for a book of 600 pages, will be about R5,000. I think I could undertake the job under these conditions, as it would compute in with my "Notices."

From H. WOODROW, Esq., Director of Public Instruction, to the Secretary to the Government of Bengal, General Department,—No. 4161, dated Fort William, the 9th August 1876.

WITH reference to your office No. 2013, dated the 3rd instant, I have the honour to inform you that the Rev. Dr. Banerjea is willing to prepare an abstract of the analytical catalogue of Sanskṛit books belonging to the Mahárája of Bikanír. He would leave to Government the amount of remuneration, as he could not himself give an opinion on the point till he saw the materials he had to deal with. He would do the work required with the utmost expedition that the nature of the case would allow.

From J. O'KINEALY, Esq., Officiating Secretary to the Government of India, to the Secretary to the Government of Bengal,—No. 12, dated Fort William, the 3rd January 1878.

WITH reference to your letter No. 2623, dated 17th August 1876, I am directed to inform you that the Governor-General in Council accepts Dr. Rájendralála Mitra's offer to prepare a properly arranged abstract of Hariśchandra Śástrí's analytical catalogue of Sanskṛit books in the possession of the Mahárája of Bikanír, and to complete the same within the period of one year, at a cost not exceeding R5,000, which it is understood includes the cost of printing.

2. The Governor-General's Agent in Rajputana will be requested to forward the materials for the work direct to the Asiatic Society, Bengal.

No. 13.

COPY forwarded to the Financial Department for the issue of the further necessary orders.

No. 14.

COPY forwarded to the Foreign Department, with reference to their endorsement No. 1079 G., dated 22nd May, for communication to the Governor-General's Agent at Rajputana.

Extract from the Proceedings of the Government of India in the Home Department (Public),—No. 7-250, dated Fort William, the 9th February 1878.

Read again—

Public Proceedings, 7th November 1868, Nos. 53 to 57.

Read—

A report on Sanskṛit Manuscripts in Native libraries by Dr. Rájendralála Mitra, dated 15th February 1875.

Read—

Public Proceedings,	8th May 1869, No. 28.	Report on Sanskṛit Manuscripts in the North-Western Provinces.
Ditto,	26th June 1869, No. 116.	
Ditto,	February 1875, Nos. 13 and 14.	
Ditto,	May 1875, Nos. 214 and 215.	

Read—

Public Proceedings,	11th September 1869, Nos. 159 to 161.	Reports from Bombay by Drs. Bühler and Kielhorn on Sanskṛit Manuscripts.
Ditto,	27th August 1870, Nos. 64 and 65.	
Ditto,	21st October 1871, Nos. 68 and 69.	
Ditto,	May 1872, No. 50.	
Ditto,	December 1872, Nos. 521 and 522.	
Ditto,	August 1874, Nos. 195 and 195 A.	
Ditto,	May 1875, Nos. 203 to 205.	
Ditto,	June 1875, No. 218.	
Ditto,	October 1875, Nos. 230 and 231.	

Read—

Public Proceedings,	22nd May 1869, No. 30.	Report on the Sanskṛit Manuscripts in the Library of the late Rájá of Tanjore.
Ditto,	October 1873, Nos. 459 to 462.	
Ditto,	December 1877, Nos. 107 to 110.	

Read—

Public Proceedings,	19th March 1870, Nos. 91 to 98.	Report on Sanskṛit Manuscripts in the Library of the Mahárája of Mysore.
Ditto,	13th August 1870, Nos. 176 to 178.	

Read—

Circular from Home Department, dated 16th March 1876, Public Proceedings, March 1876, Nos. 106 and 107, and the Circular of 5th April 1876, Public Proceedings, April 1876, No. 17.

Read—

Report from the Government of Madras, No. 391, dated 6th October 1876.

Read—

Report from the Chief Commissioner, Central Provinces, No. 3131-139, dated 15th August 1876.

Read—

Report from the Chief Commissioner of Oudh, No. 3015, dated 5th July 1876.

Read—

Correspondence regarding the Sanskṛit books in the Library of the Mahárája of Bikanír:

Public Proceedings for June 1876, Nos. 143 and 144.
Ditto ditto January 1878, Nos. 13 and 14.

RESOLUTION.—At the instance of Pandit Rádhákṛishṇa, of Lahore, a scheme was sanctioned by a Resolution in the Home Department, dated 3rd November 1868, for the discovery and preservation of the records of ancient Sanskṛit literature at an outlay of R24,000 per annum. The chief features of the scheme were as follows:—

(1) "To print uniformly all procurable unprinted lists of the Sanskṛit manuscripts in Indian libraries, and to send them to the various learned Societies of Europe, and to individual scholars in Europe and India, with an intimation that the Government will carefully attend to their suggestions as to which of the manuscripts therein mentioned should be examined, purchased, or transcribed;

(2) "to institute searches for manuscripts, and to this end to prepare lists of desirable codices; to distribute these lists among scholars and other persons willing to assist in the search, with a request that they will report their discoveries to such officer as may, from time to time, be appointed by the Government of India; and to depute competent scholars on tours through the several Presidencies and Provinces to examine the manuscripts reported upon, to seek new manuscripts, to purchase manuscripts procurable at reasonable rates, and to have copies made of such manuscripts as are unique or otherwise desirable, but which the possessors refuse to part with; and

(3) "to grant to the Asiatic Society of Bengal an additional allowance for the publication of Sanskṛit works hitherto unprinted."

The statement given in the margin shews the financial result of the scheme, *i. e.*, how the R24,000 sanctioned as the annual expense for carrying it out are distributed.

	Tour expense of competent scholars.	Purchase of manuscripts.	Transcription of manuscripts.	TOTAL.
	R	R	R	R
Bengal . .	1,000	1,000	1,200	3,200
Bombay . .	1,000	1,000	1,200	3,200
Madras and Mysore . .	1,000	1,000	1,200	3,200
North-Western Provinces .	500	500	600	1,600
Punjab . .	500	500	600	1,600
Oudh . .	500	500	600	1,600
Central Provinces . .	500	500	600	1,600
Rajputana .	1,000	1,000	1,200	3,200
	6,000	6,000	7,200	19,200
Printing Native catalogues of desirable manuscripts .	...	...	...	1,000
Additional grant to Asiatic Society . .	...	...	...	3,000
Sundries . .	...	...	...	800
				24,000

This Resolution was communicated to the several Local Governments and Administrations with instructions as to how to carry out the scheme.

The instructions were that all procurable unprinted lists of Sanskṛit manuscripts in the Native libraries, situate within the territories under the respective Local Governments and Administrations, should be printed uniformly in octavo in the Nágarí character, and under the superintendence of a competent editor, such as Babu Rájendralála Mitra in Bengal, Mr. Burnell in Madras, and Dr. Bühler in Bombay.

Competent scholars should, it was said, be sent annually on tours to examine the manuscripts named in the Native catalogues so printed; to seek new manuscripts; to explain to Native scholars at the different places visited the objects and importance of the mission; to purchase such manuscripts as the possessors were willing to sell at a reasonable rate, and to employ copyists to transcribe codices which were unique, extremely old, or otherwise desirable, but which the possessors might refuse to part with. The gentlemen sent on tours were to make reports to their respective Local Governments, and such reports to be transmitted to the Government of India in the Home Department; scholars, both in India and in Europe, to be invited to transmit lists of desiderata; those in Europe to be requested to communicate with the Government of India through the Secretary of State; those in India, through the Local Governments. From the suggestions so received, general lists of desiderata were to be prepared and circulated annually, and the notice of Local Governments and Administrations would be drawn to entries in the catalogues received from them, which seemed to refer to any work in the lists of desiderata.

Quarterly lists* of the manuscripts found during the previous quarter were directed to be submitted in the prescribed form to the Government of India in the Home Department.

* These lists are now annually prepared.

Local Governments and Administrations were to use their discretion in purchasing, or having copies made of, the manuscripts existing within their jurisdiction. Local Governments were, however, reminded of the desirability of bearing in mind the subjects which European scholars should deem most valuable, and that manuscripts of the Vedas and Vedángas, and of their commentaries, law-books, grammars, vocabularies, and philosophical treatises, should be regarded as of primary importance. When transcripts were made, these should be in the modern Devanágarí character. Copies of the Sanskṛit manuscripts existing in Southern India, if made in the Telugu or other Drávidian character, would be of little use to European Sanskṛitists and to the large majority of Native scholars.

These instructions have been carried out as follows :—

BENGAL.

In Bengal the task of collecting the lists, and purchasing and transcribing manuscripts, was entrusted to the Asiatic Society of Bengal. Dr. Rájendralála Mitra, aided by two pandits, or Sanskṛit scholars, has been engaged by the Asiatic Society in carrying out the scheme.

He has already published twelve pamphlets containing notices of Sanskṛit manuscripts extant in Bengal.

His report, dated 15th February 1875, on the operations carried on by him to the close of 1874 for collecting information regarding Sanskṛit manuscripts in Native libraries, is very interesting.

NORTH-WESTERN PROVINCES.

In May 1869, at the instance of the Government of the North-Western Provinces, the Financial Department authorised the utilisation of the saving of the annual allowance of R1,600 for five years in the cataloguing and purchase of Sanskṛit manuscripts. The period of five years expired on 31st March 1874; and in December 1874 the Government of the North-Western Provinces reported the progress made in the preparation of catalogues of Sanskṛit manuscripts existing in those Provinces.

Two hundred copies of Part I of the catalogue of Sanskṛit manuscripts examined were printed and distributed, as directed by the Government of India. Mr. Griffith was entrusted with the supervision of the work.

The Government of India sanctioned the expenditure of R2,822-9 incurred for the publication of Part I of the catalogue, and also a further grant of R2,000 for the continuance of the work of examination and cataloguing the manuscripts. The Government of the North-Western Provinces was at the same time called upon to report as to the place where any manuscripts purchased or copied were deposited, and to send a list of them.

Under date the 7th May 1875, the Government of the North-Western Provinces reported that ten manuscripts, as per list given, were purchased and deposited in the Library of the Benares Sanskṛit College.

BOMBAY.

In Bombay the results were most satisfactory. The operations commenced there in 1869. On receipt of the Home Department Resolution No. 4350 of 3rd November 1868, Drs. Bühler and Kielhorn* were entrusted with the duty of carrying out the scheme in the Bombay Presidency. Their first reports were submitted in August 1869, which shewed that their success was marked and important. They purchased several old manuscripts, *viz.*, Dr. Bühler 21 and Dr. Kielhorn 17 manuscripts; some of these works were rare, and unknown to European scholars.

* Dr. Bühler was employed in the Northern Division; Dr. Kielhorn in the Southern Division.

Consequent on the departure of Dr. Bühler to Europe on sick leave in December 1869, the work which was commenced by him in the Northern Division was carried on by Dr. Kielhorn, in addition to his own work in the Southern Division. Dr. Kielhorn submitted, in July 1870, a report on the progress made of the search for Sanskṛit manuscripts instituted by Dr. Bühler and himself. The report shews that 120 old manuscripts were bought for Government.

In October 1871 the Government of Bombay submitted copies of reports by Dr. Bühler of his and Dr. Kielhorn's proceedings in acquiring Sanskṛit manuscripts during 1870-71.

Dr. Bühler observed that on his return from leave the work was again divided between himself and Dr. Kielhorn; but in January 1871 Dr. Kielhorn obtained sick leave, and the whole charge was made over to Dr. Bühler.

On the 18th October 1871, the report for 1870-71 submitted by Dr. Bühler was sent to the Director-General of the Archæological Survey of India for perusal and return.

In returning the report, General Cunningham suggested the expediency of extending the researches by Drs. Bühler and Kielhorn beyond the limits of the Bombay Presidency; and he recommended their visiting Jesalmír and Bikanír. General Cunningham observed that "in the former place Colonel Tod mentions the existence of numerous manuscripts;" and in the latter country, in the great fortress of Bhatner, he had himself seen a room, ten or twelve feet long and about six feet broad, half filled with manuscripts, fastened up in the Native way in red cloth, and piled one on another to a height of about four feet; and from amongst the top ones he selected a palm-leaf manuscript bearing the date of Saṃvat 1200.

General Cunningham's suggestion was communicated to the Government of Bombay.

In November 1872, the Government of Bombay forwarded a report by Dr. Bühler on the results of his search for Sanskṛit manuscripts in Gujarat during the year 1871-72.

The Government of India expressed satisfaction at the results of Dr. Bühler's search.

In August 1874, the Government of Bombay submitted Dr. Bühler's report on Sanskṛit manuscripts in Gujarat for 1872-73. He stated that during the period under review he had bought or procured 200 copies of manuscripts, of which 75 belonged to Bráhmanical literature and 123 to the Jainas, and two contained Gujarati prose-works.

In May 1875, the Government of Bombay submitted an abstract report by Dr. Bühler of his operations during 1873-74 in Gujarat, Rajputana and Lahore, Delhi, Benares, and other towns of Northern and Eastern India. The results exhibited in this report were as satisfactory as those shewn in the preceding one.

In September 1875, the Government of Bombay forwarded a report by Dr. Bühler on the search of Sanskṛit manuscripts for the year 1874-75. This report also shews that copies of manuscripts were liberally supplied to *savants* in Europe and India.

Dr. Bühler has been now engaged in exploring Sanskṛit manuscripts in Kaśmír, Jaypur, and Ujjain. Instructions were issued through the Foreign Department to the Government of the Punjab, and Governor-General's Agent in Rajputana, for giving Dr. Bühler every assistance in the furtherance of the object of his mission, which had produced valuable results, as shewn in Dr. Bühler's latest report.

Sanskṛit Manuscripts in the Library of the late Rájá of Tanjore.

In May 1869, a list of the Sanskṛit works in the library of the late Rájá of Tanjore was procured from the Rev. Mr. Long, in consequence of a demi-official communication of Sir Erskine Perry, suggesting that this collection might be purchased for Government.

This list was forwarded to the Government of Bombay, with a request that Professor Bühler might be asked to give his opinion as to the propriety of purchasing the Sanskṛit works enumerated therein, or any portion thereof.

In August 1869, the Government of Bombay submitted a copy of Dr. Bühler's report containing his opinion on the propriety of purchasing the Sanskṛit works in question. Dr. Bühler said :—

"On examining the list of the Sanskṛit manuscripts which belonged to the late Rájá of Tanjore, I find that it contains a great many useful, and a number of very rare or nearly unique, books (*vide* list). I am, therefore, of opinion that it would be in the interest of Sanskṛit philology if the Government of India decided to buy the whole collection. Should this be impossible, I beg strongly to recommend that at least the works contained in the list may be bought, many of which are quite unknown, or procurable only with great trouble and expense."

On the 25th August 1873, the Government of Fort St. George submitted, as called for, their proceedings, which embodied a letter from Dr. Burnell reporting on the progress made by him with the catalogue of the Sanskṛit manuscripts in the library of the late Rájá of Tanjore. Dr. Burnell reported that the total number of manuscripts in the Tanjore Library amounted to upwards of 18,000, and these in eleven distinct alphabets, being from all parts of India; that in February 1872 the catalogue was nearly completed, but since that time he had been unable to do as much as he expected, though, on the whole, the work had advanced. The delay was due to the difficulty in procuring types, and the distance at which he lived from Tanjore.

He observed "that the Tanjore Library contains several good manuscripts of all the most important works known as yet, including a few that are new." He believed "that this library must, sooner or later, escheat to Government; the preparation of this catalogue will therefore protect property of enormous value. Sanskṛit manuscripts have long been very dear, and the cost of making proper transcripts is now very heavy." As far as he could judge, "it would not be possible to form a collection like that of Tanjore at a less cost than £50,000; but many manuscripts are unquestionably unique." He added that "as the Government has expressed a wish to promote Sanskṛit studies, he has to some extent anticipated the publication of his catalogue by procuring manuscripts for scholars. Several have been sent to Calcutta, Bombay, and Europe."

On the 31st October 1873, the Government of India expressed full concurrence in the praise bestowed on Dr. Burnell for his disinterested services, and hoped to see the catalogue soon completed.

In November 1874, the Government of Madras submitted a letter from Dr. Burnell, stating that he had not been able as yet to complete the revision of his manuscript (fair copy) of the catalogue of the Tanjore Library, but hoped to do the work much faster, provided his health permitted him to do extra work.

In June 1875, the Government of Madras forwarded a further letter from Dr. Burnell, in which he stated that he had had "the duties of a district and sessions judge to perform since three years, and that he has had very little leisure, being in charge of very heavy courts. To do such work as this properly, much time is obviously necessary." He would, however, "be glad to complete it as quickly as is consistent with the standard of completeness now required."

In November 1877, the Government of Madras submitted a further letter from Dr. Burnell, in which he states that his catalogue has been printed as far as the article "Kosha," and that he hopes to be able to finish the revision of his manuscripts up to the end of section "Technical Literature," during the leave in December and January ensuing. He expects to issue shortly the first part of his catalogue.

Sanskṛit Manuscripts in the Library of His Highness the Mahárája of Mysore.

The Chief Commissioner of Mysore submitted, in March 1870, a catalogue of Sanskṛit manuscripts in the library of His Highness the Mahárája of Mysore. This catalogue was sent to the Government of Bombay for a report thereon by Dr. Kielhorn. On the 2nd April 1870, the Government of Bombay submitted Dr. Kielhorn's report.

He said "that he compared this catalogue with those of the Sanskṛit manuscripts in the India Office Library, in the Bodleian Library at Oxford, in the Royal Library at Berlin, and with other smaller libraries in Europe."

The result of this comparison was that, of the 608 works of the catalogue under report, 468 are already in Europe, as indicated by him. He, therefore, suggested that the remaining 140 manuscripts specified might be re-catalogued. Dr. Kielhorn's suggestions were communicated to the Chief Commissioner of Mysore with a form of the catalogue sent by the Government of Bombay for adoption. Further communication has not been received from the Chief Commissioner of Mysore. But a supplementary catalogue of Sanskṛit manuscripts in the library of His Highness the Mahárája of Mysore, prepared by Dr. Kielhorn, was received in May 1874. It contains the particulars as to the age, &c., of the works which Dr. Kielhorn suggested should be exhibited in the catalogue.

CENTRAL PROVINCES.

The Chief Commissioner of the Central Provinces sent copy of a letter * from the Inspector-General of Education, who, after giving a narrative of what was done towards publishing a catalogue of Sanskṛit manuscripts discovered in those Provinces, and how the copies of the catalogue were distributed, reported as follows :—

* No. 3131-139, dated 15th August 1876.

"I have acquired, in original, no manuscripts for Government, but have obtained copies of the following manuscripts which are placed in the Museum Library, Nágpur :—

(1) Ratnamañjarí, by Rájaśekhara (drama).

(2) Púrvamímáṇsásútra, by Jaimini.

(3) Nyáyaprakáśaṭíká, by Anantadeva.

"I have also sent copies of the above manuscripts to Professor Kielhorn, together with two copies of Harikárikávyákhyána by Helárája (grammar), and I have sent two copies of manuscripts to Dr. Bühler, namely, Chandralokaṭíká (rhetoric), and Śekharanábha (drama). No other Oriental scholars have asked for any manuscripts, excepting Captain Jacob, Inspector of Army Schools, Bombay, and he will receive a copy of the manuscript he requires.

"I have not received any desiderata, though it was supposed such would from time to time be forwarded: *vide* paragraph 4 of No. 4349-4354 of 3rd November 1868. I would add that, so far as I have had copies taken of manuscripts—generally themselves copies—I have found such manuscripts to be very incorrect. I do not for a moment believe that many manuscripts, in addition to those already catalogued, exist in the Central

Provinces. There is not a single seat of ancient Sanskṛit learning in these Provinces. The few manuscripts that exist were probably brought from Northern or Western India by immigrant pandits—not, I should say, themselves very learned men, but rather adventurers, who accompanied invading Mahrattas. Even now there are only thirteen towns in the Central Provinces of more than 10,000 inhabitants. In other parts of India Sanskṛit learning is dying or dead; here it never existed, and is not likely now to commence. Dr. Haug, mentioned by the Officiating Home Secretary, is not, I believe, now in India. I have no doubt that Professors Kielhorn and Bühler do continually find fresh manuscripts of value in the Deccan, Gujarat, and Kaśmír, where Sanskṛit learning once flourished. Possibly they would be equally successful in Bengal and the North-Western Provinces; but even their learning and activity would, I am afraid, fail to detect manuscripts of value in these rudely rustic provinces, where, in some places, a bamboo guitar is esteemed a treasure, bows and arrows weapons not to be despised, and the people are not Hindus—still less Bráhmans. It might be supposed that as, of late years, the Mahánadí and Narmadá have grown in reputed sanctity, the influx of Bráhmans with pilgrims would have introduced perhaps stray Sanskṛit manuscripts. But these directors of religious ceremonies are the most illiterate of their caste; and even if they know a little Sanskṛit, only value their knowledge as it enables them to 'eat a piece of bread.' I believe it will be quite sufficient to direct Zila Inspectors to send in, once a year, reports of any Sanskṛit libraries they may have discovered and been able to examine; or when Pandit Vishṇuśástrí has finished his archæological work, he may once again be appointed to see what fresh Sanskṛit manuscripts he can bring to light. In this case, a grant of not less than R1,080 annually will be necessary; and I am much afraid that there will be no results commensurate with the outlay."

MADRAS.

Nothing appears to have been done in Madras towards carrying out the scheme. The duty of giving effect to the instructions* of the Government of India was entrusted in December 1868 to Mr. Pickford, then Professor of Sanskṛit in Madras; but that gentleman returned to Europe on sick leave, and never returned. Two native gentlemen successively officiated in his place until 1872, when Dr. Oppert arrived.

* No. 391, dated 6th October 1876.

Dr. Oppert states that the contents of the orders of the Government of India, dated 3rd November 1868, were unknown to him up to 18th May 1876, when he received a copy from the Director of Public Instruction. He remarks that, had he been acquainted with that order, he should have gladly acted according to it, the more so as he learnt there was a yearly allowance of R850 assigned to the library to fulfil the demands of that order. Mr. Pickford had stated that he had two catalogues in hand when he left India; that one of them was fairly advanced and already in process of printing at the Foster Press, and that copies of both these catalogues were deposited in the Oriental Library. Mr. Powell, however, reported that he had had a search made for these catalogues by the Native gentleman who was appointed to act for Mr. Pickford, and that they could not be found.

The Madras report also shews that Mr. Burnell's services were in November 1870 placed at the disposal of the Chief Commissiouer of Mysore, for the examination of Sanskṛit manuscripts in Mysore.

OUDH.

The Chief Commissioner submitted a letter* from Mr. Nesfield, the Director of Public Instruction in Oudh, containing the report called for.

* No. 3015, dated 5th July 1876.

It appears from the Chief Commissioner's letter that, on receipt of the Resolution of the Government of India, dated 3rd November 1868, the Deputy Commissioners of the several districts were requested to prepare, with the co-operation of learned Natives, lists of Sanskṛit manuscripts in Oudh. These lists were received in 1871, and were found very incomplete. Mr. Browning, then Director of Public Instruction in Oudh, was requested to take the necessary steps for carrying out the scheme.

Mr. Browning proposed that the scholar to be appointed to search for additional manuscripts, and prepare the quarterly lists, should be Pandit Devíprasáda, Head Master of the Model School, Lucknow; and he suggested that the sum sanctioned by the Government of India for Oudh, *viz.*, R1,600 per annum, should be drawn annually for five years and formed into a fund, and that any savings which might accrue after a lapse of five years could be returned to the treasury, after the plan adopted in the North-Western Provinces. In July 1871, the Chief Commissioner approved of the appointment of Devíprasáda for the search of manuscripts and preparation of quarterly lists. But, in regard to the financial proposal respecting the annual allotment of R1,600 made by the Government of India, Mr. Browning was informed by the Chief Commissioner that the sums sanctioned for the years 1868-69, 1869-70, and 1870-71 had lapsed, and that, in the current year's budget, only R900 had been provided.

Mr. Nesfield, the present Director of Public Instruction, reports as follows:—

"First, as to the discovery of Sanskṛit manuscripts, and the submission of lists. From June 1871 up to the end of the calendar year 1875—an interval of four years and a half—thirteen fasciculi, or lists of manuscripts, were compiled, or three on an average each year. The rule prescribed by the Government of India in their original scheme, that a new fasciculus should be sent up every quarter, was not carried out. One reason was, that the late Director could not spare Pandit Devíprasáda from his duties as Head Master of the Model School; consequently, only three fasciculi out of twelve were compiled from June 1871 up till Mr. Browning's departure from Oudh in October 1873,—a space of two years and five months; and only R830 were paid by the Chief Commissioner on account of the Pandit's travelling bills. But it would have been difficult, in any case, to send up four valuable lists-every year; for in Oudh there are no Sanskṛit ṭols (or universities, if the term may be used), such as exist, or did exist, in Lower Bengal. The libraries are not usually found in cities or in the larger towns, but have to be hunted for in villages, and the more secluded towns, in the schools or houses of pandits. The first of the thirteen lists or fasciculi alluded to, was merely a compilation of the lists furnished by Deputy Commissioners and forwarded to Mr. Browning. The rest are lists of manuscripts which have been discovered by the Educational Department through the agency of Pandit Devíprasáda. In the opinion of the late Director, Mr. Browning, the first is of less value than the two other lists which were prepared during his incumbency.

"A few remarks as to the owners of manuscripts, the authenticity of the same, and the state of preservation in which they are found, may not be out of place before proceeding further. The only possessors of manuscripts are pandits, that is, Bráhmans. These may be divided into *(a)* pandits of independent means, and *(b)* pandits who live by their profession. Of the former class, some are men of literary tastes, who preserve or collect manuscripts for the sake of studying them; others are illiterate men, who preserve the manuscripts bequeathed to them merely as sacred family furniture.

"In Oudh, the only Native libraries that had been examined up to December 1875 are those possessed by literary pandits belonging to class *(a)*. It was best to begin with these, because the owners are more accessible to reason, and their example in opening their libraries would be setting a precedent for the rest to follow. Indeed, it has already been followed, to some extent, since December 1875.

"Manuscripts are almost always found written on paper, and not on the palm-leaf. Only one manuscript has yet been found written on the palm-leaf. They are generally kept in the kind of box known as *piṭárá*. Considerable care is taken to preserve them from harm; but the constantly increasing use of the frail European paper in the place of the more durable country paper, which was formerly used universally, exposes them to much more rapid destruction by insects. There is reason to fear that as fast as existing manuscripts are destroyed or lost, their places will not always be supplied by fresh copies. The Sanskṛit *páṭhaśálás* or schools kept by professional pandits, which are the only existing means for perpetuating Sanskṛit learning, are rapidly dying out. Sanskṛit learning does not pay in these days, and lithographed manuscripts do not find a ready sale; pandits are becoming more and more ignorant; and the art of caligraphy, once so common, is now almost extinct. The natural result of all these changes is, that either fresh copies will not be taken at all, or, if they are taken, they will contain more errors than those which preceded them."

RAJPUTANA.

From Foreign Department, No. 1079G., dated 22nd May 1876, forwarding, for consideration, a letter from the Governor-General's Agent at Rajputana.

The Governor-General's Agent in Rajputana has not reported what progress had been made in acquiring Sanskṛit manuscripts in the Native States under him up to the end of 1875. He simply submitted copy of a memorandum by Dr. G. Bühler, Educational Inspector in the Bombay Presidency, on the catalogue of Sanskṛit manuscripts in the library of the Mahárája of Bikanír, compiled by Hariśchandraśástrí, which had been bought for ₨1,000.

The Governor-General's Agent stated that the materials collected by the Śástrí might be sent to Calcutta, where a competent person could be found to abstract and arrange them under supervision. He suggested that

Mr. C. Tawney might be willing to receive charge of the documents, and to direct their arrangement.

Dr. Bühler stated that he had examined both the library and the Śástrí's work, and expressed his opinion that the latter might be used as a basis for a really useful catalogue fit for publication. He observed that the library of the Maháràja contained in all about 1,400 manuscripts. Hariśchandra had prepared a large voluminous compilation, giving a catalogue, with abstract of contents, of 1,200 works. He added that to print this compilation would be very expensive, and nearly useless. He suggested that a short abstract of it be made, in which the books should be arranged under each Śástra in alphabetical order. The Śástrí was prevented by death from preparing abstracts of the remaining 200 works.

The Government of Bengal was asked whether they could recommend any one else who would undertake to bring out the works within a reasonable time, and on what terms, it being understood that Mr. Tawney was then in Europe.

On 17th August 1876, the Government of Bengal replied that either Dr. Rájendralála Mitra or the Rev. Dr. K. M. Banerjea might be relied on as being competent to perform the work in a thoroughly efficient manner. Dr. Rájendralála Mitra roughly estimated the cost of bringing out the catalogue at about ₨5,000. Dr. K. M. Banerjea observed that he could not himself give an opinion as to the amount of remuneration, till he saw the materials he had to deal with.

The Governor-General in Council has been pleased to entrust the work to Dr. Rájendralála Mitra.

Dr. Bühler, it appears, was engaged in exploring Sanskṛit manuscripts in Jaypur and Ujjain. The Governor-General's Agent does not report the result of the investigations carried on by Dr. Bühler in those places.

No report has yet been received from the Punjab.

The Governor-General in Council expresses his highest satisfaction at what has already been effected, especially by Dr. Rájendralála Mitra in Bengal, by Drs. Bühler and Kielhorn in Bombay, and by Mr. Griffith in the North-Western Provinces. His Excellency in Council regrets that no report has yet been received of what has been done in the Punjab, where there would appear to be an unusually good field for research with such places as Amritsar and Thanesar, to which may be added Rajaor, Kaśmír, and Jammu. There can be little doubt that valuable results would be gained; and the Government of India trust that His Honour the Lieutenant-

Governor will succeed in finding some person at Lahore or elsewhere, who is competent and willing to undertake the work.

The general results which have been obtained are, in the opinion of the Government of India, such as to warrant the prosecution of the search; but the reports received from the several Local Governments and Administrations appear to His Excellency in Council to point to the desirability of redistributing the work; and, in this view, the following arrangements have been suggested as appropriate :—

(*a*) that Rajputana, Central India, and the Central Provinces should be attached to the Bombay Circle;

(*b*) that Mysore and Coorg should be attached to the Madras Circle; and

(*c*) that the North-Western Provinces and Oudh should be amalgamated into one circle, and that the work should be entrusted to one officer, or, in the event of it being impossible to find such an officer, that both the North-Western Provinces and Oudh should be joined to the Bengal Circle, the grant for that circle being proportionately raised.

The Governor-General in Council desires to be furnished with the opinion of the several Local Governments and Administrations as to the suitability of the redistribution thus proposed, and to suggest that the existing list of Sanskṛit manuscripts should be re-examined by some one competent; and asks, with the view of ascertaining how far it may be worth while to acquire by purchase, where possible, or to secure copies of manuscripts known to exist, that steps be taken accordingly.

His Excellency in Council further desires that th Resolution may be circulated as widely as possible, and that Sanskṛit scholars may be invited to make suggestions to indicate desiderata for which it may be deemed expedient to make special search.

ORDER.—Ordered, that copies of this Resolution be forwarded to the several Local Governments and Administrations, and to learned institutions and *savants* in Europe, America, and India, with an intimation that a volume of SELECTIONS FROM THE RECORDS of the Government of India, embodying the papers on the subject, will be forwarded hereafter.